W9-COE-154

THE CHILDREN'S HOUR

Volume One
FIRST STORY BOOK

Volume Two
FAVORITE FAIRY TALES

Volume Three
OLD TIME FAVORITES

Volume Four
CARAVAN OF FUN

Volume Five
BEST-LOVED POEMS

Volume Six
STORIES OF TODAY

Volume Seven
FAVORITE MYSTERY STORIES

Volume Eight
MYTHS AND LEGENDS

Volume Nine
FROM MANY LANDS

Volume Ten
SCHOOL AND SPORT

Volume Eleven
ALONG BLAZED TRAILS

Volume Twelve
STORIES OF LONG AGO

Volume Thirteen
ROADS TO ADVENTURE

Volume Fourteen
FAVORITE ANIMAL STORIES

Volume Fifteen
LEADERS AND HEROES

Volume Sixteen
SCIENCE FICTION–GUIDE

Favorite Fairy Tales

A BOOK TO GROW ON

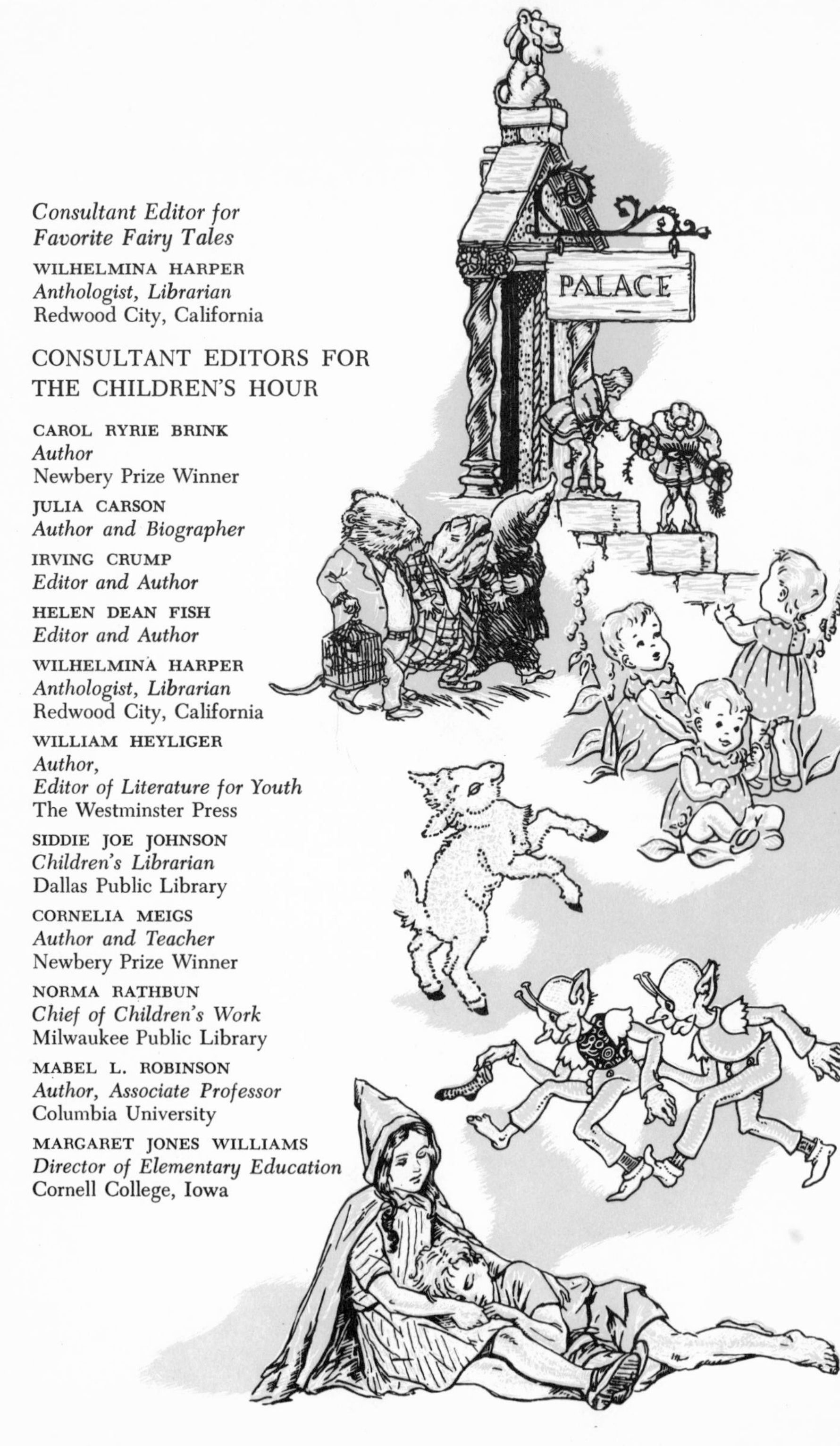

Consultant Editor for
Favorite Fairy Tales

WILHELMINA HARPER
Anthologist, Librarian
Redwood City, California

CONSULTANT EDITORS FOR THE CHILDREN'S HOUR

CAROL RYRIE BRINK
Author
Newbery Prize Winner

JULIA CARSON
Author and Biographer

IRVING CRUMP
Editor and Author

HELEN DEAN FISH
Editor and Author

WILHELMINA HARPER
Anthologist, Librarian
Redwood City, California

WILLIAM HEYLIGER
Author,
Editor of Literature for Youth
The Westminster Press

SIDDIE JOE JOHNSON
Children's Librarian
Dallas Public Library

CORNELIA MEIGS
Author and Teacher
Newbery Prize Winner

NORMA RATHBUN
Chief of Children's Work
Milwaukee Public Library

MABEL L. ROBINSON
Author, Associate Professor
Columbia University

MARGARET JONES WILLIAMS
Director of Elementary Education
Cornell College, Iowa

THE CHILDREN'S HOUR

MARJORIE BARROWS, *Editor*

Favorite Fairy Tales

MATHILDA SCHIRMER
Associate Editor

DOROTHY SHORT
Art Editor

Standard Book Number 7172–1350–1
Library of Congress Catalog Card Number: 74–76542

PRINTED IN THE UNITED STATES OF AMERICA

Acknowledgments

The editor and publishers wish to thank the following publishers, agents, authors, and artists for permission to use and reprint stories, poems, and illustrations included in this book:

CONSOLIDATED BOOK PUBLISHERS for "The Elves and the Shoemaker," "The Three Wishes," "Rumpelstiltskin," "The Lad Who Went to the North Wind," and "The Sleeping Beauty" retold by Pauline Rosenberg; "The Glass Hill" and "Cinderella" retold by Jane McHenry; "Brownie's Ride" retold by Mathilda Schirmer; and illustrations by Marie Lawson, Elise Morton, and Ruth van Tellingen.

COWARD-McCANN, INC., for illustrations for "Snow White and the Seven Dwarfs" by Wanda Gág, published by Coward-McCann, Inc. Copyright, 1938, by Wanda Gág.

DODD, MEAD & COMPANY, INC., for "Patsy and the Leprechaun" by Margaret and Mary Baker. Copyright, 1933, by Dodd, Mead & Company, Inc.

DOUBLEDAY & COMPANY, INC., for "The First Christmas Tree" from *A Little Book of Christmas* by Rose Fyleman. Copyright, 1927, by Doubleday & Company, Inc.

GREENBERG, PUBLISHERS, for "The Last of the Dragons" by E. Nesbit.

HARCOURT, BRACE & CO., for illustrations by Louis Slobodkin for James Thurber's *Many Moons.*

WILLIAM HEINEMANN, LTD., for one illustration by Arthur Rackham for "The Emperor's New Clothes" from *The Arthur Rackham Fairy Book.*

HENRY HOLT & CO., INC., for "Bluebells" from *Collected Poems* by Walter de la Mare. Copyright, 1920, by Henry Holt and Company, Inc. Copyright, 1948, by Walter de la Mare.

HOUGHTON MIFFLIN COMPANY for "The Three-Legged Stool" by Isa L. Wright.

J. B. LIPPINCOTT CO. for "Once When You Were Walking" by Annette Wynne from *For Days and Days* by Annette Wynne, copyright, 1919, by J. B. Lippincott Company; one illustration by Arthur Rackham for "The Emperor's New Clothes" from *The Arthur Rackham Fairy Book.*

LONGMANS, GREEN & CO., INC., for "Ballor's Son Goes Riding" by Ella Young, copyright, 1932, by Longman's, Green and Co., Inc., (shortened version of "Kyelins, Blue and Green" in *The Unicorn with Silver Shoes*).

THE MACMILLAN CO. for "The White Blackbird" from *The Peepshow Man* by Padraic Colum, copyright by The Macmillan Co.; "Song for Summer" from *Summer Green* by Elizabeth Coatsworth, copyright by The Macmillan Co.

METHUEN & CO., LTD., for Canadian permission to reprint "The First Christmas Tree" by Rose Fyleman.

RAND McNALLY & COMPANY for *Poppy, or, the Adventures of a Fairy* by Anne Pérez-Guerra, and illustrations by Benton West. Copyright, 1931, by Rand McNally & Company, Publishers.

CHARLES SCRIBNER'S SONS for "The Open Road" from *The Wind in the Willows* by Kenneth Grahame; copyright, 1908, 1935, by Charles Scribner's Sons; and illustrations by Ernest H. Shepard from *The Wind in the Willows* by Kenneth Grahame; copyright, 1933, by Charles Scribner's Sons; "Peter Pan and Captain Hook" from *Peter Pan and Wendy* by Sir James M. Barrie, copyright, 1911, by Charles Scribner's Sons, 1939, by Lady Cynthia Asquith and Peter Llewlyn Davies.

SOCIETY OF AUTHORS for Canadian permission to reprint "The First Christmas Tree" by Rose Fyleman.

MILDRED BOWERS ARMSTRONG for "Song for a Summer Evening" and "City Fairies."

MARGARET J. BAKER for "The Fairy Who Didn't Believe in Children" by Margaret J. Baker, published first in *Jack and Jill,* The Curtis Publishing Company.

MARJORIE BARROWS for "The Fairy School," published first in *Child Life Magazine.*

NANCY CLINTON for "The Browny."

PADRAIC COLUM for "The Man with the Bag" published first in *Child Life Magazine.*

HENRY CREW for "A Bluebird" by Helen Coale Crew.

EDWARD WADE DEVLIN for "The Dippy."

RUTH DIXON for "The Enchanted Garden."

IVY O. EASTWICK for "Sea-Shell."

FLORENCE PAGE JAQUES for "The Piping on Christmas Eve," first published in *Child Life Magazine.*

JANET LEWIS WINTERS for "The Elf" by Janet Lewis.

ANNE PÉREZ-GUERRA for "If I Were Thumbelina."

CONSTANCE SAVERY for "The Little Dragon," first published in *Child Life Magazine.*

RAY ST. CLAIR for "The Fox Ferry," first published in *The Treasure Chest*, G. A.Pflaum.

JAMES THURBER for *The Great Quillow* and *Many Moons*, both published by Harcourt, Brace & Co.

ELLA YOUNG for "Ardan's Pooka," first published in *Child Life Magazine.*

MRS. DONN P. CRANE for illustrations by Donn P. Crane from Padraic Colum's "The White Blackbird."

JOHN GEE for illustrations for Edward Wade Devlin's "The Dippy."

ALEXANDER KEY for illustrations for Ella Young's "Ballor's Son Goes Riding."

DOROTHY LATHROP for illustrations for Ella Young's "Ardan's Pooka."

ROBERT LAWSON for illustrations for Constance Savery's "The Little Dragon," Padraic Colum's "The Man with the Bag," and Florence Page Jaques' "The Piping on Christmas Eve."

Contents

Part I: FOR YOUNGER READERS

James Thurber

MANY MOONS

ILLUSTRATED BY *Louis Slobodkin*

ONCE upon a time, in a kingdom by the sea, there lived a little Princess named Lenore. She was ten years old, going on eleven. One day Lenore fell ill of a surfeit of raspberry tarts and took to her bed.

The Royal Physician came to see her and took her temperature and felt her pulse and made her stick out her tongue. The Royal Physician was worried. He sent for the King, Lenore's father, and the King came to see her.

"I will get you anything your heart desires," the King said. "Is there anything your heart desires?"

"Yes," said the Princess. "I want the moon. If I can have the moon, I will be well again."

Now the King had a great many wise men who always got for him anything he wanted, so he told his daughter that she could have the moon. Then he went to the throne room and pulled a bell cord, three long pulls and a short pull, and presently the Lord High Chamberlain came into the room.

The Lord High Chamberlain was a large, fat man who wore thick glasses which made his eyes seem twice as big as they really were. This made the Lord High Chamberlain seem twice as wise as he really was.

"I want you to get the moon," said the King. "The Princess Lenore wants the moon. If she can have the moon, she will get well again."

"The moon?" exclaimed the Lord High Chamberlain, his eyes widening. This made him look four times as wise as he really was.

"Yes, the moon," said the King. "M-o-o-n, moon. Get it tonight, tomorrow at the latest."

The Lord High Chamberlain wiped his forehead with a handkerchief and then blew his nose loudly. "I have got a great many things for you in my time, Your Majesty," he said. "It just happens that I have with me a list of the things I have got for you in my time." He pulled a long scroll of parchment out of his pocket. "Let me see, now." He glanced at the list, frowning. "I have got ivory, apes, and peacocks, rubies, opals, and emeralds, black orchids, pink elephants, and blue poodles, gold bugs, scarabs, and flies in amber, hummingbirds' tongues, angels' feathers, and unicorns' horns, giants, midgets, and mermaids, frankincense, ambergris, and myrrh, troubadours, minstrels, and dancing women, a pound of butter, two dozen eggs, and a sack of sugar—sorry, my wife wrote that in there."

"I don't remember any blue poodles," said the King.

"It says blue poodles right here on the list, and they are checked off with a little check mark," said the Lord High Chamberlain. "So there must have been blue poodles. You just forget."

"Never mind the blue poodles," said the King. "What I want now is the moon."

"I have sent as far as Samarkand and Araby and Zanzibar to get things for you, Your Majesty," said the Lord High Chamberlain. "But the moon is out of the question. It is 35,000 miles away and it is bigger than the room the Princess lies in. Furthermore, it is made of molten copper. I cannot get the moon for you. Blue poodles, yes; the moon, no."

The King flew into a rage and told the Lord High Chamberlain to leave the room and to send the Royal Wizard to the throne room.

The Royal Wizard was a little, thin man with a long face. He wore a high red peaked hat covered with silver stars, and a long blue robe covered with golden owls. His face grew very pale when the King told him that he wanted the moon for his little daughter, and that he expected the Royal Wizard to get it.

"I have worked a great deal of magic for you in my time, Your Majesty," said the Royal Wizard. "As a matter of fact, I just happen to have in my pocket a list of the wizardries I have performed for you." He drew a paper from a deep pocket of his robe. "It begins: 'Dear Royal Wizard: I am returning herewith the so-called philosopher's stone which you claimed—' no, that isn't it." The Royal Wizard brought a long scroll of parchment from another pocket of his robe. "Here it is," he said. "Now, let's see. I have squeezed blood out of turnips for you, and turnips out of blood. I have produced rabbits out of silk hats, and silk hats out of rabbits. I have conjured up flowers, tambourines, and doves out of nowhere, and nowhere out of flowers, tambourines, and doves. I have brought you divining rods, magic wands, and crystal spheres in which to behold the future. I have compounded philters, unguents, and potions, to cure heartbreak, surfeit, and ringing in the ears. I have made you my own special mixture of wolfbane, nightshade, and eagles' tears, to ward off witches, demons, and things that go bump in the night. I have given you seven league boots, the golden touch, and a cloak of invisibility—"

"It didn't work," said the King. "The cloak of invisibility didn't work."

"Yes, it did," said the Royal Wizard.

"No, it didn't," said the King. "I kept bumping into things, the same as ever."

"The cloak is supposed to make you invisible," said the Royal Wizard. "It is not to keep you from bumping into things."

"All I know is, I kept bumping into things," said the King.

The Royal Wizard looked at his list again. "I got you," he said, "horns from Elfland, sand from the Sandman, and gold from the rainbow. Also a spool of thread, a paper of needles, and a lump of beeswax—sorry, those are things my wife wrote down for me to get her."

"What I want you to do now," said the King, "is to get me the moon. The Princess Lenore wants the moon, and when she gets it, she will be well again."

"Nobody can get the moon," said the Royal Wizard. "It is 150,000 miles away, and it is made of green cheese, and it is twice as big as this palace."

The King flew into another rage and sent the Royal Wizard back to his cave. Then he rang a gong and summoned the Royal Mathematician.

The Royal Mathematician was a bald-headed, nearsighted man, with a skullcap on his head and a pencil behind each ear. He wore a black suit with white numbers on it.

"I don't want to hear a long list of all the things you have figured out for me since 1907," the King said to him. "I want you to figure out right now how to get the moon for the Princess Lenore. When she gets the moon, she will be well again."

"I am glad you mentioned all the things I have figured out for you since 1907," said the Royal Mathematician. "It so happens that I have a list of them with me."

He pulled a long scroll of parchment out of a pocket and looked at it. "Now let me see. I have figured out for you the distance between the horns of a dilemma, night and day, and A and Z. I have computed how far is Up, how long it takes to get to Away, and what becomes of Gone. I have discovered the length of the sea serpent, the price of the priceless, and the square of the hippopotamus. I know where you are when you are at Sixes and Sevens, how much Is you have to have to make an Are, and how many birds you can catch with the salt in the ocean—187,796,132, if it would interest you to know."

"There aren't that many birds," said the King.

"I didn't say there were," said the Royal Mathematician. "I said if there were."

"I don't want to hear about seven hundred million imaginary birds," said the King. "I want you to get the moon for the Princess Lenore."

"The moon is 300,000 miles away," said the Royal Mathematician. "It is round and flat like a coin, only it is made of asbestos, and it is half the size of this kingdom. Furthermore, it is pasted on the sky. Nobody can get the moon."

The King flew into still another rage and sent the Royal Mathematician away. Then he rang for the Court Jester. The Jester came bounding into the throne room in his motley and his cap and bells, and sat at the foot of the throne.

"What can I do for you, Your Majesty?" asked the Court Jester.

"Nobody can do anything for me," said the King mournfully. "The Princess Lenore wants the moon, and she cannot be well till she gets it, but nobody can get it for her. Every time I ask anybody for the moon, it gets larger and farther away. There is nothing you can do for me except play on your lute. Something sad."

"How big do they say the moon is," asked the Court Jester, "and how far away?"

"The Lord High Chamberlain says it is 35,000 miles away and bigger than the Princess Lenore's room," said the King. "The Royal Wizard says it is 150,000 miles away and twice as big as this palace. The Royal Mathematician says it is 300,000 miles away and half the size of this kingdom."

The Court Jester strummed on his lute for a little while. "They are all wise men," he said, "and so they must all be right. If they are all right, then the moon must be just as large and as far away as each person thinks it is. The thing to do is find out how big the Princess Lenore thinks it is, and how far away."

"I never thought of that," said the King.

"I will go and ask her, Your Majesty," said the Court Jester. And he crept softly into the little girl's room.

The Princess Lenore was awake, and she was glad to see the Court Jester, but her face was pale and her voice very weak.

"Have you brought the moon to me?" she asked.

"Not yet," said the Court Jester, "but I will get it for you right away. How big do you think it is?"

"It is just a little smaller than my thumbnail," she said, "for when I hold my thumbnail up at the moon, it just covers it."

"And how far away is it?" asked the Court Jester.

"It is not as high as the big tree outside my window," said the Princess, "for sometimes it gets caught in the top branches."

"It will be very easy to get the moon for you," said the Court Jester. "I will climb the tree tonight when it gets caught in the top branches and bring it to you."

Then he thought of something else. "What is the moon made of, Princess?" he asked.

"Oh," she said, "it's made of gold, of course, silly."

The Court Jester left the Princess Lenore's room and went to see the Royal Goldsmith. He had the Royal Goldsmith make a tiny round golden moon just a little smaller than the thumbnail of the Princess Lenore. Then he had him string it on a golden chain so the Princess could wear it around her neck.

"What is this thing I have made?" asked the Royal Goldsmith when he had finished it.

"You have made the moon," said the Court Jester. "That is the moon."

"But the moon," said the Royal Goldsmith, "is 500,000 miles away and is made of bronze and is round like a marble."

"That's what you think," said the Court Jester as he went away with the moon.

The Court Jester took the moon to the Princess Lenore, and she was overjoyed. The next day she was well again and could get up and go out in the gardens to play.

But the King's worries were not yet over. He knew that the moon would shine in the sky again that night, and he did not want the Princess Lenore to see it. If she did, she would know that the moon she wore on a chain around her neck was not the real moon.

So the King sent for the Lord High Chamberlain and said, "We must keep the Princess Lenore from seeing the moon

"There is nothing you can do for me except play on your lute. Something sad."

when it shines in the sky tonight. Think of something."

The Lord High Chamberlain tapped his forehead with his fingers thoughtfully and said, "I know just the thing. We can make some dark glasses for the Princess Lenore. We can make them so dark that she will not be able to see anything at all through them. Then she will not be able to see the moon when it shines in the sky."

This made the King very angry, and he shook his head from side to side. "If she wore dark glasses, she would bump into things," he said, "and then she would be ill again." So he sent the Lord High Chamberlain away and called the Royal Wizard.

"We must hide the moon," said the King, "so that the Princess Lenore will not see it when it shines in the sky tonight. How are we going to do that?"

The Royal Wizard stood on his hands and then he stood on his head and then he stood on his feet again. "I know what we can do," he said. "We can stretch some black velvet curtains on poles. The curtains will cover all the palace gardens like a circus tent, and the Princess Lenore will not be able to see through them, so she will not see the moon in the sky."

The King was so angry at this that he waved his arms around. "Black velvet curtains would keep out the air," he said. "The Princess Lenore would not be able to breathe, and she would be ill again." So he sent the Royal Wizard away and summoned the Royal Mathematician.

"We must do something," said the King, "so that the Princess Lenore will not see the moon when it shines in the sky tonight. If you know so much, figure out a way to do that."

The Royal Mathematician walked around in a circle, and then he walked around in a square, and then he stood still. "I have it!" he said. "We can set off fireworks in the gardens every night. We will make a lot of silver fountains and golden cascades, and when they go off, they will fill the sky with so many sparks that it will be as light as day and the Princess Lenore will not be able to see the moon."

The King flew into such a rage that he began jumping up and down. "Fireworks would keep the Princess Lenore awake," he said. "She would not get any sleep at all and she would be ill again." So the King sent the Royal Mathematician away.

When he looked up again, it was dark outside and he saw the bright rim of the moon just peeping over the horizon. He jumped up in a great fright and rang for the Court Jester. The Court Jester came bounding into the room and sat down at the foot of the throne.

"What can I do for you, Your Majesty?" he asked.

"Nobody can do anything for me," said the King, mournfully. "The moon is coming up again. It will shine into the Princess Lenore's bedroom, and she will know it is still in the sky and that she does not wear it on a golden chain around her neck. Play me something on your lute, something very sad, for when the Princess sees the moon, she will be ill again."

The Court Jester strummed on his lute. "What do your wise men say?" he asked.

"They can think of no way to hide the moon that will not make the Princess Lenore ill," said the King.

The Court Jester played another song, very softly. "Your wise men know everything," he said, "and if they cannot hide the moon, then it cannot be hidden."

The King put his head in his hands again and sighed. Suddenly he jumped up from his throne and pointed to the windows. "Look!" he cried. "The moon is already shining into the Princess Lenore's bedroom. Who can explain how the moon can be shining in the sky when it is hanging on a golden chain around her neck?"

The Court Jester stopped playing on his lute. "Who could explain how to get the moon when your wise men said it was too large and too far away? It was the Princess Lenore. Therefore the Princess Lenore is wiser than your wise men and knows more about the moon than they do. So I will ask *her*." And before the King could stop him, the Court Jester slipped quietly out of the throne room and up the wide marble staircase to the Princess Lenore's bedroom.

The Princess was lying in bed, but she was wide awake and she was looking out the window at the moon shining in the sky. Shining in her hand was the moon the Court Jester had got for her. He looked very sad, and there seemed to be tears in his eyes.

"Tell me, Princess Lenore," he said mournfully, "how can the moon be shining in the sky when it is hanging on a golden chain around your neck?"

The Princess looked at him and laughed. "That is easy, silly," she said. "When I lose a tooth, a new one grows in its place, doesn't it?"

"Of course," said the Court Jester. "And when the unicorn loses his horn in the forest, a new one grows in the middle of his forehead."

"That is right," said the Princess. "And when the Royal Gardener cuts the flowers in the garden, other flowers come to take their place."

"I should have thought of that," said the Court Jester, "for it is the same way with the daylight."

"And it is the same way with the moon," said the Princess Lenore. "I guess it is the same way with everything." Her voice became very low and faded away, and the Court Jester saw that she was asleep. Gently he tucked the covers in around the sleeping Princess.

But before he left the room, he went over to the window and winked at the moon, for it seemed to the Court Jester that the moon had winked at him.

E. Nesbit

THE LAST OF THE DRAGONS

ILLUSTRATED BY *Esther Friend*

OF COURSE you know that dragons were once as common as motorbuses are now, and almost as dangerous. But as every well-brought-up prince was expected to kill a dragon and rescue a princess, the dragons grew fewer and fewer, till it was often quite hard for a princess to find a dragon to be rescued from. And at last there were no more dragons in France and no more dragons in Germany, or Spain, or Italy, or Russia. There were some left in China, and are still, but they are cold and bronzy, and there never were any, of course, in America. But the last real live dragon left was in England, and of course that was a very long time ago, before what you call English History began. This dragon lived in Cornwall in the big caves amidst the rocks, and a very fine big dragon, quite seventy feet long from the tip of its fearful snout to the end of its terrible tail. It breathed fire and smoke, and rattled when it walked, because its scales were made of iron. Its wings were like half-umbrellas—or like bat's wings, only several thousand times bigger. Everyone was very frightened of it, and well they might be.

Now the King of Cornwall had one daughter, and when she was sixteen, of course, she would have to go and face the dragon. Such tales are always told in royal nurseries at twilight, so the Princess knew what she had to expect. The dragon would not eat her, of course—because the prince would come and rescue her. But the Princess could not help thinking it would be much pleasanter to have nothing to do with the dragon at all—not even to be rescued from him.

"All the princes I know are such very silly little boys," she told her father. "Why must I be rescued by a prince?"

"It's always done, my dear," said the King, taking his crown off and putting it on the grass, for they were alone in the garden, and even kings must unbend sometimes.

"Father, darling," said the Princess presently, when she had made a daisy chain and put it on the King's head, where the crown ought to have been. "Father, darling, couldn't we tie up one of the silly little princes for the dragon to look at—and then I could go and kill the dragon and rescue the Prince? I fence much better than any of the princes we know."

"What an unladylike idea!" said the King, and put his crown on again, for he saw the Prime Minister coming with a basket of new-laid Bills for him to sign. "Dismiss the thought, my child. I rescued your mother from a dragon, and you don't want to set yourself up above her, I should hope?"

"But this is the *last* dragon. It is different from all other dragons."

"How?" asked the King.

"Because it *is* the last," said the Princess, and went off to her fencing lesson, with which she took great pains. She took great pains with all her lessons—for she could not give up the idea of fighting the dragon. She took such pains that she became the strongest and boldest and most skillful and most sensible princess in Europe. She had always been the prettiest and nicest.

And the days and years went on, till at last the day came which was the day before the Princess was to be rescued from the dragon. The prince who was to do this deed of valor was a pale prince, with large eyes and a head full of mathematics and philosophy, but he had unfortunately neglected his fencing lessons. He was to stay the night at the palace, and there was a banquet.

After supper the Princess sent her pet parrot to the Prince with a note. It said:

"Please, Prince, come on to the terrace. I want to talk to you without anybody else hearing.—The Princess."

So, of course, he went—and he saw her gown of silver a long way off shining among the shadows of the trees like water in starlight. And when he came quite close to her he said:

"Princess, at your service," and bent his cloth-of-gold-covered knee and put his hand on his cloth-of-gold-covered heart.

"Do you think," said the Princess earnestly, "that you will be able to kill the dragon?"

"I will kill the dragon," said the Prince firmly, "or perish in the attempt."

"It's no use your perishing," said the Princess.

"It's the least I can do," said the Prince.

"What I'm afraid of is that it'll be the most you can do," said the Princess.

"It's the only thing I can do," said he, "unless I kill the dragon."

"Why you should do anything for me is what I can't see," said she.

"But I want to," he said. "You must know that I love you better than anything in the world."

When he said that he looked so kind that the Princess began to like him a little.

"Look here," she said, "no one else will go out tomorrow. You know they tie me to a rock, and leave me—and then everybody scurries home and puts up the shutters and keeps them shut till you ride through the town in triumph shouting that you've killed the dragon, and I ride on the horse behind you weeping for joy."

"I've heard that that is how it is done," said he.

"Well, do you love me well enough to come very quickly and set me free—and we'll fight the dragon together?"

"It wouldn't be safe for you."

"Much safer for both of us for me to be free, with a sword in my hand, than tied up and helpless. *Do* agree."

He could refuse her nothing. So he agreed. And next day everything happened as she had said.

When he had cut the cords that tied her to the rocks they stood on the lonely mountainside looking at each other.

"It seems to me," said the Prince, "that this ceremony could have been arranged without the dragon."

"Yes," said the Princess, "but since it has been arranged with the dragon—"

"It seems such a pity to kill the dragon—the last in the world," said the Prince.

"Well, then, don't let's," said the Princess. "Let's tame it not to eat princesses but to eat out of their hands. They say everything can be tamed by kindness."

"Tamed by kindness means giving them things to eat," said the Prince. "Have you got anything to eat?"

She hadn't, but the Prince owned that he had a few biscuits. "Breakfast was so very early," said he, "and I thought you might have felt faint after the fight."

"How clever," said the Princess, and they took a biscuit in each hand. And they looked here and they looked there, but never a dragon could they see.

"But here's its trail," said the Prince, and pointed to where the rock was scarred and scratched so as to make a track leading to the mouth of a dark cave. It was like cart ruts in a Sussex road, mixed with the marks of sea gulls' feet on the sea sand. "Look, that's where it's dragged its brass tail and planted its steel claws."

"Don't let's think how hard its tail and its claws are," said the Princess, "or I shall begin to be frightened—and I know you can't tame anything, even by kindness, if you're frightened of it. Come on. Now or never."

She caught the Prince's hand in hers, and they ran along the path towards the dark mouth of the cave. But they did not run into it. It really was so very *dark*.

So they stood outside, and the Prince shouted: "What ho!

Dragon there! What ho within!" And from the cave they heard an answering voice and great clattering and creaking. It sounded as though a rather large cotton mill were stretching itself and waking up out of its sleep.

The Prince and the Princess trembled, but they stood firm.

"Dragon—I say, Dragon!" said the Princess. "Do come out and talk to us. We've brought you a present."

"Oh, yes—I know your presents," growled the dragon in a huge rumbling voice. "One of those precious princesses, I suppose? And I've got to come out and fight for her. Well, I tell you straight, I'm not going to do it. A fair fight I wouldn't say no to—a fair fight and no favor—but one of these put-up fights where you've got to lose— No. So I tell you. If I wanted a princess I'd come and take her, in my own time—but I don't. What do you suppose I'd do with her, if I'd got her?"

"Eat her, wouldn't you?" said the Princess in a voice that trembled a little.

"Eat a fiddlestick end," said the dragon very rudely. "I wouldn't touch the horrid thing."

The Princess's voice grew firmer.

"Do you like biscuits?" she asked.

"No," growled the dragon.

"Not the nice little expensive ones with sugar on the top?"

"*No*," growled the dragon.

"Then what *do* you like?" asked the Prince.

"You go away and don't bother me," growled the dragon, and they could hear it turn over, and the clang and clatter of its turning echoed in the cave like the sound of the steam hammers in the arsenal at Woolwich.

The Prince and Princess looked at each other. What *were* they to do? Of course it was no use going home and telling the King that the dragon didn't want princesses—because His Majesty was very old-fashioned and would never have believed that a new-fashioned dragon could ever be at all different from an old-fashioned dragon. They could not go into the cave and kill the dragon. Indeed, unless it attacked the Princess it did not seem fair to kill it at all.

"It must like something," whispered the Princess, and she called out in a voice as sweet as honey and sugar cane:

"Dragon! Dragon, dear!"

"WHAT?" shouted the dragon coming towards them through the darkness of the cave. The Princess shivered, and said in a very small voice:

"Dragon—Dragon, dear!"

And then the dragon came out. The Prince drew his sword and the Princess drew hers—the beautiful silver-handled one that the Prince had brought in his motor-car. But they did not attack; they moved slowly back as the dragon came out, all the vast scaly length of it, and lay along the rock—its great wings half spread and its golden sheen gleaming and sparkling in the sun. At last they could retreat no farther—the dark rock behind them stopped their way—and with their backs to the rock they stood swords in hand and waited.

The dragon drew nearer and nearer—and now they could see that it was not breathing fire and smoke as they had expected—it came crawling slowly towards them wriggling a little as a puppy does when it wants to play and isn't quite sure whether you're not cross with it.

And then they saw that great tears were coursing down its brazen cheeks.

"Whatever's the matter?" said the Prince.

"Nobody," sobbed the dragon, "ever called me 'dear' before!"

"Don't cry, dragon dear," said the Princess. "We'll call you 'dear' as often as you like. We want to tame you."

"I *am* tame," said the dragon. "That's just it. That's what nobody but you has ever found out. I'm so tame that I'd eat out of your hands."

"Eat what, dragon dear?" said the Princess. "Not biscuits?"

The dragon slowly shook its heavy head.

"Not biscuits?" said the Princess tenderly. "What, then, dragon dear?"

"Your kindness quite undragons me," it said. "No one has ever asked any of us what we like to eat—always offering us princesses, and then rescuing them—and never once, 'What'll

you take to drink the King's health in?' Cruel hard I call it," and it wept again.

"But what would you like to drink our health in?" said the Prince. "We're going to be married today, aren't we, Princess?"

She said that she supposed so.

"What'll I take to drink your health in?" asked the dragon. "Ah, you're something like a gentleman, you are, sir. I don't mind if I do, sir. I'll be proud to drink your and your good lady's health in a tiddy drop of"—its voice faltered—"to think of you asking me so friendly like," it said. "Yes, sir, just a tiddy drop of puppuppuppuppupetrol—that—that's what does a dragon good, sir—"

"I've lots in the car," said the Prince, and was off down the mountain like a flash. He was a good judge of character, and he knew that with this dragon the Princess would be safe.

"If I might make so bold," said the dragon, "while the gentleman's away—p'raps just to pass the time you'd be so kind as to call me 'dear' again, and if you'd shake claws with a poor old dragon that's never been anybody's enemy but its own—well, the last of the dragons'll be the proudest dragon there's ever been since the first of them."

It held out an enormous paw, and the great steel hooks that were its claws closed over the Princess's hand as softly as the claws of the Himalayan bear will close over the bit of bun you hand it through the bars at the zoo.

And so the Prince and Princess went back to the palace in triumph, the dragon following them like a pet dog. And all through the wedding festivities no one drank more earnestly to the happiness of the bride and bridegroom than the Princess's pet dragon, whom she had at once named Fido.

And when the happy pair were settled in their own kingdom, Fido came to them and begged to be allowed to make itself useful.

"There must be some little thing I can do," it said, rattling its wings and stretching its claws. "My wings and claws and so on ought to be turned to some account—to say nothing of my grateful heart."

So the Prince had a special saddle or howdah made for it—very long it was—like the tops of many tramcars fitted together. One hundred and fifty seats were fitted to this, and the dragon, whose greatest pleasure was now to give pleasure to others, delighted in taking parties of children to the seaside. It flew through the air quite easily with its hundred and fifty little passengers, and would lie on the sand patiently waiting till they were ready to return. The children were very fond of it and used to call it Dear, a word which never failed to bring tears of affection and gratitude to its eyes. So it lived, useful and respected, till quite the other day—when someone happened to say, in its hearing, that dragons were out of date, now so much new machinery had come. This so distressed it that it asked the King to change it into something less old-fashioned, and the kindly monarch at once changed it into a mechanical contrivance. The dragon, indeed, became the first airplane.

THE LITTLE ELF

John Kendrick Bangs

I met a little Elf-man, once,
  Down where the lilies blow.
I asked him why he was so small
  And why he didn't grow.

He slightly frowned, and with his eye
  He looked me through and through.
"I'm quite as big for me," said he,
  "As you are big for you."

Kenneth Grahame

THE OPEN ROAD

ILLUSTRATED BY *Ernest H. Shepard*

"RATTY," said the Mole suddenly, one bright summer morning, "if you please, I want to ask you a favor."

The Rat was sitting on the river bank, singing a little song. He had just composed it himself, so he was very taken up with it, and would not pay proper attention to Mole or anything else. Since early morning he had been swimming in the river, in company with his friends, the ducks. And when the ducks stood on their heads suddenly, as ducks will, he would dive down and tickle their necks, just under where their chins would be if ducks had chins, till they were forced to come to the surface again in a hurry, spluttering and angry and shaking their feathers at him, for it is impossible to say quite *all* you feel when your head is under water. At last they implored him to go away and attend to his own affairs and leave them to mind theirs. So the Rat went away, and sat on the river bank in the sun, and made up a song about them, which he called:

"DUCKS' DITTY."

All along the backwater,
Through the rushes tall,
Ducks are a-dabbling,
Up tails all!

Ducks' tails, drakes' tails,
Yellow feet a-quiver,
Yellow bills all out of sight
Busy in the river!

Slushy green undergrowth
Where the roach swim—
Here we keep our larder,
Cool and full and dim.

Everyone for what he likes!
We like to be
Heads down, tails up,
Dabbling free!

High in the blue above
Swifts whirl and call—
We are down a-dabbling
Up tails all!

"I don't know that I think so *very* much of that little song, Rat," observed the Mole cautiously. He was no poet himself and didn't care who knew it; and he had a candid nature.

"Nor don't the ducks neither," replied the Rat cheerfully. "They say, '*Why* can't fellows be allowed to do what they like *when* they like and *as* they like, instead of other fellows sitting on banks and watching them all the time and making remarks and poetry and things about them? What *nonsense* it all is!' That's what the ducks say."

"So it is, so it is," said the Mole, with great heartiness.

"No, it isn't!" cried the Rat indignantly.

"Well then, it isn't, it isn't," replied the Mole soothingly. "But what I wanted to ask you was, won't you take me to call on Mr. Toad? I've heard so much about him, and I do so want to make his acquaintance."

"Why, certainly," said the good-natured Rat, jumping to his feet and dismissing poetry from his mind for the day. "Get the boat out, and we'll paddle up there at once. It's never the wrong time to call on Toad. Early or late, he's always the same fellow. Always good-tempered, always glad to see you, always sorry when you go!"

"He must be a very nice animal," observed the Mole, as he got into the boat and took the sculls, while the Rat settled himself comfortably in the stern.

"He is indeed the best of animals," replied Rat. "So simple, so good-natured, and so affectionate. Perhaps he's not very clever—we can't all be geniuses; and it may be that he is both

boastful and conceited. But he has got some great qualities, has Toady."

Rounding a bend in the river, they came in sight of a handsome, dignified old house of mellowed red brick, with well-kept lawns reaching down to the water's edge.

"There's Toad Hall," said the Rat; "and that creek on the left, where the notice-board says, 'Private. No landing allowed,' leads to his boathouse, where we'll leave the boat. The stables are over there to the right. That's the banqueting-hall you're looking at now—very old, that is. Toad is rather rich, you know, and this is really one of the nicest houses in these parts, though we never admit as much to Toad."

They glided up the creek, and the Mole shipped his sculls as they passed into the shadow of a large boathouse. Here they saw many handsome boats, slung from the crossbeams or hauled up on a slip, but none in the water; and the place had an unused and a deserted air.

The Rat looked around him. "I understand," said he. "Boating is played out. He's tired of it, and done with it. I wonder what new fad he has taken up now? Come along and let's look him up. We shall hear all about it quite soon enough."

They disembarked and strolled across the gay flower-decked lawns in search of Toad, whom they presently happened upon resting in a wicker garden-chair, with a preoccupied expression of face, and a large map spread out on his knees.

"Hooray!" he cried, jumping up on seeing them, "this is splendid!" He shook the paws of both of them warmly, never waiting for an introduction to the Mole. "How *kind* of you!" he went on, dancing round them. "I was just going to send a boat down the river for you, Ratty, with strict orders that you were to be fetched up here at once, whatever you were doing. I want you badly—both of you. Now what will you take? Come inside and have something! You don't know how lucky it is, your turning up just now!"

"Let's sit quiet a bit, Toady!" said the Rat, throwing himself into an easy chair, while the Mole took another by the side of him and made some civil remark about Toad's "delightful residence."

"Finest house on the whole river," cried Toad boisterously. "Or anywhere else, for that matter," he could not help adding.

Here the Rat nudged the Mole. Unfortunately the Toad saw him do it and turned very red. There was a moment's painful silence. Then Toad burst out laughing. "All right, Ratty," he said. "It's only my way, you know. And it's not such a very bad house, is it? You know, you rather like it yourself. Now, look here. Let's be sensible. You are the very animals I wanted. You've got to help me. It's most important!"

"It's about your rowing, I suppose," said the Rat, with an innocent air. "You're getting on fairly well, though you splash a good bit still. With a great deal of patience and any quantity of coaching, you may—"

"O, pooh! boating!" interrupted the Toad, in great disgust. "Silly boyish amusement. I've given that up *long* ago. Sheer waste of time, that's what it is. It makes me downright sorry

to see you fellows, who ought to know better, spending all your energies in that aimless manner. No, I've discovered the real thing, the only genuine occupation for a lifetime. I propose to devote the remainder of mine to it and can only regret the wasted years that lie behind me, squandered in trivialities. Come with me, dear Ratty, and your amiable friend also, if he will be so very good, just as far as the stable-yard, and you shall see what you shall see!"

He led the way to the stable-yard accordingly, the Rat following with a most mistrustful expression; and there, drawn out of the coachhouse into the open, they saw a gipsy caravan, shining with newness, painted a canary-yellow picked out with green, and red wheels.

"There you are!" cried the Toad, straddling and expanding himself. "There's real life for you, embodied in that little cart. The open road, the dusty highway, the heath, the common, the hedgerows, the rolling downs! Camps, villages, towns, cities! Here today, up and off to somewhere else tomorrow! Travel, change, interest, excitement! The whole world before you, and a horizon that's always changing! And mind! this is the very finest cart of its sort that was ever built, without any exception. Come inside and look at the arrangements. Planned 'em all myself, I did!"

The Mole was tremendously interested and excited, and followed him eagerly up the steps and into the interior of the

caravan. The Rat only snorted and thrust his hands deep into his pockets, remaining where he was.

It was indeed very compact and comfortable. Little sleeping bunks—a little table that folded up against the wall—a cooking-stove, lockers, bookshelves, a birdcage with a bird in it; and pots, pans, jugs, and kettles of every size and variety.

"All complete!" said the Toad triumphantly, pulling open a locker. "You see—biscuits, potted lobster, sardines—everything you can possibly want. Soda water here—baccy there—letter paper, bacon, jam, cards, and dominoes—you'll find," he continued, as they descended the steps again, "you'll find that nothing whatever has been forgotten, when we make our start this afternoon."

"I beg your pardon," said the Rat slowly, as he chewed a straw, "but did I overhear you say something about '*we*,' and '*start*,' and '*this afternoon*'?"

"Now, you dear good old Ratty," said Toad imploringly, "don't begin talking in that stiff and sniffy sort of way, because you know you've *got* to come. I can't possibly manage without you, so please consider it settled, and don't argue—it's the one thing I can't stand. You surely don't mean to stick to your dull fusty old river all your life, and just live in a hole in a bank, and *boat*? I want to show you the world! I'm going to make an *animal* of you, my boy!"

"I don't care," said the Rat doggedly. "I'm not coming, and that's flat. And I *am* going to stick to my old river, *and* live in a hole, *and* boat, as I've always done. And what's more, Mole's going to stick to me and do as I do, aren't you, Mole?"

"Of course I am," said the Mole, loyally. "I'll always stick to you, Rat, and what you say is to be—has got to be. All the same, it sounds as if it might have been—well, rather fun, you know!" he added wistfully. Poor Mole! The Life Adventurous was so new a thing to him, and so thrilling; and this fresh aspect of it was so tempting; and he had fallen in love at first sight with the canary-colored cart and all its little fitments.

The Rat saw what was passing in his mind and wavered. He hated disappointing people, and he was fond of the Mole

and would do almost anything to oblige him. Toad was watching both of them closely.

"Come along in and have some lunch," he said, diplomatically, "and we'll talk it over. We needn't decide anything in a hurry. Of course, *I* don't really care. I only want to give pleasure to you fellows. 'Live for others!' That's my motto in life."

During luncheon—which was excellent, of course, as everything at Toad Hall always was—the Toad simply let himself go. Disregarding the Rat, he proceeded to play upon the inexperienced Mole as on a harp. Naturally a voluble animal, and always mastered by his imagination, he painted the prospects of the trip and the joys of the open life and the roadside in such glowing colors that the Mole could hardly sit in his chair for excitement. Somehow, it soon seemed taken for granted by all three of them that the trip was a settled thing; and the Rat, though still unconvinced in his mind, allowed his good nature to override his personal objections. He could not bear to disappoint his two friends, who were already deep in schemes and anticipations, planning out each day's separate occupation for several weeks ahead.

When they were quite ready, the now triumphant Toad led his companions to the paddock and set them to capture the old gray horse, who, without having been consulted, and to his own extreme annoyance, had been told off by Toad for the dustiest job in this dusty expedition. He frankly preferred the paddock, and took a deal of catching. Meantime Toad packed the lockers still tighter with necessaries, and hung nose bags, nets of onions, bundles of hay, and baskets from the bottom of the cart. At last the horse was caught and harnessed, and they set off, all talking at once, each animal either trudging by the side of the cart or sitting on the shaft, as the humor took him. It was a golden afternoon. The smell of the dust they kicked up was rich and satisfying; out of thick orchards on either side the road, birds called and whistled to them cheerily; good-natured wayfarers, passing them, gave them "Good day," or stopped to say nice things about their beautiful cart; and rabbits, sitting at their front doors in the hedgerows, held up their forepaws, and said, "O my! O my! O my!"

Late in the evening, tired and happy and miles from home, they drew up on a remote common far from habitations, turned the horse loose to graze, and ate their simple supper sitting on the grass by the side of the cart. Toad talked big about all he was going to do in the days to come, while stars grew fuller and larger all around them, and a yellow moon, appearing suddenly and silently from nowhere in particular, came to keep them company and listen to their talk. At last they turned in to their little bunks in the cart; and Toad, kicking out his legs, sleepily said, "Well, good night, you fellows! This is the real life for a gentleman! Talk about your old river!"

"I *don't* talk about my river," replied the patient Rat. "You *know* I don't, Toad. But I *think* about it," he added pathetically, in a lower tone: "I think about it—all the time!"

The Mole reached out from under his blanket, felt for the Rat's paw in the darkness, and gave it a squeeze. "I'll do whatever you like, Ratty," he whispered. "Shall we run away tomorrow morning, quite early—*very* early—and go back to our dear old hole on the river?"

"No, no, we'll see it out," whispered back the Rat. "Thanks awfully, but I ought to stick by Toad till this trip is ended. It wouldn't be safe for him to be left to himself. It won't take very long. His fads never do. Good night!"

The end was indeed nearer than even the Rat suspected.

After so much open air and excitement the Toad slept very soundly, and no amount of shaking could rouse him out of bed next morning. So the Mole and Rat turned to, quietly and manfully, and while the Rat saw to the horse, and lit a fire, and cleaned last night's cups and platters, and got things ready for breakfast, the Mole trudged off to the nearest village, a long way off, for milk and eggs and various necessaries the Toad had, of course, forgotten to provide. The hard work had all been done, and the two animals were resting, thoroughly exhausted, by the time Toad appeared on the scene, fresh and gay, remarking what a pleasant, easy life it was they were all leading now, after the cares and worries and fatigues of housekeeping at home.

They had a pleasant ramble that day over grassy downs and along narrow by-lanes, and camped, as before, on a common; only this time the two guests took care that Toad should do his fair share of work. In consequence, when the time came for starting next morning, Toad was by no means so rapturous about the simplicity of the primitive life, and indeed attempted to resume his place in his bunk, whence he was hauled by force. Their way lay, as before, across country by narrow lanes, and it was not till the afternoon that they came out on the highroad, their first highroad; and there disaster, fleet and unforeseen, sprang out on them—disaster momentous indeed to their expedition, but simply overwhelming in its effect on the after-career of Toad.

They were strolling along the highroad easily, the Mole by the horse's head, talking to him, since the horse had complained that he was being frightfully left out of it, and nobody considered him in the least; the Toad and the Water Rat walking

behind the cart talking together—at least Toad was talking, and Rat was saying at intervals, "Yes, precisely; and what did *you* say to *him?*"—and thinking all the time of something very different, when far behind them they heard a faint warning hum, like the drone of a distant bee. Glancing back, they saw a small cloud of dust, with a dark center of energy, advancing on them at incredible speed, while from out the dust a faint "Poop-poop!" wailed like an uneasy animal in pain. Hardly regarding it, they turned to resume their conversation, when in an instant (as it seemed) the peaceful scene was changed, and with a blast of wind and a whirl of sound that made them jump for the nearest ditch, It was on them! The "Poop-poop" rang with a brazen shout in their ears, they had a moment's glimpse of an interior of glittering plate glass and rich morocco, and the magnificent motorcar, immense, breath-snatching, passionate, with its pilot tense and hugging his wheel, possessed all earth and air for the fraction of a second, flung an enveloping cloud of dust that blinded and enwrapped them utterly, and then dwindled to a speck in the far distance, changed back into a droning bee once more.

The old gray horse, dreaming, as he plodded along, of his quiet paddock, in a new raw situation such as this, simply abandoned himself to his natural emotions. Rearing, plunging, backing steadily, in spite of all the Mole's efforts at his head, and all the Mole's lively language directed at his better feelings, he drove the cart backward towards the deep ditch at the side of the road. It wavered an instant—then there was a heart-rending crash—and the canary-colored cart, their pride and their joy, lay on its side in the ditch, an irredeemable wreck.

The Rat danced up and down in the road, simply transported with passion. "You villains!" he shouted, shaking both fists. "You scoundrels, you highwaymen, you—you—roadhogs!—I'll have the law of you! I'll report you! I'll take you through all the Courts!" His homesickness had quite slipped away from him, and for the moment he was the skipper of the canary-colored vessel driven on a shoal by the reckless jockeying of rival mariners, and he was trying to recollect all the fine and biting things he used to say to masters of steamlaunches when their wash, as they drove too near the bank, used to flood his parlor carpet at home.

Toad sat straight down in the middle of the dusty road, his legs stretched out before him, and stared fixedly in the direction of the disappearing motorcar. He breathed short, his face wore a placid, satisfied expression, and at intervals he faintly murmured "Poop-poop!"

The Mole was busy trying to quiet the horse, which he succeeded in doing after a time. Then he went to look at the cart, on its side in the ditch. It was indeed a sorry sight. Panels and windows smashed, axles hopelessly bent, one wheel off, sardine tins scattered over the wide world, and the bird in the birdcage sobbing pitifully and calling to be let out.

The Rat came to help him, but their united efforts were not sufficient to right the cart. "Hi! Toad!" they cried. "Come and bear a hand, can't you!"

The Toad never answered a word, or budged from his seat in the road; so they went to see what was the matter with him. They found him in a sort of a trance, a happy smile on his face, his eyes still fixed on the dusty wake of their destroyer. At intervals he was still heard to murmur "Poop-poop!"

The Rat shook him by the shoulder. "Are you coming to help us, Toad?" he demanded sternly.

"Glorious, stirring sight!" murmured Toad, never offering to move. "The poetry of motion! The *real* way to travel! The *only* way to travel! Here today—in next week tomorrow! Villages skipped, towns and cities jumped—always somebody else's horizon! O bliss! O poop-poop! O my! O my!"

"O *stop* being an ass, Toad!" cried the Mole despairingly.

"And to think I never *knew!*" went on the Toad in a dreamy monotone. "All those wasted years that lie behind me, I never knew, never even *dreamt!* But *now*—but now that I know, now that I fully realize! O what a flowery track lies spread before me, henceforth! What dustclouds shall spring up behind me as I speed on my reckless way! What carts I shall fling carelessly into the ditch in the wake of my magnificent onset! Horrid little carts—common carts—canary-colored carts!"

"What are we to do with him?" asked the Mole of the Water Rat.

"Nothing at all," replied the Rat firmly. "Because there is really nothing to be done. You see, I know him from of old. He is now possessed. He has got a new craze, and it always takes him that way, in its first stage. He'll continue like that for days now, like an animal walking in a happy dream, quite useless for all practical purposes. Never mind him. Let's go and see what there is to be done about the cart."

A careful inspection showed them that, even if they succeeded in righting it by themselves, the cart would travel no longer. The axles were in a hopeless state, and the missing wheel was shattered into pieces.

The Rat knotted the horse's reins over his back and took him by the head, carrying the birdcage and its hysterical occupant in the other hand. "Come on!" he said grimly to the Mole. "It's five or six miles to the nearest town, and we shall just have to walk it. The sooner we make a start the better."

"But what about Toad?" asked the Mole anxiously, as they set off together. "We can't leave him here, sitting in the middle of the road by himself, in the distracted state he's in! It's not safe. Supposing another Thing were to come along?"

"O, *bother* Toad," said the Rat savagely; "I've done with him."

They had not proceeded very far on their way, however, when there was a pattering of feet behind them, and Toad caught up and thrust a paw inside the elbow of each of them; still breathing short and staring into vacancy.

"Now, look here, Toad!" said the Rat sharply: "as soon as we get to the town, you'll have to go straight to the police station and see if they know anything about that motorcar and who it belongs to, and lodge a complaint against it. And then you'll have to go to a blacksmith's or a wheelwright's and arrange for the cart to be fetched and mended and put to rights. It'll take time, but it's not quite a hopeless smash. Meanwhile, the Mole and I will go to an inn and find comfortable rooms where we can stay till the cart's ready, and till your nerves have recovered their shock."

"Police station! Complaint!" murmured Toad dreamily. "Me *complain* of that beautiful, that heavenly vision that has been vouchsafed me! *Mend* the *cart!* I've done with carts forever. I never want to see the cart, or to hear of it, again. O Ratty! You can't think how obliged I am to you for consenting to come on this trip! I wouldn't have gone without you, and then I might never have seen that—that swan, that sunbeam, that thunderbolt! I might never have heard that entrancing sound, or smelt that bewitching smell! I owe it all to you, my best of friends!"

The Rat turned from him in despair. "You see what it is?" he said to the Mole, addressing him across Toad's head: "He's quite hopeless. I give it up—when we get to the town we'll go to the railway station, and with luck we may pick up a train there that'll get us back to River Bank tonight. And if ever you catch me going a-pleasuring with this provoking animal again!"

He snorted, and during the rest of that weary trudge addressed his remarks exclusively to Mole.

On reaching the town they went straight to the station and deposited Toad in the second-class waiting room, giving a porter twopence to keep a strict eye on him. They then left the horse at an inn stable, and gave what directions they could about the cart and its contents. Eventually, a slow train having landed them at a station not very far from Toad Hall, they escorted the spellbound, sleep-walking Toad to his door, put him inside it, and instructed his housekeeper to feed him, undress him, and put him to bed. Then they got out their boat from the boathouse, sculled down the river home, and at a very late hour sat down to supper in their own cosy riverside parlor, to the Rat's great joy and contentment.

The following evening the Mole, who had risen late and taken things very easy all day, was sitting on the bank fishing, when the Rat, who had been looking up his friends and gossiping, came strolling along to find him. "Heard the news?" he said. "There's nothing else being talked about, all along the river bank. Toad went up to Town by an early train this morning. And he has ordered a large and very expensive motorcar."

SONG FOR A SUMMER EVENING

Mildred Bowers Armstrong

Fireflies in the twilight—
The fairies might be there—
Each with a little winking star
Showing in her hair.
And when the trees are still, and one
Leaf alone is blowing,
Perhaps a pixie flew from it,
Going where he was going.

Padraic Colum

THE WHITE BLACKBIRD

ILLUSTRATED BY *Donn P. Crane*

"OH, NO, it cannot be," said all the creatures of the farmyard when the little wren told them what she had seen.

"Yes, yes, yes," said the little wren excitedly, "I flew and I fluttered along the hedges, and I saw it, just as I tell you."

"What did you see, O what did you see?" asked the foolish pigeons. They came to where the cock with the hens was standing, and they stretched out their necks to hear what was being said.

"Something too terrible to talk to foolish creatures about," said the cock as he went away.

"Too terrible, too terrible," said the robin redbreast mournfully, as she went hopping under the hedge.

Inside the house the Boy was standing, and he was looking into a cage. Within that cage was a bird he had caught. It was the most wonderful of all birds, for it was a white Blackbird. Now you might live a whole lifetime and never once see a white Blackbird. But this Boy had not only seen a white Blackbird—he had caught one.

He had put the white Blackbird into a cage, and he was going to keep it forever. It would be his very own. He was often lonely, this Boy. His father and his mother had gone into another world, and he lived in the house of his grandmother, his mother's mother.

He had once, a long, long time ago, an elder brother who had lived in the house with him. But his brother had gone, and no one thought that he would be in that house again. For he had gone to be a soldier, and he had been away long, and no one had ever heard from him since he had gone. The Boy, then, had no one to take him by the hand as other boys had. He used to tell his grandmother about seeing boys with their elder brothers, the boys holding their brothers' hands. But he had given up telling her about such sights, for she sighed when he talked about brothers together.

Now the Boy had a bird for his very own. That was a joy to him. The night before he had been at an uncle's house. He came out of the barn with a man who carried a lantern. The man held the lantern into a bush. The light came upon a bird that was resting there. Dazzled by the light the bird did not move, and the man put his hand upon the bird, caught it, and gave it to the Boy to keep. This was the white Blackbird. The next day he carried the bird home.

He put the bird into an empty cage. Now that he had something of his own, he would not be lonely when he saw such and such a boy walking with his brother on the Easter Sunday that was coming. All day he watched the strange white bird. And that night as he sat by the fire his eyes were upon the cage, and he watched the stirring of the white Blackbird within.

The robin redbreast that in the winter goes along under the hedge and the little wren that flies along the top of the hedge were talking to each other. "Always, on Easter Sunday," said the wren, "I sing my first song of the year. My first song is for the Risen Lord."

"And mine, too," said the robin redbreast. "But now we will not know that it is Easter morning and that it is time to sing for the Risen Lord. For the white Blackbird always showed itself to us in times before, and when it showed itself we knew it was Easter indeed."

"O now we know what has happened," said the foolish pigeons. "The Boy has caught the white Blackbird that used to appear just before the sun was up every Easter morning. He has brought the white Blackbird into the house and he has put it into a cage. Now it will not be able to show itself. Dear, dear! We are truly sorry."

"The songs that the robin and the wren sing are not so very important," said the cock. "But think of the proclamation that I have made every Easter morning, *Mok an o-ee slaun*, 'the Son of the virgin is safe.' I made it when the white Blackbird showed himself. Now men will not know that they may be rejoiceful."

"I—I—" said the wren, looking around very bravely.

"The world will be the worse for not hearing my tidings," said the cock.

"I—I—" said the wren again.

"The wren is trying to say something, and no one will listen to her," said robin redbreast.

"Oh, by all means let the wren keep on talking," said the cock, and he went away.

"Tell us, tell us—" said the pigeons.

"I," said the little wren, "will try to set the white Blackbird free."

"How, how—," said the foolish pigeons.

"I might fly into the house when no one is watching," said the wren. "I can really slip into and out of places without being seen. I might manage to open the door of the cage that the white Blackbird is in."

"Oh, it is terrible in the house," said the foolish pigeons; "we went in once, picking grains. The door was closed on us. It was dark in there. And we saw the eyes of the cat watching us." Then the pigeons flew away.

"I should be afraid to go in," said the robin redbreast, "now that they have mentioned the eyes of the cat."

"I *am* afraid," said the little wren. "And there is no one that would miss me if anything befell me. I really am so afraid that I want to fly right away from this place."

But then, although her little heart was beating very fast, the wren flew up on the thatched porch. There was no one could see her there, so small and so brown she was. When darkness came outside she fluttered into the house. She hid in a corner of the dresser behind a little luster jug. She watched the cage that had the white Blackbird in it. She saw the door of the house closed and bolted for the night.

O all in a flutter was the little brown wren as she hid in one of the houses of men. She saw the cat sleeping by the hearth. She saw, when the fire burned low, how the cat rose and stretched herself, and looked all around the house with her eyes. The Boy and his grandmother had now gone up to bed. The wren could still see by the light that blazed up on the hearth. The cat went up one step of the stairs. But only a step. For as the wren fluttered up and alighted on the top of the cage the cat heard the sound that she made, light and all as it was, and she turned back and looked at the cage, and the little wren knew that the cat saw her and would watch her.

There was a little catch on the door of the cage. The wren pulled at it. She said to the bird within, "O white messenger!"

"How will I fly out of the house—tell me, tell me—" said the white Blackbird.

"We will fly up the chimney and away," said the little wren as she opened the door.

Before the darkness had quite gone a young man came along the road that went by that house. He had on the clothes of a soldier. He stood and looked at the house as he came before it. But he would not stay after he had looked upon it. His years of service in the army were over, but he would go on to the town and join in the army again.

For he had joined the army and gone into the war against the wish of his mother and his grandmother. His mother he could never see again, and his grandmother he did not want to see. He had looked upon the house he was born in, and now he would go on again.

It was near daylight now. Out of the hedge came a thin little song. It was the song of the wren, he knew, and he smiled as he listened to it. He heard another song, a song with joyous notes in it, the first song that the robin sings from the hedge-tops. All the times before she had been going under the hedges without a song.

And then he heard the cock crow. Loudly, loudly, the cock cried, "*Mok an o-ee slaun, Mok an o-ee slaun,*" and when he heard that call the young man remembered that this was Easter morning. He did not go on now. He waited and he stood looking at the house.

And then upon the thatch of the porch he saw a strange bird—a strange white bird. The young man could not go on now. Once only in a lifetime might one see a white Blackbird. And this was the second time he had seen one. Once before, and on an Easter morning too, he had seen a white Blackbird. He had come out of this house a little boy. His young mother was in it then. She had called him early in the morning, so that he might see the sun rise on Easter morning. And just as soon as he had gone outside he had seen a strange bird on the thatch of the porch—he had seen the white Blackbird then as he saw it now.

He did not go. He remembered that there was a baby in the house that would be a boy now—a boy such as he was when he had gone outside that Easter morning and had stood watching the bird and whispering to his mother so that she might not frighten it. And his mother had seen the white Blackbird too, and she had told him about it being the messenger to the birds to tell them that it is Easter.

He did not go.

Then out of the house came a little boy. He held an empty cage in his hand. He looked all around. He saw the white Blackbird upon the thatch of the porch, and he held his hands to the bird as if trying to draw it down to him.

The young man went to the Boy. And the Boy, knowing him, caught the hand that was held to him. The Boy drew the young man within. There was an old woman at the hearth. She turned and saw the young man, and for a long time she remained looking on him.

"Safe, safe," cried the cock outside.

"And you are safe, my daughter's son," said the woman, "safe, thanks to the Risen Lord. And now this child will have a brother to take him by the hand this Easter."

The Boy felt that never again would he have a lonely thought. His great brother was holding him by the hand. He heard the robin singing. He heard the wren singing. He heard the cock telling all the world about the Risen Lord. And without any sorrow he watched the white Blackbird flying away.

A BLUEBIRD

Helen Coale Crew

A bluebird is lovelier
Than any other thing.
He's like a bit of blue sky
That has taken wing.
And many bluebirds make you think
The sky's begun to sing.

Jacob and Wilhelm Grimm

THE ELVES AND THE SHOEMAKER

ADAPTED BY *Pauline Rosenberg*

ILLUSTRATED BY *Marie Lawson*

THERE was once a shoemaker, who, through no fault of his own, became so poor that he had nothing left but leather for one pair of shoes. In the evening he cut out the shoes so they would be ready to work on the next morning. Then he said his prayers, lay down, and fell asleep.

In the morning he said his prayers again and sat down to work. But to his surprise he saw a pair of shoes all finished on the table. He looked them over carefully and found them so well made that every stitch was perfect.

Soon a customer came in, and because the shoes pleased him well he paid more than the usual price for them.

With this money the shoemaker was able to buy leather for two pairs of shoes. He cut them out in the evening, and in the morning he was about to go to work again. But there was no need for him to work, for two pairs of shoes stood on the table, already finished.

Before long people came in to buy the shoes, and they paid so well for them that the shoemaker was able to buy leather for four pairs. Again he cut out the shoes in the evening, and again in the morning he found them all beautifully made.

So it went on. Whatever the shoemaker cut out at night was finished in the morning. Soon he was making plenty of money, and at last was becoming rich.

One evening, not long before Christmas, the shoemaker said to his wife:

"How would it be if we stayed up tonight and watched to see who is helping us?"

The wife agreed. She lighted a candle, and they hid behind some coats that were hanging in the corner. They waited and watched.

At midnight they saw two little men come in and seat themselves at the shoemaker's table. They had scarcely any clothes on. They took up the leather that was cut out and set to work with their nimble little fingers, stitching and hammering so quickly that the shoemaker's eyes could scarcely follow them. And they didn't stop until everything was finished and the shoes stood ready on the table. Then the little men jumped up and ran away.

The next day the wife said to her husband, "Those little men have made us rich, and we ought to do something for them. They must be very cold, running about without any clothes on. I'll tell you what we'll do. I will make them little shirts and vests and trousers, and knit each of them a pair of stockings, and you shall make each of them a pair of shoes."

The husband thought this was a good plan. Everything was made ready, and on Christmas eve the presents were laid out on the table instead of the usual work. Then the shoemaker and his wife hid in the corner where they could watch the little men.

When midnight came, the elves rushed in, ready to set to work. When they found instead of pieces of leather the neat little clothes laid ready for them, at first they were astonished and then they were delighted. Quickly they put on the pretty clothes, and as they dressed they sang:

> "We're well-dressed boys as all can see;
> No longer shoemakers are we!"

Then they skipped and danced about, jumping over chairs and tables, and at last they danced out at the door.

From that time they never came back, but all went well with the shoemaker, and he succeeded in everything he did.

PUCK'S SONG

William Shakespeare

Over hill, over dale,
  Through bush, through brier,
Over park, over pale,
  Through flood, through fire,
  I do wander everywhere,
  Swifter than the moone's sphere,
  And I serve the fairy queen,
  To dew her orbs upon the green.
  The cowslips tall her pensioners be;
  In their gold coats spots you see;
  Those be rubies, fairy favors,
  In those freckles live their savors;
I must go seek some dewdrops here,
And hang a pearl in every cowslip's ear.

THE GLASS HILL

ADAPTED BY *Jane McHenry*

ILLUSTRATED BY *Elise Morton*

ONCE there was a forest of great beauty, where often in the hush of night the nightingales sang and stirred sleepy smiles on the lips of those who slumbered. During the busy days great pine trees were felled, tied into rafts, and taken down the river to Holland. Of the scraps of wood, some of the forest people made charcoal, while others fashioned cuckoo clocks and toys.

Deep in the Black Forest (for this was its name) lived a charcoal burner who had three sons. Two were lazy, selfish oafs; but the youngest, Peter, was merry and industrious, with a heart of gold. They lived in a hut made of pine logs. The thatched roof hung low over the eaves. In a little wooden cage by the front door their pet linnet welcomed them each morning. When the day's work was done and the forest darkness pressed close, he sang a good-night song into the scented stillness.

Young Peter chopped the wood, fed the geese, and more often than not, did his brother's chores as well as his own. But though his hands were always busy, he hummed sprightly tunes and dreamed dreams.

Now the most remarkable thing about this part of the world was a hill—*a hill made entirely of glass!* It loomed like a giant bubble in the King's meadow just at the edge of the forest. Strangers emerging from the leafy darkness would exclaim,

"What wonder do we behold?" and, blinded for a moment, would rub their eyes.

All the woods people knew its purpose, even Peter. They had waited many years for the eighteenth birthday of the King's youngest daughter. For on that day, this is what was to happen —in fact, what *did* happen:

On the morning of her birthday the princess was with her handmaidens. A pine log whispered to itself on the hearth in her dressing room, while she rinsed her hands and face in scented water from a silver basin. She put on a satin gown the color of poppies and tied her hair in a net of gold. Then slowly she twirled about while the fluttering maids exclaimed, "Your Highness is bewitching!"

"Don't forget the golden apple!"

"Come, we shall keep your royal father waiting!" Then with a rustling of silks and shrill laughter and a tip-tapping of heels, they ran down the marble staircase.

Now the King had placed upon the summit of the glass hill a throne, delicately carved. On this the Princess was seated, holding an apple of solid gold. Long since it had been proclaimed that she was to marry the knight, who, clad in full armor and mounted upon a horse of his choice, could climb the glass hill and receive the golden apple from her own hand.

And since the great day had arrived, the people of the forest ceased their work. The meadow was teeming with townsfolk and countryfolk all in their gayest and best, craning, gaping, gazing, and shouting with impatience for the first rider to begin. The glass hill gleamed like a sheer wall of ice, and the assembled noblemen nervously paced their mounts.

All of this Peter's brothers watched. But Peter was at home watching the charcoal fires. They had to be constantly tended, sometimes for several days, lest all of their work be lost. A thick white smoke poured from the peak of the fire. The pine sticks could not burn too quickly, nor smother and go out. So poor Peter, smudged with soot, did not *dream* of seeing the wonderful tournament. He was busily piling sods and wet ashes on the fires, when suddenly a voice spoke to him.

"Son, may I trouble you for a drink of water?"

Peter turned on his heels and saw a bent old man. He had frightened the geese half out of their wits by his sudden, silent appearance.

"Now here's a silly, lost fellow on his way to the meet," thought the boy, but he politely bade him rest under a tree while he fetched him a drink from the well.

"The glass hill is but half a league away," Peter told him.

"Well, then why aren't you there?" cackled the old one, wiping his rusty mustache on a tattered green sleeve.

Peter laughed with some bitterness. "On what shall I ride, good Sir, a broom? And of what shall I make a coat of mail—stalks of grass?"

"Pray, look in the old toolshed yonder," answered the man.

"What nonsense be this?" mumbled Peter. His heavy boots clacked on the cobblestones as he crossed the court.

Then a most wonderful thing happened!

The old latch on the shed door lifted with a snap, quite by itself, and out trotted a shining roan stallion, saddled and bridled and carrying a suit, all of copper!

Peter leaped with joy!

Quickly he donned the armor and mounted the horse, while the old man said, "Now, Son, gallop as fast as you can to the meadow and try your luck. I shall tend your fires."

At that, the horse vaulted the gate and disappeared into the forest.

As they neared the clearing, Peter's heart pounded with excitement. The crystal arch shimmered beyond the tops of the ancient trees. With difficulty the crowds were held back. All of the nobles, men of high courage and honor, had failed!

Suddenly a strange copper-clad knight dashed past the sentries and headed straight for the shining slope. Up and up he went, while silence hung over the multitude. Halfway up, the horse's hoofs began to slip and chip on the glass, and he could

gain no further. The Princess leaned far out as if to help, but in a flash the horse turned, skimmed down the hill and vanished into the forest.

A tremendous cry went up! He had gone higher than all the others! The trumpeters trumpeted until their cheeks were purple and their feathered hats askew. But the handsome knight did not return. The little Princess privately prayed he would—next day . . !

That night, while a pot of porridge bubbled on the hearth, Peter's two brothers both talked at once, relating the curious story. Somehow Peter was drowsy and sad. He crawled up into his loft bed almost before they had finished.

"What a dull bumpkin that Peter is!" they snorted, shaking their heads.

On the following morning the two brothers left early to take the best places at the meet for themselves. Peter again watched the fires with no heart for a song. Yet a linnet trilled, the geese honked, and the world *seemed* merry enough.

Then, just as before, the old man appeared, requested a drink and sent Peter to the shed. *This* time, out pranced a horse as white as sea foam with brilliant trappings of silver! Peter lost no time in dressing himself and away they raced through the sun and shadow.

Again he arrived as the last rider descended. Spurring his horse, he sped toward the hill and went up and up and up and UP—nearly two-thirds of the way—close enough to catch sight of the Princess' face (with no line of scorn or vanity to mar its beauty). And he tried valiantly to reach the top! But, alas, the steed began to lose footing, and as before, it turned, descended, and swooped out of sight! By now, this knight was everyone's favorite, and they all sighed a mighty sigh. Poor King, poor Princess, and trumpeters, and people! But then, Peter felt even worse!

It was the third and final day of the trials. Word of the two previous days had brought spectators and contestants from the ends of the kingdom. Gaily hued groups moved toward the glass hill; vendors cried out, banners waved, dogs barked.

Alone in the forest, Peter hoped—and then, did not *dare* to—that the strange old man would help him again. He kicked stones, muttered, and squinted into the trees where a pine-needle path led into familiar darkness. Then, he heard the cackly voice before seeing its owner!

Peter was so happy, he fell over his own feet hastening to fill the dipper and hurrying to unlatch the shed. But again, the latch flew up of its own accord—right under his nose—and from the shadows stepped a great stallion, black as a thunderbolt!

Its nimble hoofs chinked on the cobblestones. The golden trappings jingled impatiently till Peter leaped to the saddle, gleaming from head to toe in a suit of purest gold. With the speed of wind they raced and swerved through the wood, and as they came into view, the light flashed upon them.

The crowd held its breath . . . and waited!

In a trice they covered the field, and as a great "Ah . . h!" arose from the crowd, they went up and up and UP AND UP AND UP—one-third, then two-thirds of the way. And now, since the hill had suffered so many riders, the surface was roughed just enough to carry the flashing, slashing hoofs to the VERY VERY TOP!

With a radiant smile the Princess tossed him the golden

apple. In a twinkling Peter caught it and dropped it into his shoe, for he needed both hands to manage his steed and at the same time whisk the waiting Princess right up onto his saddle.

She cried, "Oh, mercy!"—but she didn't really mean it!

A few moments later Peter placed her gently on the dais by the King. He then dismounted and bowed as mannerly as his armor would permit.

"Noble Lord," bellowed the beaming King, "you have won the Princess and half my kingdom!"

Peter, tall as a heron among tadpoles (almost!), kissed the Princess' hand.

"And now," spoke the King, thumping his royal chest, "since all my subjects are assembled and so handsomely dressed, I command that we celebrate the wedding this very day!"

And they did!

SONG FOR SUMMER

Elizabeth Coatsworth

I like birds, said the Dryad,
And the murmuring of the trees,
And the stars seen through dark branches,
And mumbling, tumbling bees,
I like the forest and its smells and its shadows,
I like all these.

And I like fish, said the Mermaid,
And the sharp rustle of waves,
And the branching shapes of corals
That grow on seamen's graves,
I like the wetness and the depth and the silence,
I like green caves.

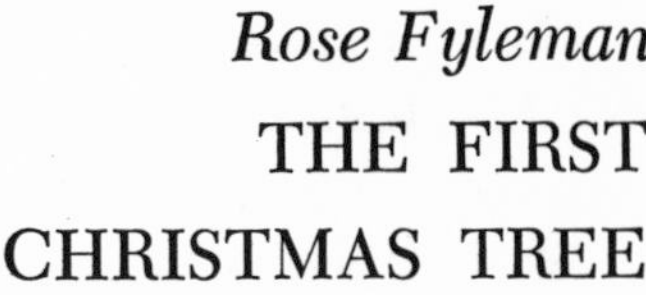

Rose Fyleman

THE FIRST CHRISTMAS TREE

ILLUSTRATED BY *Ruth van Tellingen*

THIS story of the First Christmas Tree was told me by the Fairy Queen herself, so you may be quite sure it is a true one. Here it is.

Once upon a time there lived in the middle of a forest a poor woodcutter.

He had one little daughter called Annis, whom he loved dearly. Annis was a dear little girl, kind and gentle.

She was very fond of all the woodland creatures, and they in turn knew and loved her well. The fairies loved her also. They used to dance on the top of the low stone wall that went round the little garden in front of the cottage.

"Annis! Annis!" they would call to her while she was busy helping her mother in the kitchen. But she would shake her head.

"I can't come. I'm busy," she would answer.

But at nighttime, when she was fast asleep under her red quilt, they would come tapping at the little window.

"Annis! Annis!"

Then she would slip out of bed and run quickly downstairs in her bare feet, and off with the fairies into the moonshining woods.

But the next day she was never sure whether it had been a dream or reality.

That was in the summer.

It was winter now and very cold. The sky was dark and heavy with coming snow.

Every evening, all through the winter, Annis would hang a little lantern with a candle in it on the small fir tree that grew just inside the garden gate. Her father could see it as he came home through the trees. It was a little, bright welcome for him, even before he reached home.

On Christmas Eve he went to work as usual. He came home for his dinner at midday and started back early. He was at work quite a long way off.

"I shall finish there today," he said to his wife as he left the house. "Then I shall come nearer home. If the snow comes, it will be difficult to find the way in the dark evenings."

And that very day the snow began. All the afternoon it fell in great, soft flakes.

Down, down, down. . . . It seemed as if the whole sky were falling in little bits.

The woodcutter worked hard in the fading light.

It was quite dark by the time he had finished, and he had to keep shaking the snow from his shoulders and from his old hat.

The wood was all neatly stacked in the little shed which had been built up there to house it.

He started off home with a sigh of relief, smiling to himself as he thought of his warm hearth and the bowl of hot porridge waiting for him on the hob, and of little Annis knitting in the chimney corner.

But presently—how it happened I know not, for he knew the forest well, and the snow had almost stopped falling, and the moon was shining—he found that he had lost his way.

He was quite cheerful at first. "In a minute I shall find the path again," he said. But many minutes passed, and he did not find it. A cloud came over the moon; the snow began to fall again more thickly. It was like a moving, whirling mist where the trees stood less close together.

The woodcutter began to lose heart.

Then, suddenly, he saw a light ahead of him on one of the fir trees.

"Can I be so near home?" he said, half-bewildered. But when he came near he found that it was not the fir tree in his own garden that was lit up, but an ordinary forest tree. Little lights twinkled and glittered on its branches, burning brightly and steadily in spite of the falling snow. The woodcutter rubbed his eyes. "Is this wicked magic?" he thought. But the lights burned more brightly than ever, and as he looked about he saw

in the distance another tree lit up in the same way. Then he understood.

"It is the good fairies helping me," he said, and trudged off cheerily in the direction of the second tree.

And when he looked back, the first one had already grown dark again. But when he reached the second tree, another was shining ahead to show him the way.

And so he went on from tree to tree until at last he was guided safely home to Annis's little lantern in his own garden.

And always after that he used to put lights on a little fir tree on Christmas Eve in memory of the time when the fairies saved him from being lost in the forest. And so the custom began, and because it was such a pretty one, and because the fairies so willed it, it spread, and today the fairy Christmas tree is to be found all over the world in houses where there are children and where the fairies come. . . .

Anne Pérez-Guerra

POPPY

ILLUSTRATED BY *Benton West*

POPPY was a fairy, a four-inch fairy, who had lost her way in the World of People. She never knew quite how it happened. All she could remember was that she awakened one morning in the fuzzy toe of a great big slipper.

But the slipper proved to be a very poor place to take a nap. For while Poppy was lying there, half awake and half asleep, five huge toes slid down and pushed her into the darkest corner of it. She squirmed and she wriggled, but she couldn't get out of their way. Finally, she took a sharp little nip with her tiny teeth from the very biggest toe.

"O-o-o-ow!" rumbled the loudest voice she had ever heard. The toes backed out, and two long fingers reached in after her.

Poppy stared up at an enormous creature who was dangling her by a tiny arm.

"Are—are you a giant?" she gasped.

"A Gentleman Giant," shouted the creature, trying to balance her on the end of a finger.

"Gentleman!" cried Poppy. "If you were a gentleman, you wouldn't hold me out here like this."

At that the Gentleman Giant laughed and let Poppy run down into the palm of his hand.

"And what are you, if I may ask?" he chuckled.

"I'm Poppy," she answered proudly.

"But how did you get here?" persisted the Gentleman Giant.

Poppy hung her head. "I—I forget," she said.

"Never mind," said the Gentleman Giant. "I know, the cat brought you in."

"That must have been it," agreed Poppy, "the cat brought me in."

She stood in his palm looking so serious that the Gentleman Giant shook with laughter. Poppy had to throw both arms about his thumb to keep from tumbling off.

"Wait till the kids see you," he roared.

"Kids?" repeated Poppy, with a puzzled expression in her wide black eyes. "What are they?"

"Children," replied the Gentleman Giant, lifting one of her wee red curls with a clumsy finger. "Don't you know what children are?"

"Are they as big as you are?" cried Poppy miserably.

"Not quite," laughed the Gentleman Giant.

"Maybe they'll eat me," wailed Poppy. And two shining tears ran down her pretty cheeks.

"Oh, no, no! Oh, my, no!" comforted the Gentleman Giant. "Eat you? Why, they'll be simply crazy about you."

He cradled her softly in his big hand. Poppy felt better. The Gentleman Giant seemed kind enough, and probably the children would be good to her. She hopped onto the dresser, and the Gentleman Giant gave her a tiny mirror to play with. But she amused herself by digging in a box of powder with a long nail file while he dressed.

Presently he had finished and was ready to go.

"Wouldn't you like to come down to breakfast with me?" he asked. "I suppose you eat occasionally."

"I'm really hungry," began Poppy, "but—"

"But what?"

"You're sure you won't put me in the soup?" she asked cautiously.

"Why, you poor little midget!" laughed the Gentleman Giant. "Are you as frightened as that?"

"Well, wouldn't *you* be frightened," demanded Poppy, "if someone as big as you are hauled somebody as little as I am out of a slipper, and you were the little somebody?"

"It's very likely," admitted the Gentleman Giant seriously. "But you needn't be afraid, little Poppy-seed. I'll take care of you. We aren't giants. We are people, and people never hurt fairies. And would you believe it? I never saw a fairy before!"

"*Never before?*" asked Poppy, brushing her tears away with a wee fist.

"Never before," affirmed the Gentleman Giant.

So they went downstairs together.

Poppy was still rather bewildered and frightened as the Gentleman Giant put her on the table beside the cream pitcher. Three pairs of eyes turned upon her. They seemed to grow larger as she watched them, until there wasn't one of them smaller than her own curly head.

"Daddy," cried one of the little girls, "where did you find her?"

"In my slipper," replied the Gentleman Giant, as if he were accustomed to finding a fairy in his bedroom slipper every morning of the week.

"But how did she get there?" asked the little girl.

"Oh, I know," cried Poppy, eagerly, "the cat brought me in."

The three children giggled, and the boy who sat next to the Gentleman Giant looked as if he didn't believe it at all.

"Well, it *did*," repeated Poppy, turning up her saucy little nose. "The Gentleman Giant said so."

"Gentleman Giant!" shrieked the boy. "Ha, ha, ha! Who's that?"

Poppy pointed a wee finger at the Gentleman Giant, and the children laughed more heartily than ever.

"And is she going to stay here?" gasped the smaller girl, who was so excited that she had not even begun to eat her breakfast.

"That is up to you," replied the Gentleman Giant. "I fancy she will stay as long as you are kind to her."

"Oh, but we will be!" exclaimed the little girl, clapping her hands. "We will be, and she can live in the dollhouse."

"We shall have to make some new furniture for it," suggested the other girl.

"She is just the right size to ride in my mechanical train," volunteered the boy who had laughed at her.

"Right now," interrupted the Gentleman Giant, "I think she would like a bite to eat. How about it, Poppity?"

Poppy smiled a little half-smile. They did seem to like her, even if they had laughed at her.

Ellen, who was the older girl, went to the dollhouse and came back with a tiny green table and chair. Poppy was delighted; they fitted her exactly. Ellen placed the little table and chair right on the big table, so that everyone could see Poppy while she ate.

Amy, who had disappeared, returned presently with a beautiful little salt dish. In it there was a slice of banana for Poppy's breakfast. It made a rather large bowl for the little fairy, but it was the smallest dish in the house. Poppy was fascinated with her new bowl; for it was decorated with tiny blue forget-me-nots and wee pink rosebuds. She was given a piece of toothpick for a spoon, and she began to dig out bits of the banana in a very awkward manner. Poppy would have preferred using her fingers, but nobody else did; so she continued to use the toothpick.

She was getting along very nicely when the children cried, "Look, Mumsey, look!"

A tall woman was standing in the doorway, staring at Poppy.

"Daddy found her in his slipper," explained Amy.

"But—but how in the world—" began Mumsey. She stopped right there, too much astonished to believe her eyes.

Poppy took a mouthful of banana.

"I dode thig id badders," she sighed, "how I cabe. I reedy dode."

She paused a moment to swallow the banana. "I thought the cat brought me in. The Gentleman Giant said it did. But they laughed," she waved her toothpick at the grinning children, "so maybe it didn't. I don't know how I came."

She went on eating.

"You're not sorry you're here, are you, Poppy?" asked the Gentleman Giant.

"Not if you like me," replied Poppy. "I'd love to stay as long as you like me."

"*Like* you," echoed the children. "We'll do anything to keep you here—anything."

And Poppy knew that they meant it!

Amy had spent the entire day making nightgowns for Poppy. They were simple affairs, cut out of bits of soft silk and fine cotton which the little girl had gathered from the scrap bag.

Poppy watched Amy patiently sewing up the tiny seams, and she *did* wish she could help. It looked as if it would be fun to sew.

She tried on each nightgown as it was finished; then she folded it neatly and put it in the little pill box that Amy had given to her. There was one that Poppy liked particularly. Its soft pale green folds hung so beautifully that she spent a long time strutting up and down in front of her little pocket mirror admiring herself.

Poppy had never given any thought to clothing. It had been unnecessary in Fairyland, where a new dress meant simply a matter of begging a couple of petals from a hollyhock. But there was nothing individual about a hollyhock dress, for any fairy in Fairyland could have one exactly like it.

Poppy took off the little green nightie, smoothed out the wrinkles, and lovingly folded it. She would wear it that very night.

"How many have I now?" she asked, as Amy gave her the last one and began picking up the scraps and threads.

"Six," replied Amy. "Can't you count? That's quite enough for anyone as small as you are."

"I love you, Amy," said Poppy suddenly. "Do you really want me to stay with you?"

"What a silly question!" exclaimed Amy. "Of course I do. Do you think I would sew all day for you if I didn't? You little darling!"

"Now are you going to show me the dollhouse?" asked Poppy excitedly.

"Oh, yes, I'd forgotten," cried Amy. "Hop into this box, and I'll take you up right this minute."

Poppy climbed into the box and sat down on top of all the new nighties, and upstairs they went.

"Oh!" she exclaimed, as Amy put her down in front of a pretty little house. "Is this it?"

"This is it," replied Amy, "and you may just wander around and look at everything. I'm going downstairs a minute to show these nightgowns to Mumsey."

Poppy roamed through the tiny hall and into the living room. There was a piano, a sofa, some chairs, and a table.

She ran to the piano and touched the keys. They made no sound. They were not keys at all.

The very first chair she sat in collapsed! When she looked at it closely, she saw that it was made of paper.

"I wonder if it is all like this!" sighed Poppy, wandering from room to room.

The dining room was practically empty, because she was using the table and one chair in the family dining room. The stove in the kitchen looked all right until you came close to it, and then you just knew that you couldn't have a fire in it and cook anything.

The stairway was a dangerous affair, but Poppy ran up it so swiftly that it didn't have time to fall through.

She looked into the bedroom. The drawers in the dresser were merely lines drawn there to look like drawers. Here, too, the chairs were paper. The bed was as hard as stone, being a metal affair with no mattress.

The bathroom was somewhat better than the rest of the house, but the tub threatened to tip over when she climbed in. Nor was there any water, though perhaps Ellen or Amy would bring that when she needed it.

But the whole thing was such a tremendous disappointment that Poppy threw herself on the floor and cried and cried.

Amy found her there when she came back.

"Why, Poppy darling, what is the matter?" she cried. "Don't you like it?"

"No, I don't," wailed Poppy. "The piano won't play, and I sat in a chair and it broke right down, and the mirror in the dresser isn't a mirror at all. It's just a piece of shiny paper, and it makes me look all wrinkly. I don't want to live in the dollhouse."

"Then, you don't have to live in the dollhouse, precious," consoled Amy, softly. "I forgot that it was made for dolls and not for fairies."

It was nighttime. Amy had scoured the house for something out of which she could make a bed for Poppy. She had tested ever so many things, but like the beds of the Father Bear and the Mother Bear, they were either too hard or too soft. She couldn't seem to find anything that was just right.

"Oh," she cried, suddenly. "I know something."

"What?" asked Poppy, with enthusiasm.

"The rubber bath sponge. It's flat and smooth and soft and springy, just like a real bed. It's just the right size, too."

Amy ran to the bathroom and returned with it. She squeezed it together, and then Poppy bounced up and down on it.

"How it is?" asked Amy eagerly.

"Just right," announced Poppy, out of breath.

"I'll get a hot-dish holder from the kitchen for a mattress and two of my little white linen handkerchiefs for sheets. But what can you use for a pillow?"

Amy looked all around the room.

"The pincushion is too hard and too big. A sachet is too smelly. You wouldn't like that—"

"Oh, yes," interrupted Poppy. "I used to sleep in a rose."

"Really?" said Amy. "Then I'll get the green one."

"To match my green nightie," beamed Poppy, and she danced a fairy jig.

"These little squares of white wool will make beautiful blankets," went on Amy, spreading them over the bed, "and tomorrow I shall buttonhole all around the edges with green silk thread. Do you want to take a bath, Poppy? We always do."

"Well—" Poppy hesitated. She was thinking of that rickety little bathtub in the dollhouse.

"Oh," said Amy, guessing her thoughts. "You don't have to take it in that old tub. I know it tips and spills everything. I'll find something better. We used to have a canary, and you could use the little tub that he had. I'll get it."

Poppy began taking off her little garments. They looked old and stringy to her now. She hoped that Amy or Ellen would make her some new ones. They had such pretty dresses themselves that they might be ashamed of hers.

"Look, Poppy!" Amy stood in the doorway. "I couldn't find the bird's bathtub, but Mumsey gave me this. Isn't it lovely?"

She held up, for Poppy to see, a most beautiful little glass bowl. It was oval in shape and edged in gold, and the inside was decorated with lovely little flower sprays, painted in very delicate colors.

"Beautiful!" gasped Poppy. There were advantages in being only four inches tall! Certainly no one in all the world could have as beautiful a bathtub as she had.

Amy filled it with sparkling water and placed it beside the candle on the bedside table. She brought two soap flakes from the box on the bathroom shelf and gave them to Poppy, who was already splashing happily in her lovely tub.

"Don't do that, Poppy, you'll get your hair wet!" exclaimed Amy anxiously, as Poppy held up the tiny washcloth and squeezed it over her head. "It takes too long to dry."

"I don't care," giggled Poppy. "I don't have to go right to bed, do I?"

"No," replied Amy. "I suppose not right away, but what do you expect to do?"

"Oh, I don't know, but it wouldn't matter if my hair did get wet. It dries fast because there is such a little bit of it. I used to sleep in a rose. When it rained, I never worried."

"Then I won't, either," laughed Amy. "Could I help you?"

Poppy looked at Amy's hands and shook her head. "Not until I have to get out," she said. She dried herself on a scrap of towel, and Amy helped her get into her little green nightie.

"Well, how is Poppy tonight?" rumbled someone from the doorway.

"Come and see my bed," called Poppy to the Gentleman Giant. She jumped upon it and began springing up and down. The fact that she was but four inches tall made not a speck of difference in her fun. By the time she had finished exercising, the whole family had gathered to watch her.

Amy seized her wriggling little body and wrapped her in a blanket.

"I can't tell you how much we love you, Poppy. I'm so happy that you want to stay with us," she said softly.

"And I love you, too," whispered Poppy. "I'm not afraid of you any more."

Poppy slept very well on the bath sponge. It was soft and cushiony, and her little body sank into it as if it were a featherbed.

When she awoke in the morning, she sat up and looked for Amy, but Amy's bed was empty. Poppy rubbed her eyes. This wasn't fair, she thought. Amy should have called her. Her clothes had been taken away, and there she was in a nightgown with nothing else to put on. She took a tremendous leap from the edge of the table down to Amy's bed, hoping she could get to the floor from there.

She walked around on the bed, stumbling over the wrinkles in the sheets and blankets. Then she noticed that the cane panels in the end of the bed reached nearly to the floor. She swung around to the other side, and down she went, hand under hand, till she came to the bottom and dropped to the floor. Trailing her little nightie, which was much too long to walk in comfortably, she went out into the upper hall.

"Yooo-o-o hoo-o-o!" she called, but her little voice seemed to run in a small circle around her head. "Yoo-o-o hoo-o-o-o!" she called again.

"It's Poppy," she heard someone say, and Ellen bounded up the stairs.

"Why didn't you call me when you were getting up?" asked Poppy, accusingly.

"Well, you see, precious," began Ellen picking her up, "Amy and I had to get up early because we wanted to make you a new dress before breakfast."

"Oh!" exclaimed Poppy with shining eyes. "Is that why?"

Ellen ran downstairs with Poppy in her hand.

"Where is my new dress?" asked Poppy, with her usual impatience. "What color is it?"

"Green," answered Amy. "You look so sweet in green with those little red curls of yours."

"Let me put it on!" cried Poppy when she saw it. "Let me put it on. How did you know it would fit me?"

There were new undergarments and a dainty little petticoat. Poppy slipped them on and danced a fairy fling around the table top, over the embroidered cloth, and under the lamp.

"Shall we have breakfast now?" asked Ellen.

"I forgot about eating," confessed Poppy, "with this new dress 'n' everything."

"Do you like cornflakes?" asked Ellen.

"Of course," replied Poppy, trying to tie a bit of green ribbon to one of her curls. "What are they?"

Ellen laughed.

"How do you know you like them, if you don't know what they are?"

"Do *you* like them?" asked Poppy.

"Of course I do," said Ellen.

"Well, I like everything you do," replied Poppy.

The table was set with the same dishes as before, and Poppy ran around to see what each person was having for breakfast. Her own little table was under a large bouquet of sweet peas; so when her curiosity was satisfied, she sat down before her own meal.

On her plate, which was the wee glass cover of a candy jar, were two very large cornflakes and a sweet green grape.

Poppy bit into the grape, which was a breakfast in itself for her. She found it rather awkward and asked Ellen to cut it for her. When Ellen brought it back, it looked exactly like a tiny melon cut in half, with the seeds removed. Poppy attacked it with her toothpick spoon. She enjoyed every mouthful.

The cornflakes were delicious. She loved their crisp crunchiness, but after eating an entire grape, she could eat only one of them. So Amy washed the little glass plate, put the remaining cornflake on it, and set it away in the cupboard for Poppy's lunch.

"Dear, dear!" wailed Poppy one morning. "Ellen has forgotten to take me off the mantel, and now she has gone to school, and Mumsey isn't anywhere about. What shall I ever do?"

She stood on the very edge of the mantel and looked down. The distance to the floor was so great that she would most certainly be killed if she jumped, and Poppy didn't want to be killed. She didn't even want to be hurt.

Two minutes later, she had forgotten her troubles and was having a very gay time sliding down the smooth, shining side of the mahogany mantel clock. That she was scratching it up frightfully made not the slightest difference to her. She was having more fun than she had had in a long time. She did find it a bit difficult to climb up each time, but the long thrilling slide was worth the effort.

When she grew tired of that, she played pirate in the antique ship model. Here she could not do quite so much damage, as the scratches didn't show at all. Nevertheless the Gentleman Giant would not have approved of her game.

But, after all, being a pirate isn't so very much fun when you have to play alone, so Poppy began to look for other amusement. In the back of the clock was a door, and because it was open a tiny crack, she couldn't resist one little peep inside. Before her towered the most beautiful wheels and wires and springs that she had ever set eyes on.

She caught the pendulum as it swung by and rode back and forth a few times. Above her head was a brass plate with odd-shaped windows in it, covering the works of the clock. As the pendulum swung past, Poppy caught the bottom of this and climbed up. From her perch on the top of it, she could look over this fascinating machinery to better advantage.

She began to investigate, touching things here and there. One little wheel turned quite swiftly. Another she could turn with her busy little hands—and she did. One she could not move at all. Behind her was a large heavy spring, on which rested a little hammer. Poppy tried to lift the hammer, but one end of it was attached somewhere and it dropped on the spring. To Poppy's great delight the clock struck one. But no little mouse ran down. Poppy lifted the hammer again, and the clock struck two.

By the time the clock had struck fifteen rather haphazardly, Mumsey stood before it with a puzzled frown on her forehead.

It couldn't be out of order. It had been put in first-class condition only a month before. What on earth had happened to it?

The clock struck sixteen. A happy little giggle came from the interior, and Mumsey knew at once what was the matter with the clock.

"Poppy!" she cried. "What are you doing?"

"I'm waiting for you, Mumsey," replied Poppy. "Listen."

The clock struck seventeen.

"Poppy," cried Mumsey impatiently. "Stop that this minute and come right down. Do you hear?"

"Yes, Mumsey," said Poppy obediently, "I'm coming." And she started to climb down. "Oh, help me, I'm caught," she cried, as her little dress caught on a screw and refused to let go.

Mumsey unhooked it and lifted her out of the clock.

"You listen to me, Poppy," she scolded. "That isn't the place for you to play, and I don't want you ever to go into the clock again. Do you understand?"

"Yes, Mumsey," said Poppy in a wee, small voice. "But what can I do?"

"Well, we'll find something. I think a tea party would be fun. Would you like a cake crumb and some milk?"

"Oh, Mumsey," cried Poppy. "You are so nice to me, even

when I'm naughty. But I didn't know I shouldn't play in the clock, and I didn't know where you were."

"That's all right, Poppy, as long as you never do it again. Promise me you won't."

"I won't," promised Poppy. And she kept her word.

It was a busy morning, and Mumsey was making gingerbread. Poppy sat beside the mixing bowl on the cover of the baking-powder can. She hated sitting still.

"May I wash this spoon, Mumsey?" she begged. "I want to help."

"But I am not through with that spoon yet, Poppy. When I am, you may wash it," answered Mumsey.

Suddenly Poppy scrambled off from her seat and picked up a speck of something from the table. It looked good, so she popped it into her mouth.

"Oh, oh, oh, oh!" she cried. "Give me a drink, quick, Mumsey! I'm burning."

"Poppy," scolded Mumsey. "You tasted that ginger and I told you not to." She patiently stopped her mixing and gave Poppy a drink. Before she had finished, the doorbell rang, and she had to leave the kitchen.

Poppy waited impatiently for her return, but the time went very slowly. She began to build a stairway to the top of the lard pail, so that she could see what was in it.

First she pulled up the raisin box; then she pushed up the ginger jar; then, the empty soda box. This she turned over on its side to make it just the right height. There! She had the nicest little stairs right up to the top, and she lost no time in flying up them.

Before her lay a sea of snowy whiteness.

"Wouldn't it be fun to jump into that," she cried, clapping her hands, and in she jumped.

And there she stuck!

She could lift one foot at a time, but not both. It was awful. What would Mumsey say now?

"Poppy!" Mumsey stood in the doorway, shaking her head at the sight. "What am I *ever* going to do with you? You get into more mischief in two minutes than a puppy gets into in a year."

"Please take me out of here," begged Poppy. "I didn't know what it was. It looked so soft and white that I just jumped in. Ugh, what a mess!"

"This means another bath, I suppose," said Mumsey, lifting her out onto a plate. "Poppy, will you never learn to mind your own business?"

"But you aren't going to feed me to the cat, are you?" pleaded Poppy. "Really, Mumsey, I do try to be good, but I just do things before I think."

Mumsey smiled in spite of her impatience. "No," she said, "I am not going to feed you to the cat."

She dropped a few soap flakes into the nearest sauce dish and filled it with warm water.

"Now, you wash all that lard off, Miss Midget, while I get you some clean clothes."

Poppy stripped off her greasy little garments, left them in a heap on the plate and jumped into the nice warm suds. She sang a pert little song and used her shirt for a washcloth.

That gave her an idea. She reached over the side of her tiny tub and pulled in all her clothes.

"I'll wash them," she announced to herself, "and maybe Mumsey will forgive me." She hummed busily and soused her tiny gown up and down in the suds. She swished her wee petticoat around so energetically that the water splashed overboard on all sides.

"Mercy!" shrieked Mumsey. "Poppy, stop that this minute. If you weren't so little, I'd spank you."

"But what have I done, Mumsey?" asked the bewildered Poppy. "I'm only washing my clothes. I'm trying to help."

"Well, if you are trying to help, for goodness' sake, stop it and do something else." Mumsey's patience was completely gone.

"I'll wipe up the water," offered Poppy.

"You needn't," snapped Mumsey. "You might start sliding and break your little neck." She sopped up the spilled suds with the dishcloth.

"What shall I do, then?" asked Poppy, looking very penitent. "I'm all washed, and I really don't want to make any more work for you."

"Dress yourself. I've put your clothes on the other end of the table, and here is a towel." She handed Poppy a small scrap of an old washcloth and helped her out of her tub.

"And here's a raisin, and a lump of brown sugar for a tea party. When you get dressed, take them in to your little table, and please, oh please, stay away from my kitchen. I'll never get anything done, if you bother me again this morning."

The days flew by for Poppy, because she was so busy discovering things. But she never could learn to keep out of mischief. The children grew fonder of her every day and tried to do everything she wished them to do. If she wanted candy, they gave her huge pieces. They even taught her to chew gum. But when Mumsey noticed that Poppy wasn't eating her meals properly, she scolded the children soundly for giving her candy.

"The very idea!" she exclaimed. "Do you want to make her sick, giving her two big chocolates at once!"

After that, Poppy didn't like Mumsey quite so well; for the candy was given her in pieces the size of a bean, and it didn't last half long enough.

The Gentleman Giant was much nicer. Once he gave her a whole peanut, and it didn't make her the least bit sick, as Mumsey had said it would. Of course, she could taste it long after she had eaten it, and that wasn't as pleasant as it might have been.

Jack was a terrible tease, but sometimes he was so nice to her that she could almost forgive him for his pranks. Most of the time, however, he was hatching up some sort of trick to play on her.

Once he put Poppy into a fruit jar and didn't let her out until she cried, and another time he fastened her to the chandelier, with the chain that came off Amy's little pocketbook, and left her hanging there for half an hour. And half an hour is an eternity to a four-inch fairy.

But Poppy liked to think of the nice things that he did for her, for sometimes he honestly did try to make her happy. He gave her wild rides in his electric train and even let her whirl around the track astride the engine, clinging fast to the smokestack. She played in his little racer without even asking, and he made marvelous palaces for her out of his stone blocks.

At such times Amy or Ellen would dress her in the garments of a little queen, and they would set up the entire army of leaden soldiers to guard her castle. The children pretended to be giants who owned the neighboring kingdoms.

Jack would build wonderful towers and bridges with his construction toys, and what grand fun they would all have!

Amy and Ellen were like two little mothers. They saw that Poppy had a bath each night and tucked her into bed. It used to worry them that she had no toothbrush, but since they could not ever find anything small enough to substitute, they finally stopped thinking any more about it.

They washed her little clothes in their toy washing machine, which was a real electric one that Aunt Jane had given them for Christmas. They rinsed them in their little tubs and wrung them through a wee wringer into a little wicker clothesbasket. Then they would stretch a line between two chairs and hang them up to dry.

Poppy often helped. If they put her right into the tub with the clothes, she could rinse them, otherwise she couldn't reach. But Amy or Ellen always hung the line too high for her to hang them up.

"Don't you wish—" began Ellen one day, while they were busily at work with the washing, "don't you wish that it took as little material to make our dresses as it takes to make Poppy's?"

"We'd have a lot more," agreed Amy.

"Oh, well," said Ellen, "we don't need as many."

"I should say we don't," exclaimed Amy. "Poppy is always losing or spoiling something. Is this the dress you wore when you fell in the molasses?" Amy held up a sticky little wad.

Poppy nodded. She hoped they wouldn't scold about that

again. It was entirely accidental, as was everything that happened to her. She was sorry, but that didn't help after it was done.

"It was one of your best, too," sighed Amy. "It took me longer to make that than it did any other dress that you have."

"Won't it come out?" asked Poppy.

"We can try. Oh, I suppose it will. Yes, it is," said Amy, washing it all the while she was talking.

Poppy breathed more easily. The whole thing would very likely be forgotten, now that the molasses had come out of the dress.

"Why can't I learn to sew?" she asked.

"Mercy!" exclaimed Amy. "With a needle as big as a sword!" She stopped her rinsing in consternation.

"We can do all the sewing that needs to be done," said Ellen, maternally. "All you need to do is play."

"And that *is* all I do," sighed Poppy.

Poppy was in jail. She had been so very, very mischievous that out of sheer self-preservation Mumsey had turned the colander over on top of her. It wasn't such a very bad prison, really. It had plenty of air holes, and she could see out of any

one of them. In fact, Poppy was quite enjoying her captivity.

Mumsey had been kind enough to put in a few things for her to play with, such as the small celluloid duck, and the little hammock, and a very tiny doll, which in spite of its smallness was half as tall as Poppy herself.

The holes in the colander let in the light and made a hundred little round dots on the floor of her prison. At least, Poppy had counted a hundred. Then, too, she could talk to Mumsey just as well as if she were right out where Mumsey was. And even though Mumsey didn't answer most of the time, she could talk *at* her, and there was so much to talk about.

"Mumsey, could I have my clay to play with?" she asked, after Mumsey had been silent for a long time.

"Anything to stop your chatter," answered Mumsey, though she knew that nothing short of a miracle could do that, and she brought Poppy a lump of clay.

"Thank you, Mumsey," said Poppy, and she began to punch holes in it with her little fists. This side, that side, and all around the top she pounded, until the lump looked like a piece of Swiss cheese.

Then Poppy had an idea. She was always getting ideas, but this one was particularly good. It had come to her when she discovered that by plastering a large handful of clay over one of the holes in the side of the colander, one of the little white dots disappeared from the floor of her prison. If she could fill all the holes, there wouldn't be any little white dots left. She could make it just like night. So, dropping everything else, she proceeded with the idea.

"One, four, seven," counted Poppy, though it really made only three. "Two, eleven, six," she went on. "Eight, twenty-one, thirty," and that made nine.

It was hard work. Clay was heavy, especially when you had to lift it high over your head. Besides, she had smeared so much of it on her dress that she felt as if she weighed a pound. But the work was progressing, and she didn't want to stop until she had finished. The interior was getting darker and darker.

Just a little circle of dots remained on the floor, and they came through the holes in the top, the very top. Try as she might, Poppy could not reach them.

"Oh, well," she sighed, "I did all I could." And because she was tired, she dropped into the little hammock beside the tiny doll and fell asleep.

"I might have known," said Mumsey, half an hour later, as she tried desperately to get the clay out of the holes in the colander, "I might have known that you would make me more work than usual, if I tried to stop you."

Poppy, still asleep from exhaustion, didn't hear, but she felt, in her own busy little soul, that she had accomplished a good morning's work.

"I wish you didn't have to go to school every day," said Poppy one morning, while the children were eating breakfast. "I get so lonesome. I wish you could stay home and play with me."

"So do we," said Ellen, "but if we did, we'd never learn anything."

"Why—" began the Gentleman Giant, and Poppy put down her toothpick spoon to listen, "why don't you youngsters get busy and build a playground for Poppy? Give the poor little midget something to do while you are away. It's no wonder she gets lonesome."

"We never thought of it," confessed Ellen.

"It could be on the window seat," suggested Amy, "and she could have a sand pile and a swing and everything, just like a regular playground."

"I could make a sliding board for her," said Jack enthusiastically, "and a teeter-totter."

"But I haven't anybody to teeter with," interrupted Poppy, and everybody laughed.

"Well, she could have a little swimming pool and all sorts of things to play on," said Ellen.

"That's it," said the Gentleman Giant. "I see Mumsey looks pleased."

"She'll be glad to have me out of her way," said Poppy meekly, feeling rather uncomfortable.

When Jack came home that night, he had a small box in his hand.

"What is it?" asked Amy and Ellen together.

"Nothing for you," he replied loftily. "It's for Poppy," and Poppy was brought to the window seat to unwrap a box of the tiniest blocks the girls had ever seen. There were dozens of them, all shapes and sizes. Poppy was delighted.

"Now I can build things for myself," she announced happily, and she settled down to work busily, filling the little truck that had come from the ten-cent store.

The children laughed at her industry. But that was the beginning of the playground. Night after night, when he came home from school, Jack worked at the little sliding board, and the swing and trapeze, and the horizontal bars, smoothing and painting them until they fairly shone.

Sometimes Poppy went to the basement with him to watch the work that went on, but more often not. She was such a nuisance! Once she stepped on a drop of glue and couldn't budge until Jack had washed his hands and pulled her off again. Another time she stumbled over a shaving and fell on a piece of sandpaper, scratching her little knees. Jack found that he could accomplish a great deal more, if Poppy remained upstairs.

"It is no wonder Mumsey wanted something to keep Poppy busy while we are gone," he sputtered to himself. "If she is as much bother to her as she is to me, I don't see how she ever gets anything done."

They made a bathing pool for Poppy out of Mumsey's best white-enamel cake pan, promising Mumsey that if she ever really needed the pan at any time, she might take it.

"It looks exactly like tile," said Amy.

"I wish I were Poppy," said Ellen. "Then I could have a playground all my own."

"Don't you think we could build her a little dressing room out of blocks?" asked Amy.

"Oh, let's do," cried Ellen, "and paint it white."

With a tube of strong glue, they put a little house together out of blocks, laying them up in rows and rows, just like bricks. They left a little window and a door and made steps for the tiny porch. When they had finished, they stood back to admire their work.

"Isn't it darling?" sighed Amy.

"Jack isn't the only one who can make things," said Ellen. "I'm going to get the paint."

"Look, Mumsey," cried Amy as her mother came into the room. "This is the little dressing room that we made to stand beside the swimming pool. Isn't it dear?"

"No white paint," announced Ellen, returning. "But I thought green would do as well, so I brought it. This is the kind that dries in half an hour."

They stirred it well, and with a little brush that kept shedding its hairs, they painted the little house.

"I think it is just as cunning as it can be," said Amy, for the fortieth time. "Shall we show it to Poppy now, or shall we wait until it is dry?"

"Oh, wait until it is dry," cried Ellen. "She has on her best dress, and you know Poppy! She'd be covered with green paint before we could say 'Jack Robinson.'"

"Are you ready, Poppy?" called Amy. "It is dinnertime."

Amy put her on the table in her customary place. Poppy squinted at the meal laid out on her own little table. There was one very large red bean, two grains of cooked rice that had been dipped in butter, a very tiny square of crisp, crisp bacon, and a little leaf from the very heart of a crisp head of lettuce.

As she had been taught that it was not polite to begin eating until everyone had been seated at the table, Poppy sat for a moment, waiting for the rest of the family.

Suddenly the doorbell rang noisily, and voices told her that company had arrived unexpectedly. She waited and she waited, but Mumsey and the girls kept right on talking, apparently having forgotten her. Finally, she concluded that it would be all right to forget them, too, and have her own dinner.

"I hate beans," she sputtered, and with great care she dropped the large red bean into Jack's soup. With a grain of

rice in each hand, she approached Amy's bowl. Here she threw one. The other she bestowed upon the Gentleman Giant.

"They'll never notice," she giggled, "and they'll think I ate them. Now, I'll have a sandwich."

Carefully she pried open a little oyster cracker, smeared it with butter, and inserted the bacon and the lettuce leaf. It was a flat-tasting sandwich, however. So Poppy stood beside Amy's tomato salad and dug out little bits of it with her toothpick spoon to accompany her lunch. It made a vast improvement.

As yet, no one had appeared at the table. There was still much noise coming from the direction of the living room and hall.

Poppy was never long in finding something to do. With an air of unconcern, she started marching around the table. Her march was halted by the observation that olives looked very much like little green footballs. She picked one up, with some difficulty to be sure, and attempted to roll it over the table. It rolled very well, but slowly, and Poppy wanted speed. For excitement, she lifted the olive to the edge of the cream pitcher and dropped it in. It made the most delightful splash. She dropped in another. This brought the cream up so high that she thought it best to stop.

Next Poppy climbed the mound of celery, much as most

children scrambled over a woodpile, except that she got her dress wet instead of dirty; for there were still drops of water on the celery. In jumping off the celery plate, she bumped into the electric percolator which was terribly hot, and she burned her little arm.

"*OOOO-oooooo!*" she whispered. For if she cried aloud, some one would be sure to hear her and come running. Quick as a flash, Poppy smeared a handful of butter on the burn. She had seen Mumsey put butter on her hand once when she had burned it.

The burn put an end to heavy activity. However, with her other arm Poppy placed an oyster cracker in Amy's soup and watched it grow. This was quite fascinating. It grew to twice its normal size. When it had stopped swelling, Poppy threw in another.

"You rascal," cried Amy, bursting through the doorway. "I thought you would get into mischief, if you were left alone. I know where you'd better be, and that's in bed. I wonder what Mumsey will say when she sees how you've tracked butter all over the tablecloth. Mercy! It is even in your hair. Oh, oh, oh! Whatever did you do to your arm?"

"I burned it," replied Poppy, hanging her head and feeling very much ashamed. "I bumped into the coffeepot."

"Oh, you poor little angel," crooned Amy, "and to think I scolded you! You'll forgive me, won't you?"

And Poppy was taken up to bed.

"Is the company going to stay for supper?" she asked, when her arm had been bandaged and she was tucked in between the cool sheets.

"Oh, no," said Amy. "Why?"

"Just because," answered Poppy. "I don't like company. I always get into trouble when they come."

Mumsey had a birthday. Aside from the beautiful cake which he sent home from the bakery, the Gentleman Giant brought her a quaint little Japanese garden in a bowl.

Poppy didn't quite understand what a birthday was. She never remembered having any herself. Years didn't mean much in Fairyland, where nobody ever was really old.

Since there was room on the broad window seat for both the garden and Poppy's playground, the bowl was placed there the next day. When Poppy saw it so near at hand, she thought that naturally there would be no objection to her playing in it, and she climbed up onto the mossy ground.

"Now I can play giant," she giggled, softly stepping all around. "I wish I had someone to play with."

There was a tiny little pond in the middle of the garden. Its sides were all lined with pebbles. Poppy pulled off her shoes and stockings and stuck a wriggling pink toe into the glassy water. It had been warmed by the sunshine that came through the window, and she went in wading. There wasn't much space for wading, really. It was just a little pond, no bigger than the cover of a fruit jar. But it was great fun, and she played with the tiny brown boat that had a little fisherman in it.

Then it occurred to Poppy that things might be arranged a bit differently. For instance, the houses were too far apart, and there wasn't even a path between them. Besides, they were on opposite sides of the pond. With much work she pushed one over the least little bit, and finding it terribly hard to move, she tried the other. And with the first shove, over it went!

Not over toward the other house, but over on its poor little windows. The house fell upon a slender little bird who had been standing rather uncertainly on one red leg.

Poppy sighed disgustedly and stood him up on his one leg again. She tried to lift the house, but she couldn't. It was far too heavy, for the house was as high as she was. To lift a house as big as one's self, is no small task.

"Well, anyway," thought Poppy, "at least I can make the path. But what does one make paths of?"

Poppy sat down upon the delicate little bridge that spanned the pond and felt more like a giant than ever. Paths in real gardens are sometimes made of cinders, Poppy remembered. But then she hadn't any cinders.

"But I have sand," she said, and she scrambled over to her little playground and filled her wee apron with it. The sand was a heavy load, but somehow she managed to get it back to the garden and scatter it along in a straggling path.

The sand didn't go very far, so she went back after another load. And that didn't go much farther, so Poppy brought two more apronfuls. By the time she had scattered the last handful in the moss, she was too tired to get any more. So she sat down in front of the little tipped-over house and rested. The moss was soft. Poppy pulled some of it into a little pillow and lay down. She was so very comfortable that she went to sleep.

Poppy didn't even wake up when Ellen lifted her gently and put her into the little hammock that swung between two poles in the playground. Poor Ellen! She could have cried at the wreck Poppy had made of Mumsey's beautiful garden.

Ellen set the little house right side up and straightened the trellis that Poppy had put in crooked. The sand was a frightful problem, and it was almost impossible to get it out of the moss. But after picking out what she could, Ellen blew out a great deal more. The garden looked almost as good as new, now. Maybe Mumsey wouldn't notice anything wrong.

"You little mischief," Ellen whispered to Poppy, who slept soundly. "Don't you ever get into Mumsey's garden again."

And when Poppy awoke, she honestly thought she never *had* been in it!

The very next day, Poppy was accidentally shut up in the icebox. For hours and hours and hours, with never a soul to hear when she called and called and called.

I suppose you wonder how she ever happened to get there in the first place. She really hadn't meant to, at all, but, then, she never meant to have any of the terrible things happen to her that did. They just happened, that's all.

Just because she thought it would be fun to hide in the egg carton and was slipped into the refrigerator before she realized where she was going, she had to sit in a cramped little hole until she almost froze to death.

To make matters worse than that, Mumsey had put something heavy on top of the egg carton, and she couldn't get the cover open. After calling until her little throat ached, she tried to tear a hole in the heavy cardboard, but her little fingers could not even make a pinhole, though they worked and worked and worked.

She began to cry, then, when she saw how utterly impossible it was for her to get out, and gave up completely to her sorrow. How long she stayed there, she didn't know. She only knew that she was getting more chilled every second, and she wondered bravely just how long it would be before she stiffened into gelatin.

Mercifully, she did not have to stay there until dinnertime, for at three o'clock Mumsey took the eggs out again, because she needed some to make a cake. There sat Poppy, as forlorn and pale as she could be.

"Why, how did this ever happen?" gasped Mumsey, but Poppy only looked at her with a sick little smile and tumbled into a queer heap on the kitchen table.

Mumsey picked her up gently, oh, very gently. Her first impulse was to call the doctor, but the absurdity of the idea almost made her laugh, in spite of the problem that was before her. The picture of the family doctor bending over Poppy and listening to the rattle in her chest with an instrument big enough to swallow her was, indeed, funny. And what sort of medicine could he give her? Poppy couldn't possibly swallow a pill if her life depended upon it.

So Mumsey undressed her very carefully and held her in a little bowl of warm water, rubbing her tenderly with the tip of a gentle finger, until the life came back into her cold little body. Then she wrapped her up in one of the little white woolen blankets and laid her in the hammock.

There was no cake for dinner that night, for Mumsey was still watching the sleeping Poppy when Amy and Ellen came in from school.

How happy they were when Poppy opened one small eye and told them weakly that she was all right. By dinnertime, she had revived enough to drink a whole teaspoonful of milk and a few drops of sugar water. After this she felt much better and would have eaten a potato chip, if Mumsey hadn't thought it would be too much for her digestion.

Nobody ever told Mumsey that Jack hid one under her pillow that night, which she ate after she went to bed.

"Poppy, darlingest," whispered Amy, with a kiss that she planted on her little red curls. "Please think before you do such terrible things. Can't you see how empty everything would be if we lost you?"

"Fairies can't think, I guess," Poppy answered. "I want to sleep."

Amy blew out the candle, and Poppy reached under her pillow for the potato chip, which she devoured greedily. It didn't make her sick, but she dreamed that night of having been cut into bits, along with bananas, oranges, pineapples, and cherries, and put into a fruit salad that was eaten at a picnic.

It was late afternoon. Poppy sat in the flower box that hung from Amy's bedroom window. She was feeling very sad and lonely. There was a big lump in her throat that she couldn't seem to swallow and that ached desperately. It was all on account of Mumsey, too. She had been so terribly, terribly cross.

"I didn't mean to spill the vinegar," sighed Poppy to herself. "I didn't mean to. I only wanted to see what it tasted like, and Mumsey shouted at me so loudly that I jumped and the whole thing tipped over.

"And I didn't mean to spoil the cake, but salt looks just like sugar, and I was only trying to help."

She dug her little bare toes into the soft, warm earth, and two big tears rolled down her cheeks.

"Mumsey doesn't like me," she cried softly. "I'm always, always doing something that I shouldn't, and I can't help it."

With her little hands, she picked up a bit of dirt and rolled it over the edge of the box. She heard it drop far, far below and leaned over to see where it had struck.

Then she noticed that the vines which grew over the sides of the box reached almost to the ground. She had a sudden wild desire to get away. She could, too. She could climb as well as anybody. Maybe better!

Poppy swung over the side of the box and grasped a strong vine tightly in her little arms. Slip, slide! She went a little way. The leaves bothered her. Sometimes they got in the way, and then she couldn't see a thing. The ground seemed farther and farther away. There was a breeze, too, and she had to hang on ever so tightly for fear of being blown off.

"I shall go away and never come back, when I get down there," she promised herself. "Never come back. I wish Amy could go with me, though. I hate to leave Amy. Amy was so good to me. And Ellen, too. I know Ellen likes me, and the

Gentleman Giant, and Jack, too—even if he does tease me."

Slip, slide, hand under hand, down she went, till at last she reached the end of the swinging vine. From there she dropped to a little pile of drying grass that Jack had raked up after mowing the lawn. She sat there, blinking, and looked up at the distance she had traveled. The vine flew out in the breeze. Poppy shivered. She was glad it was over.

She trotted through a field of grass that was as high as she was, not knowing quite where to go. If she only knew the way back to Fairyland—but she didn't, so that was that.

She wandered out into the garden. It was a long walk, and she grew very tired. She sat down after a while under a queer, thick, little white umbrella that was growing right out of the ground. It was entirely too comfortable, and in spite of all her worries, she fell asleep.

It was almost dusk, when she was awakened by something stirring near by.

"Who is it?" she cried, a little alarmed.

"Who is it yourself, sleepyhead!" cried a gay little voice. "Don't you know your old friends?"

"Poco!" exclaimed Poppy, running to him. "It's you!"

"It certainly is," answered Poco, thrusting his head out of a mass of forget-me-nots. "I've been wandering about here for days, hoping I'd see somebody I knew. How do you happen to be here?" He caught Poppy's hand. "We've missed you so, Poppy darling."

"And I'm happy to see you, Poco. You see I live here now. You ought to see where I live. I have everything I want to play with—a playground with a swimming pool and a sliding board and swings and a hammock and a sand pile, and blocks and—oh, everything!"

"Then, why are you out here, looking so lonesome?" asked Poco sensibly.

"I—I was running away," remembered Poppy, feeling very foolish. "I was running away because I—" She stopped. She had forgotten why she was running away.

"Do you suppose—" began Poco.

"Suppose what?" asked Poppy. "Do you want to come and stay with me?" she cried hospitably. "Then I'd have someone to play pirate with in the big boat that stands on the mantel." She hugged Poco vigorously. "You'll love it here, and we can take the new bath sponge for a bed for you. Are you lost, too?"

"Well, not exactly." Nevertheless, Poco looked around as if he weren't very sure of his surroundings. "I caught a ride with a swallow, and the rascal left me behind the first time I dropped off. I was too heavy, I guess."

"Do you know the way back?" asked Poppy.

"Back where?"

"Why, back to Fairyland."

"Isn't this Fairyland?" asked Poco in astonishment.

"No, this isn't Fairyland," answered Poppy. "Giants live here. But they are kind giants," she added, not wishing to frighten him. "They have taken good care of me. Come on, I'll show you."

Down the path danced Poppy and Poco, hand in hand, shoulder to shoulder, like two little sprites. Poppy's red curls were bobbing up and down beside Poco's black ringlets.

Suddenly Poppy stopped short.

"We can't go in the way I came out," she laughed. "I'd almost forgotten."

"Why can't we?" asked Poco.

"Well, you see," Poppy explained, "I slid down the vine from the window box, and it doesn't reach all the way to the ground. We shall have to wait until the Gentleman Giant comes home."

"We could try knocking," suggested Poco.

"So we could," nodded Poppy. "As Ellen would say, two heads are better than one."

"Are they?" asked Poco, doubtfully. "I wouldn't want to have two heads."

"Neither would I," agreed Poppy.

They skipped along over the pebbles and through the tall grass, gossiping and giggling all the while.

"Well, what shall we knock with?" asked Poppy, when they had reached the steps. "Our heads?"

"Heavens, no!" exclaimed Poco. "Here's a burnt match. We'll ram that against the door."

"They wouldn't even hear it," chuckled Poppy.

"Let's kick, then," suggested Poco.

"But I'm barefooted!" protested Poppy.

"Then, we'll have to wait until somebody comes along." Poco sighed heavily. "How long will it be?"

"I don't know," answered Poppy, with her usual careless air. "Any time now."

They sat down in the dusk on the floor of the veranda.

"Tomorrow is my birthday," remarked Poppy, in a confidential tone.

"What is a birthday?" asked Poco.

"Oh, I don't really know," said Poppy, "except that everybody has them here, and they get a lot of nice presents. So I thought I'd have mine tomorrow. You'd better have one, too, some day."

"Oh, I will!" Poco assured her. "But, if you are having a birthday tomorrow, why were you running away?"

"Well, that was why," remembered Poppy, or thought she did. "I wanted to see the present Jack was making me, and he wouldn't show it to me, so I was angry."

"What is that noise, Poppy?" cried Poco, as a terrific commotion arose in the living room.

"It's my family," shrieked Poppy. "There is a glass door there that comes all the way to the floor, and we might be able to make them hear if we try."

"Let's get some pebbles," said Poco.

"Let's," agreed Poppy, and they gathered several about the size of a pinhead and carried them around to the terrace. Standing on their tiptoes, they could barely see over the base of the door, but uncomfortable as their position was, they were fascinated with the sight within.

Amy and Ellen were crying bitterly.

"I've looked everywhere," sobbed Amy. "Just everywhere, and I can't find her."

"She'll turn up," said the Gentleman Giant, trying to comfort her. "She's probably hiding for a joke."

Mumsey was very quiet, and Poppy wondered if it was because she was glad or sorry that they couldn't find her.

But that didn't concern her long, for in Jack's hands was the most delightful little merry-go-round that anyone had ever seen. It was about seven inches in diameter, and upon it were six little animals, all different. There were a cow, an elephant, a giraffe, a tiger, a bear, and a horse, all painted in brilliant colors. In the very middle over a tiny hole was a little ladder, about an inch wide and three inches tall, standing straight up in the air.

"He bought the animals at the ten-cent store," remarked Poppy. "I wonder if it will run."

"What?" asked Poco, stupidly.

"Why, the merry-go-round, silly. It's my present, the one he wouldn't show me. Can't you see it?"

Jack knelt down in front of the phonograph and put the merry-go-round on the floor very carefully. Then he took one of the largest records from the cabinet and put it on the phonograph. Poppy was spellbound as she watched him set the little merry-go-round on the record and start the machine. Round and round it went, to the tune of a rollicking march.

"Get the pebbles, quick," screamed Poppy. "I can't wait. It does run, just like a real one."

But before they had thrown any pebbles, Amy had heard her scream, and the door flew open.

"Here she is!" cried several voices at once.

"Here we are," amended Poppy. "This is my friend, Poco. I found him in the garden."

Poco bowed with the grace of a gentleman, and Poppy was extremely proud of him.

"I found him in the garden," repeated Poppy. "A swallow brought him, and he's going to live with me, and he'll be very, very good."

"As good as you are?" asked the Gentleman Giant with a wide grin.

"Well—" Poppy thought a moment. "He'll *try* to be very, very good."

"That's more like it," the Gentleman Giant laughed.

Poppy was full of apologies for running away and frightening them so, and she promised over and over that she would never do it again, but all the while her mind was on the jolly little merry-go-round.

"Let me ride it now, Jack!" she begged. "I was fooling when I said that tomorrow would be my birthday. It's today."

"Poppy!" exclaimed the Gentleman Giant, but she winked so cunningly that her falsehood was forgiven, and she and Poco were hoisted to the merry-go-round.

"Now make it go," she shrieked, and off they went round and round screaming in glee, Poppy clinging to the neck of the giraffe and Poco perched on the elephant.

Jack was as happy as Poppy and Poco, and Mumsey and the Gentleman Giant beamed with pleasure.

"And now," announced Poppy, when their glorious ride had come to an end, "I know you'll be glad that we have Poco, Jack, because at last you can make me a teeter-totter, and I'll have someone to teeter with!"

IF I WERE THUMBELINA

Anne Pérez-Guerra

If I were Thumbelina,
  I'd marry Thomas Thumb.
I'd serve a grape for breakfast,
  For lunch a cookie crumb.
And we'd live in the dollhouse
  Where beds are just our size,
We'd travel on electric trains
  And sail on dragonflies.
And we could have a bathing pool
  Made from a pudding pan—
But what's the good of wishing it?
  I know I never can.

Ella Young

ARDAN'S POOKA

ILLUSTRATED BY *Dorothy Lathrop*

THERE was a great brightness outside, made by the moon. That is why Ardan was awake. Sitting up in bed, he was, and craning his neck to look at that part of the sky where the moon showed herself. The moon was a friend of his, and she would be floating upwards soon, floating slowly, slowly, like a white bubble in the sky. Ardan had to crane his head to see her because the bedroom window was meager in size and set deep in the thickness of the wall. Windows and walls were like that in the place where Ardan lived. They had to be, because a wind swept down from the hills now and then and caught the low-crouching houses and shook them, strong as they were, the way a cat would shake a mouse! Tonight the wind was nowhere at all, and the sea, that roared and shouted and trampled day in and day out beyond the sand dunes, made only a quiet soft whispering sound.

Tomorrow would be Ardan's birthday. Tomorrow he would be eight years old. It is likely that his mother had something carefully hidden away—something to surprise him with tomorrow, but he was not thinking of what his mother would give him tomorrow. He was thinking of the lake. It was not many steps away from the house, the lake, and it had white water lilies and little purple tufted reeds in it, things one would like to touch, but Ardan was not allowed to go close to it, ever, or touch one of the reeds.

Even grown-up folk kept away from the lake. There was a faery horse deep down in the waters. He was white and very big and at night he came out of the lake. Sometimes in daylight he came out, and people who saw him ran away. Ardan thought it was silly of folk to run away. He said to himself that he would not run away if the white horse came out. He said to himself that he would take a handful of young sweet grass and offer it to the white horse. He had said as much to his father one time, and his father had said,—

"The white water horse is a Pooka, and no one knows what thoughts a Pooka has in his mind. He might not even be shaped like a horse when he came out of the water. He might be like a goat or a cat or a dog, for a Pooka can be any shape."

"Can he be the shape of a little boy like me?" asked Ardan.

"He can so," said his father, "and think of something sensible now and don't be talking of the Pooka, for it might bring him."

Ardan sat up in bed and craned his neck to look at the moon. She was quite round and of a most pure whiteness, a whiteness to light the world. The little blossoms on the reeds would show themselves plainly. The dark pool would be silver—how silver-white the horse would be if he came out of the lake with the water dripping off him!

All at once Ardan remembered something. You could have a wish if you woke up at night and saw the moon looking in your window at the time when she was a little slender sickle,

or at the time when she was round and white. She was round now and very white as she looked in the window, so Ardan clapped his hands to her and cried out,

"O Moon, tomorrow is my birthday. You can see the lake with the lilies. You can see the big white horse come out of it, the horse that is a Pooka. My father says that all the Pookas know you. Ask the white Pooka to make himself very small, small enough to come through my window. Maybe he would stand on the floor for a moment. Ask him, White Moon. You see him every night. Ask him, White Moon. Tomorrow is my birthday."

Ardan sat quiet with his eyes fixed on the moon. He thought that she might twinkle a little to show that she had heard him, but though his own eyes winked he did not see any change in the moon. He clambered out of bed and opened his window, then he hurried back and lay with his eyes fixed on the bright open space. No Pooka came.

"It is likely it will take him a while," said Ardan to himself. "It will take him more than a little while to come up from the deep part of the lake and across the meadows and past the three willow trees to my window. It will take him a good many minutes, I think."

He began to count slowly, "*One; two; three; four; five,*" till he came to "*sixty.*" Then he stopped and began again. When he had done so a good many times he forgot how many "*sixties*" he had counted.

"I'd better get something with words in it," thought Ardan, and he began,

> "*Eena deena dina dass,*
> *Bottle of weena wina wass.*"

"*Bottle of weena,*" he repeated sleepily. "I wonder is he out of the lake yet. I wonder, will he know my window? *Eena, deena*—I wonder why I forget the rest of it. I wonder why words are so hard to say."

Ardan's eyelids weighed heavily on his eyes. They weighed very heavily. He felt that he had not strength enough to open

his eyes. He had not strength enough to go on counting, but the moon was his friend, and he had asked for a Pooka. He must keep awake. He tugged his hair and pinched himself. "*Archangel Michael at my bedhead, my bedhead.*" He must be out of the lake by this time—he must be crossing the meadows. Oh, I wish he would hurry! "*Archangel Michael, my bed—head my . . .*" Ardan was asleep.

He never knew whether it was a long time that he slept or a short time. He awakened all of a sudden because he felt a living thing moving on the bed. He felt the weight of it, for it had climbed on his body and was moving up close to his face.

"Why, it's Gray Puss!" he said to himself, thinking of his little striped cat. He reached out delighted hands to touch the soft fur and the warm body, but the animal moved away from his touch. And suddenly when his hands searched for it on both sides, it brought down its two front feet on his shoulder; brought them down with a sharp stamp, and what Ardan felt was not the padded claws of a cat or the rough paws of a dog but the delicate cloven hoofs of a very small kid—the tiniest, faeriest of little kids!

"It's the Pooka," cried Ardan, sitting up in bed and clutching at nothingness. For one moment he saw it in the moonlight, airy, slender, and delicate, silver-white like the moon herself, shaped like a goat with little budding horns of gold. The next moment it was gone! Ardan leaped out of bed and ran to the window. He stretched his hands into the blue, star-powdered night and cried, "Come back, Silver-Foot! Come back, I want to play with you."

But there was only the wind moving softly outside and moonlight everywhere. Ardan felt his shoulder. He never could be quite sure about it afterwards, but just then he knew that his shoulder had a little dent in it. He laughed with joy and leaned far out of the window. The moon had grown smaller and whiter. She seemed to be smiling in secret. She seemed to be staring at Ardan, just as Ardan was staring at her.

"O Moon," he cried, "you sent him after all. You called him from the lake for me. He was the smallest, dinkyest, darlingest Pooka in the world."

Ardan slid down from the window. He danced and capered round the room, inventing new steps and new gestures and new abandonments till he could hardly stand on his feet. Then he turned three somersaults on the floor and went to bed.

THE BROWNY

Nancy Clinton

Today when it was raining I tiptoed over where
Beneath a toadstool parasol a browny combed his hair.
But when he saw me looking he flew up in a tree,
Then turned into a little wren and winked at me.

Edward Wade Devlin

THE DIPPY

ILLUSTRATED BY *John Gee*

IN A HILL near the little town of Taradiddle was a deep cave; and in the cave lived a dragon, called the Dippy, who was very old and bad-tempered. Once, long ago, he asked the King of the town for his daughter to eat; but as the King would not let her go, the Dippy came down to the town and ate up every living soul in it in two large gulps. So the story ran; but the Dippy never appeared again, so that in time he became no more than a name that mothers used to make their children obedient.

Now my story starts on a May Day, when the Fair was held in Taradiddle. At the bottom of the street leading to the King's castle was a large pleasant meadow, and here the Fair was held. The first person to be up in the town on this morning was Robin, the fat bellringer; and such a noise he made with his ringing and his singing, it was a shame for folk to hear. When he reached the Fairground, he found there a mountebank whose name was Antic. He had come, he said, from a town near by to see what luck he might have. Robin left him swinging his heels and went on with his song and his clanging; and the country people heard him as they came in their heavy carts, bringing their eggs and cheese and honey to the Fair.

At length the King came down the street, with his gold crown and long green cloak. With him was his daughter, the Princess Arabella, who was as pretty as a daffodil, but very naughty, as we shall see.

When the royal ruler was seated, Thomas Treacle, the Master Mayor, unrolled a long parchment scroll and commenced to read a very dull speech of welcome. But before he was halfway through, the Princess clapped her hands and cried, "Enough, Master Thomas; we declare the Fair open." Then the fiddlers and pipers struck up a dance for the young people, while the old ones gossiped or looked about at the stalls. Antic, the clown, juggled red and gold balls, which so pleased the Princess, that she called him to her and bade him give her a song. When it was ended, she threw him the gold ring she wore on her finger. Antic bowed, swallowed the ring, brought it out of his ear, and turned three somersaults.

Dame Turbot, the King's cook, enticed the fat Beadle, Nicholas Nitwit, to join her in the dance, and very gayly they went at it, too. Everywhere was merriment; Master Cracknel and his Dancing Bear were very well liked. The Princess went about among the people, joining in the fun here, helping an old woman there, as though she were anybody's daughter but the King's. She sought out Antic and begged another song of him; so he sang "The Fair-haired Ploughboy":

"The Fair-haired Ploughboy swings down the lane,
And he whistles right merrilie-O!
For the Fair-haired Ploughboy is going to marry Jane,
And very well pleased is he-O!

As the Fair-haired Ploughboy goes he sings
A gay merry snatch of song-O!
For the world is full of beautiful things;
So he sings as he goes along-O!"

And no sooner was the song done, than there came a boy running up to where the King was. He pointed a trembling hand to the gates and gasped, "The Dippy is coming, sire! The sentinels have seen it coming down from the hills!"

When the people heard this, there was a fearful hubbub. The King called the Princess; people scattered like frightened rabbits; some ran to the King, others hurried to the housetops. Bells began to ring, soldiers ran to bar the gates, the men took up their knives and scythes and rakes and stood before the King and Princess. The Mayor now came forward hesitatingly.

"Your Majesty knows," he said, "that this dragon wants only one thing in the town."

"And what is that?" said the King.

"Why," said Treacle, "what else but the King's daughter? So if we but give him the Princess, he will go away satisfied!"

The King turned purple with anger when he heard this, and Dame Turbot ran to Princess Arabella and petted and kissed her.

"It is not for myself that I fear," protested the Mayor. "I think only of the people of the town."

At that, Antic, the clown, stepped up to him and said, "Then if it is only for the people of the town that you fear, I will tell you how you can save them. This Dippy, you say, is old; then he will have lost his teeth and so will swallow his food whole without tasting it. Therefore, if you, Master Mayor, will put on the Princess's cloak and go forth to meet the Dippy, he will gobble you up and go away satisfied; and we shall put a statue of you in the market place."

The Mayor turned pale and said that he was too tall for the cloak; the Princess said that she had larger ones at the castle, but this was too much; the Mayor fled away and was never seen from that day onwards.

So the people awaited the coming of the Dippy. At last there was a knock at the town gate; the bars fell away, the gates opened slowly—and in walked a very, very small dragon, carrying a large basket in his right front paw. He came timidly up to the King and said in a meek voice, "Be you the King?"

The King smiled and said, "Yes. Are you the Dippy?"

"Oh Lawks no!" said the little dragon. "I'm only Gemeril; the Dippy was my grandfather. He died hundreds of years ago because he was very bad."

How everyone hurried down from the housetops, and how they laughed with relief, and how they wondered at the little dragon! When he had been told what a to-do he had caused, he was very much upset and said, "I'm sure I'm very harmless; indeed my mother always says I wouldn't so much as pull the cat's tail, and I wouldn't either. Now my grandfather that I told you of, he used to eat Princesses whenever he could, but they weren't half so tasty as plum jam. No, I be just come to the Fair to see the dancing and maybe eat some cakes. My mother had

FRUIT

a heap of jam to make so she couldn't take me herself, but I runned away, I did, and here I be. My mother always says I can't take care of myself, being only three hundred years old."

Then the people brought the little dragon all manner of good things—raisin cakes and gingerbread men and sweet apples, and up came good Dame Turbot with a basket full of pots of rich plum jam and many other goodies.

"Thank ye kindly, ma'am," he said. "I'm greatly fond of plum jam, though I do often swallow the stones. But then my mother always says that maybe in another hundred years I'll learn some sense."

Just then there was a fearful snorting and stamping outside the gates; and in rushed a very large green dragon with a white apron about her waist. Gemeril turned sadly to the King and said, "That is my mother, and now I will be spanked."

The large dragon stormed up to him. "Ah, little wretch!" she cried. "I told you not to come, and you disobeyed me deliberate, me with all my jamming to do! Come away home, little monster, and it's the back of the cave and a good stick for you!"

"Come now, Dame Dragon," said the King, "let your son stay and have his pleasure, and we'll see that no harm comes to him."

"Oho!" cried the mother dragon, "and who may you be, old nanny-goat?"

"Oh," said he mildly, "only the King."

At that she became very humble; and when Gemeril showed her all the jam and dainties that he had been given, she was very much pleased and said that he might stay. Then she bought some milk jars and butter bowls and a piece of marchpane to suck and went off happily to finish her jamming.

Then the King made Nitwit Mayor of Taradiddle; and not many days later Dame Turbot became Mayoress. Arabella thought so highly of Antic, for all he was a clown, that he was made a knight, and after many feats of arms he married the Princess. As for little Gemeril, he came often to the town all by himself, and a better-liked little dragon you couldn't find, however hard you searched. And that is the end of this story.

THE THREE WISHES

ADAPTED BY *Pauline Rosenberg*

ILLUSTRATED BY *Marie Lawson*

ONE cold winter's night many years ago, an old man named Pedro sat by the fire talking with his wife Maria. Now Pedro had worked hard all his life but had never made much money. Still he had much to be thankful for. He had a good little piece of ground to farm, a comfortable cottage, and a donkey to carry his burdens. But tonight, instead of giving thanks to God for the many good things they enjoyed, he and his wife spent the time wishing they had some of the things that belonged to their neighbors.

"This little hut is only fit to house a donkey in," said Pedro, "and this land is the poorest around here. I wish we had the house and farm of our neighbor Carlos."

"Carlos' house and farm are better than ours, to be sure," answered Maria, "but what I'd like to have is the fine mansion of Don Francisco."

"And I," continued her husband, "instead of our old donkey, which can scarcely carry an empty sack, would like to have Carlos' mule!"

"Well, if I had my wish," exclaimed Maria, "I'd have the fine white horse with silver-studded harness that draws the carriage of Donna Clara. Some people have only to wish for a thing in order to get it. How I should like to see my wishes come true!"

Scarcely had she finished speaking, when they saw a most beautiful little woman standing in front of the fire. She was not more than eighteen inches tall, but on her head was a crown like a queen's. She wore a filmy dress and veil that seemed made of white smoke. Sparks from the fire leaped about her like fireworks and shone on her dress like glittering spangles. In her hand she carried a little golden wand, at the end of which a single bright spark gleamed like a ruby.

"I am the Fairy Fortunata," she said. "I was passing by and heard your complaints and I have come to help you. I shall give you three wishes: one to you, Maria, one to you, Pedro, and the third must be something that you both want. This third wish I will grant you tomorrow when I return at this time."

So saying, the beautiful fairy sprang through the flames and disappeared in a cloud of smoke.

The old couple were delighted. How wonderful to have three wishes come true! They talked over all their wishes, but they had so many that they didn't know which to select. They decided to wait until the next day. In the meantime they began to talk about entirely different things, and, as usual, spoke of their wealthy neighbors.

"I was at Carlos' house this morning," said Pedro, "and they were making black puddings. Ah, such black puddings! It would have done you good to see them!"

"I wish I had one of those puddings right now," said his wife, "to roast on the ashes for supper!"

Just as she uttered these words there appeared on the ashes the most delicious-looking black pudding that could be imagined.

Maria's eyes almost popped out of her head. But Pedro jumped up in rage.

"You greedy woman!" he cried. "To use up one of our precious wishes on nothing but a pudding! I wish the black pudding were stuck on your nose!"

No sooner had he spoken than the black pudding was actually hanging from the end of her nose! She tried to get it off, but it was stuck fast.

"See what you have done!" she cried. "If I used my wish badly, at least it hurt no one but myself, but you—just look what you have done to me!"

Just then the dog and cat, having sniffed the pudding, jumped up and tried to get a bite of what was now a part of her nose.

"There is only one thing we can do now," said Maria. "We must use the third wish to get this pudding off my nose."

"Wife, for Heaven's sake! What of the new farm?" cried Pedro.

"It does not matter," said Maria.

"But Maria, think of the fine house you wanted!"

"I don't care about that now."

"My dear, let us wish for a fortune. Then you can have a golden case set with jewels to cover the pudding."

"I will not hear of it."

"Then you would have us left just as we were before?"

"That is all I wish for."

Nothing the old man could say would change his wife's mind, so at last they agreed to use their third wish to remove the pudding.

The next night when the fairy appeared and asked what was their last wish, they said,

"We only wish to be as we were before."

The fairy smiled and vanished. The pudding tumbled off the wife's nose. And from that time the old couple lived content with what they had.

Dinah Maria Mulock

BROWNIE'S RIDE

RETOLD BY *Mathilda Schirmer*

ILLUSTRATED BY *Ruth van Tellingen*

SIX little children got a present one day—something they had longed for all their lives.

It was a real live Shetland pony. No one in the neighborhood had seen such an animal for years and years and years.

Jess—that was the pony's name—was no bigger than a donkey, and her coat was shaggy like a young bear's. She had a long tail and a great deal of hair in her mane and over her eyes.

Jess was very gentle. She loved the children and followed them about. She ate corn out of the bowl they held out to her and would even nibble from their hands.

She soon became a great pet of everyone. Cook liked her so much that she would let Jess walk in at the back door and warm her nose at the kitchen fire for a minute or two. Then Jess would turn around and politely walk out again.

Gardener was the only one who complained. He said that he was not used to groom's work, and the pony needed a lot of grooming because of her long hair. So the family looked for a boy to take care of her.

They found a boy in the village, a great rough, red-headed boy named Bill. He was a lazy fellow who liked best to lie in the sun all day and do nothing. He agreed to take care of Jess because she was such a very little pony and he thought he wouldn't have much to do.

But he soon found out that there was a lot of work to do. It took a long time to clean her and to comb her tangled hair. If he handled her roughly, she kicked and bounced about giving Bill a great deal of trouble.

. . . one of them said, "Perhaps it's the Brownie!"

He had to keep within call, too, for the children wanted their pony at all hours. She was their very own, and they wanted to learn to ride even before they got a saddle.

It was hard to stay on Jess's bare back, but little by little they did it. The boys learned first, and then they taught their sisters. They all took turns riding Jess although sometimes it was hard to remember whose turn came next.

But they did not squabble much about it. If ever they did, something very strange happened. They would hear in the air right over their heads the crack of an unseen whip. It was not their whip, for none of them had a whip yet. The sound always startled Jess so that she galloped away and could not be caught again for many minutes.

This happened several times until one of them said, "Perhaps it's the Brownie!" And they were very good for a few days. Then, one day, the two eldest boys couldn't agree which should ride foremost and which hindmost on Jess's back. *"Crick, crack,"* went the whip. Jess kicked up her heels, tossed both boys over her head and scampered off.

The two boys fell into a large nettlebed. When they crawled out, rubbing their arms and legs, they tried to catch her; but she took a skittish fit and could not be caught until the schoolbell rang, and then it was too late for another ride.

From then on Jess was thought to be a special friend of the Brownie. With good care and gentle treatment her coat became silky and her limbs graceful and her head full of intelligence so that everyone admired her. But she had her own taste as to her riders and liked the little people. Bill once thought he should like a ride; but when he got on her back she quickly ducked her head down, and he tumbled over it.

One day Gardener said, "I think I'll ride Jess to the village." She carried him, but his feet nearly touched the ground; so it looked as if the man were carrying the pony and not the pony the man. The children laughed and laughed, and Gardener never tried it again.

At last Jess got a saddle—and she was as proud as the boys and girls were. That day they took her into the village and everybody said what a beautiful pony she was.

After this Gardener spent more time with Bill and showed him how to groom her. Bill did not like it because he was such a very lazy lad. Often when the children wanted Jess, he was not there to saddle her; or she had not been properly groomed; or Bill was away at his dinner. The children disliked him very much.

"I wish," said one of the boys, "the Brownie would punish you."

"The Brownie!" cried Bill. "If I caught him I'd kick him up in the air, like this."

And he kicked his cap up in the air, but it didn't come down again. It caught at the top of a tree where it dangled for weeks and weeks while Bill had to go bareheaded.

One day the mother of the children was called away on business. When she left, all the children and the servants felt very sad—all but Bill.

"What a jolly time I'll have!" he said. "I'll do nothing all day long. Those troublesome children shan't have Jess to

ride; I'll keep her in the stable and then she won't get dirty, and I shan't have to clean her. Hurrah! What fun!"

He put his hands in his pockets and sat whistling the best part of the afternoon.

The children had been so busy that for that day they quite forgot Jess; but next morning after lessons were over, they came, begging for a ride.

"You can't get one. The stable door's locked, and I've lost the key." (He had it in his pocket all the time.)

"How is poor Jess to get her dinner?" cried the littlest girl. "Oh, how hungry she will be!"

The three little girls were quite upset, but the boys were more angry than sorry.

"It was very stupid of you, Bill, to lose the key. Look about and find it, or else break open the door."

"I won't," said Bill. "The key may turn up before night, and if it doesn't—who cares? You get riding enough and too much. I'll not bother myself about it, or Jess either."

Bill left then; but as he walked away, the key in his pocket felt so heavy that he expected it to fall out any minute. He put his hand on it and his fingers felt pinched, as if there was a lobster in his pocket. This happened again and again until he grew frightened. He went into the cow shed and hid the key in a corner under some hay. As he did so, he heard someone laugh—"Ha! ha!"; and as he went out of the shed, he felt a pinch at his ankles.

Jess, when she heard the children's voices, whinnied behind the locked stable door. The dog barked, the hens cackled, and the guinea fowls cried. There was such an uproar that the children ran out of the farmyard so that Gardener would not think they were up to some mischief. This left Bill all alone.

What an idle day he had! He sat on the wall with his hands in his pockets and lounged upon the fence and wandered round the garden.

He went and talked with Gardener's wife while she was hanging out her clothes. Gardener had gone to the lower field with the children so he knew nothing of Bill's idling, or it might have come to an end.

By and by Bill thought it was time to go home to his supper. "But first I'll give Jess her corn," said he. "I'll give her twice as much, and I need not come back to give her her breakfast so early in the morning."

He went to the cow shed to get the key. But when he looked in the corner, the key was not there. "The key—what on earth did I do with the key?" cried Bill. "You can't have eaten it, you wild old cow! Or you, you stupid old hen!" But the key was gone.

Bill didn't know what to do; but when he heard Gardener come into the farmyard with the children after him, Bill bolted over the wall like a flash of lightning and ran away home.

All the way he seemed to hear a little dog yelping at his heels, and then a swarm of gnats buzzing around his head, and it made him so dizzy that when he got to his cottage he jumped into bed and pulled the covers over his ears. But he could hear someone laughing, "Ha! ha!"

Gardener and the children were in the farmyard, and he let them watch him milk Dolly, the old cow. None of them thought of riding Jess, but the youngest girl remembered that she was locked up and went to see her. Peeping through a crack, she saw Jess munching at a large bowl full of corn—but she saw something else, too.

There on the manger squatted a small brown man! She was happy that the pony was fed and went back to the other children.

In the middle of the night, when the children were fast asleep, a little old brown man carrying a lantern went to Jess's stable and unlocked it. He patted her pretty head and rubbed her down. "Isn't it nice to be clean?" said the wee man. "And I dare say your poor little legs ache with standing still so long. Shall we have a run together? The moon shines bright in the clear, cold night. Dear me! I'm talking poetry."

But Brownies can recite poetry and work at the same time; so while he was talking, Brownie saddled and bridled Jess. Then he jumped on her back.

" 'Off,' " said the stranger; " 'off, off and away!' " sang Brownie, mimicking a song of Cook's. And Jess galloped, and the Brownie sat on her back as merrily as if they did this every night. Such a chase it was! They cleared the farmyard at a single bound and went flying down the road, across the field, into the wood, then out into the open country, and by and by into a dark, muddy lane.

"Let's go into the water to wash ourselves," said Brownie, and he coaxed Jess into a deep stream. Up the bank she scrambled, her long hair dripping as if she had been a water dog instead of a pony. Then back they went through the lane and the wood and the field, galloping like the wind.

But when she reached her stable, her sides were white with foam, and the mud was sticking all over her like a plaster. Her beautiful long hair was caked together in a tangle, and her mane was tied into knots.

Gardener got up at dawn and looked into the farmyard. His sharp eye caught sight of the stable door wide open.

"Good Bill," he shouted, "up early at last."

But when Gardener came up to the stable, such a sight greeted his eyes! Jess was trembling and shaking, all in a foam, and muddy from head to foot.

Such a scolding Bill got when he came an hour after breakfast time! But Bill could not say a word, especially since the key was hanging in its proper place by the kitchen door. All he could do was to make himself as busy as could be. He cleaned Jess. Then he took the children for a ride and afterwards put the stable in good order. He was such a changed Bill that Gardener told him he must have left himself at home and brought back somebody else.

Jess lived to be quite an old pony and carried a great many people—little people always, for she never grew any bigger. But she never carried a Brownie again.

Margaret and Mary Baker

PATSY AND THE LEPRECHAUN

ILLUSTRATED BY *Barbara Fitzgerald*

THERE once was a boy called Patsy O'Flatherty, and he lived in Ireland. He could run races and turn somersaults and whistle better than any boy in the village. But in spite of that he had his faults, and the worst of them was that he did not like work.

Patsy's father was a cobbler. "Come, my boy," he would say, "it's time you learnt to be helping me, for I've more work than I can manage, and that's the truth."

But Patsy came so unwillingly, and had so little mind to try his best, that all he did was to spoil the leather and lose the cobbler's wax and prick his finger with the awl.

"I know a way to make money quicker than by earning it," he thought, but he did not say anything about that to his father and mother. They would have shaken their heads over such ideas, and would have shaken Patsy too, perhaps.

His sister Katie was always so busy getting into mischief that it was no use trying to talk to *her*, so he went to tell his plans to the pig.

The pig's name was Biddy, and she was a very good listener. As long as Patsy rubbed her and tickled her with the end of a stick she was quite pleased to listen.

"Why should I bother learning to make shoes when I'll be catching a leprechaun one of these days?" he said. "Many's the time I've heard them up on the hillside, tip-tap, tip-tap, hammer, hammer, hammer, making wee shoes for themselves, and there's never a leprechaun but has crocks of gold buried in the ground."

The old pig turned her head and winked an eye.

"You needn't look at me that way," said Patsy, grinning. "I know what to do when I've caught one! I must hold him tight

and never take my eyes off him till he's told me where his treasure is hidden, or else he'll slip away and I'll never find him again. I know their tricks, the cunning creatures," said Patsy wisely and waggled his head. "They'll not be getting the better of me!"

The old pig's sides began to shake.

"Ara!" said Patsy, "don't you believe me? Then see what I've got all ready in my pocket!" And he pulled out a watch chain. "It's every bit of it pure gold, for it's the very chain Uncle Dennis sent home when he made his fortune across the sea. And what am I going to do with it? Sure, and you've never forgotten the tale of Thomas FitzPatrick! But maybe you've never had the chance to hear it, since you're only a pig, so I'll tell you about it."

Biddy grunted and stuck up her chin; perhaps because her feelings were hurt, or perhaps because she wanted Patsy to tickle under it with his stick.

"Well," said Patsy, "there was once a boy called Thomas FitzPatrick, and what should he do but catch a leprechaun.

" 'My fortune's made and all!' cried Tom. 'I'll not be letting you go till you've told me where your gold is buried.'

"The leprechaun, he twisted and he wriggled, and he talked and he begged; but Tom held him fast and never took his eyes off the wee wrinkled face of him. In the end the leprechaun took him to a field of ragwort.

" 'Dig up that plant, that plant over there,' says he, 'and you'll find a crock of gold, and much good may it do you!'

"Tom let him go, and so that he wouldn't forget the place while he ran home for a spade, he took off his red garter and tied it round the ragwort stalk. 'I'll be knowing you again,' says he; but not a bit of it!

"When he came back what should he find but a red garter tied round every plant in the field!

"So that's the tale of Thomas FitzPatrick," said Patsy, "and if a leprechaun tries any such tricks on me I'll not mark the place with my garter—no, not I—I'll use the chain. A field full of gold chains would be as good a fortune as finding a crock of money!"

Just then the cobbler's wife came out of the house. "Patsy!" she called. "If you've nothing better to do than talk to the pig, you can be minding Katie while I get on with my work."

Patsy got to his feet. "The first thing I'll do with my fortune is to get someone to mind Katie for me," he said. "It's harder to keep her out of mischief than it is to learn cobbling. Are you laughing at me? Just let me get my hands on one of the wee creatures and you'll feed on taties from morning till night. Then perhaps you'll believe that Patsy O'Flatherty has an idea or two in his head!"

But it seemed as if Patsy's fortune might be a long time in coming. He had left the chain hanging out of his pocket and one of the hens had walked away with it.

Next day was as fine a summer day as anyone could wish to see. The sun was shining just warm enough, and the wind was blowing just safely enough, and Patsy did not mean to spend the time in the cobbler's workshop if he could help it. He tried to slip away without being heard, but his mother's ears were sharper than he thought.

"Patsy! Patsy!" she called, "don't forget it's market-day and you must be minding Katie, the darling, while I'm away at the town."

Patsy turned back, sighing a little louder than he need have done, and lifted Katie on to his shoulders. She bounced up and down with delight and made poor Patsy's eyes water as she clutched his hair.

"Whist now! Whist now!" he cried. "We'll never get anywhere if you treat me like that!"

But even when Katie sat still they did not get far, and when they came to the place where the foxgloves were growing on the hillside he put her on the ground and wiped his hot face on his sleeve.

"I might find a leprechaun here as well as anywhere," he said.

And, wonder of wonders, they had hardly been there any time at all before they heard a tip-tap, tip-tap that could be nothing else than a leprechaun busy at his shoemaking.

"Hush! hush!" whispered Patsy. With Katie behind him he crept towards the sound, and there, sitting comfortably in the shadow of a foxglove, was a leprechaun. He had silver buckles on his shoes and silver buttons on his long-tailed coat, and there was a bit of shamrock pinned in his hat to show what a good Irishman he was.

Katie shrieked with delight when she saw him and he jumped to his feet; but Patsy was too quick for him and caught him before he could run away.

"It's the lucky boy I am!" cried Patsy, hardly able to believe his good fortune.

"And it's myself has no luck at all!" whimpered the leprechaun. "Let me go now, Patsy darling; why should you want to tease a poor little creature like myself? For shame on you, and you so big and strong!"

"Never a bit of harm will I do you," said Patsy, "but you must tell me where to find your gold."

"Gold!" shrieked the leprechaun. "What should I be doing with gold?"

"It's no use talking like that," said Patsy wisely. "Tell me where there's enough to keep me idle all my days and I'll let you go."

"I'll be ruined entirely!" sighed the leprechaun. " 'Tis only one wee crock of gold I've got, and that's the truth. But, lack-a-day, Patsy, look there!" he shouted suddenly. " 'Tis your father, poor man, being chased by Michael O'Rory's big black bull!"

Patsy nearly turned his head, but he remembered just in time. "Do you think I'll let myself be caught with a trick as old as that?" he asked, grinning.

"It's the smart boy you are, Patsy," said the leprechaun, "and it's no use at all to try to deceive you. Just dig under that foxglove where I was sitting, and you'll find as much treasure as you can carry away. Let me go, Patsy darling, and get home for a spade."

But Patsy grinned wider than ever. "I'll mark the foxglove before I do," he said, "but I'll not mark it with a red garter! And now, since you've behaved like a gentleman, I'll set you at liberty and thank you kindly."

As soon as he was free the wee mannie swept off his hat. "I'd be saving my thanks for a while, Patsy, if I were you," he said with a wink; and picking up his stool and his work he turned a somersault and disappeared.

All this time Katie had been standing with her thumb in her mouth, staring with all her eyes; but when the leprechaun vanished so suddenly she was frightened and ran crying to Patsy.

He knelt down to comfort her.

"Not a bit of harm will he do you, mavourneen!" he said

gently. "And if you'll stop crying I'll buy you a doll and a wooden horse, and you shall have a stick of sugar candy every day, that you shall!"

Katie's tears dried away when he spoke of sugar candy, and she wanted Patsy to get her some then and there.

"Ah, but you must be giving me a bit of time," said Patsy. "I must get the fortune first."

And if he had not been so sure it was only a bird twittering, he would have said he heard a tiny cackling laugh behind him.

"I'll tie the gold chain around the foxglove," said Patsy, "and then we'll go home for the spade. If the wee mannie leaves things alone I'll know the foxglove again for certain and I'll dig the treasure out in no time; and if he tries to trick me and puts a gold chain round every foxglove on the hillside, I'll have made my fortune just the same. It's the clever boy I am," said Patsy, and waggled his head.

But when he felt in his pockets the chain was not to be found; as a matter of fact, the hens at home were quarrelling over it at that very moment.

Here was a fine end to all his plans! He turned his pockets inside out, but there was nothing in them except a piece of string and his knife. Katie began to whimper again at sight of his doleful face.

"I'll tell you what it is!" he cried suddenly. "You must stay here, Katie darling, while I run home. Sit down by that foxglove, that's my jewel, and if you don't stir till Patsy comes back he'll bring you a pocketful of sugar!"

Katie did as she was told; but to make sure that she should not spoil everything by forgetting to sit still, he took the string out of his pocket and tied her to the foxglove before he ran down the hillside.

The old pig and her family were outside the gate when he reached home.

"There'll be no need for you to go looking for roots now, Biddy!" he cried. "I've caught a leprechaun, and I've come for a spade to dig up the gold and a basket to hold it!"

But Biddy only winked an eye.

Patsy ran into the house, filled his pockets from the sugar jar, emptied the potato-basket on to the floor, took the spade from the shed and hurried away again, forgetting to shut either doors or gates behind him.

Biddy watched him go; then she squeezed through the gate into the garden. After that she squeezed through the door into the house, where she found the potatoes Patsy had rolled all over the floor.

"Grumph! grumph!" she called, and all the little pigs came squealing and pushing through the doorway. Even if Patsy should not make his fortune, it was clear that they thought some good had come from finding the leprechaun.

With the spade and basket to carry, Patsy found it much harder up the hill than it had been down, and at every step he grew redder and hotter and more out of breath. But what did that matter? He would have plenty of time after this to take things at his ease.

At last he came to the foxglove patch, and no sooner did he set eyes on it than he stopped short in dismay, for tied to every foxglove was a baby shouting "Patsy! Patsy! Patsy!" at the top of her voice. With his eyes nearly rolling out of his head, he looked wildly from one foxglove to another—the babies were all exactly alike!

"The leprechaun has been too many for me after all!" he wailed. "I've lost the fortune, and whatever can I do with fifty babies? I'll never be able to tell which is Katie!"

"Patsy! Patsy!" they shouted. "Patsy! Patsy! Patsy!"

He held his hands over his ears. "How can I think what to do in such a noise?" he cried.

Then he had a fine idea and he began to laugh.

"Why didn't I think of it before?" he exclaimed. "Even if I can't tell which is Katie, to be sure Katie will know which is herself!"

So he took out his penknife and ran in and out among the foxgloves and cut the strings as fast as he could, and all the babies began to run about and stumble and roll and pick themselves up again. Then he stooped down and held out his arms.

“Katie, Katie darling! Come to your old Patsy!” he called.

But all the babies must have been called Katie, for they all tried to get into his arms at once, and pushed and struggled till he was almost knocked over.

He got quickly to his feet. “Let the leprechaun keep his gold and his babies! I’ll have none of them!” he cried, and he took to his heels.

It was easy to leave the gold behind, but the babies did not mean to stay where they were without Patsy, and they all began to cry at once. The sound would have softened a much harder heart than his, and when he stopped and looked back he saw them all hurrying after him as fast as their plump little legs could carry them.

"What must I do?" cried Patsy, ready to tear out his hair in despair. "How can I run away and leave Katie? And how can I be sure it's Katie I'm taking home unless I take them all?"

In the end they all went down the hillside together, but they took half the morning over it. Some of the babies kept tumbling down and had to be picked up and comforted, some wanted to be carried, some would not keep to the path and had to be brought back over and over again, some tried to walk in all the puddles, and some wanted to sit down and pick flowers and had to be coaxed to walk along with the rest. "If we never find which is Katie, shall I have to mind them like this every day till they're grown up?" sighed Patsy.

The pigs were wakened from their morning nap by the sound of so many little voices and the pattering of so many little feet.

"Humph-grumph!" said Biddy, as much as to say, "Is that the fortune you've been digging out of the ground? I could have done better myself!" But Patsy paid no attention to her.

"Father!" he called. "Come and tell me which is Katie."

"What's that?" said the cobbler, coming to the door of his workshop. "Whatever are you wanting with so many babies?"

"I'm not wanting them," said Patsy, "but I've lost Katie among them all and now I can't find her."

"Did you ever hear the like?" gasped the cobbler. He looked at the children with his spectacles on, and he looked at them with his spectacles off, but he was no cleverer than Patsy at telling one baby from another.

"And there are fifty of them," sighed Patsy. "Where can we be putting them all to sleep?"

"Was any man in such a fix before?" groaned the cobbler. "I'd be dead in a week with such a family to plague me!" By this time the neighbors had come running up to see what the noise could mean. When they had been told the trouble they were all ready with offers of help. Some thought this baby was Katie and some thought that. The cobbler, poor man, could only hold his head in his hands and groan.

But he soon had something else to do, for the babies were getting into every kind of mischief.

"They'll pull all the feathers out of the hens!" shouted someone.

"Look you yonder!" cried another, "there's one of them climbing the ladder into the loft, and she'll fall down and break her little neck."

"Father! Father!" shouted Patsy, "come and help me or they'll all be drowning themselves in the duckpond!"

As fast as they rescued one baby from trouble there were half a dozen more of them in mischief. They pulled the tails of the little pigs; they tried to ride on Biddy's back; they sat down on the flower beds and swung on the pump handle. The cobbler and Patsy and the neighbors were worn out with running after them.

"But to be sure, Mr. O'Flatherty," said the neighbors, "what else can you expect when there's only one real baby among them and the rest are only changelings?"

The cobbler's wife, coming back from market, did not call out in surprise when she reached the gate and saw all the

crowd of babies. She did not stop and look from one to the other as Patsy and his father had done. She put down her basket, ran through the gateway and snatched one of them up in her arms.

"I'll be glad if someone will tell me why you're letting all these strange children tease my own wee Katie!" she cried.

"Indeed, and we couldn't tell which *was* Katie," everyone began; but before they could say another word there was a burst of cackling laughter. In the twinkling of an eye the babies turned into leprechauns, each with his buckled shoes and long-tailed coat, and they wriggled through the fence and were away up the hillside before anyone could draw a breath.

The cobbler and Patsy and the neighbors stood staring after them, and then they turned to stare at Katie safe in her mother's arms.

"If that isn't the biggest wonder of all!" cried the cobbler. "How could you tell her?"

"And everyone of them her very picture!" cried Patsy.

"Indeed they were not!" said the cobbler's wife. "There wasn't one to be compared with her! Other folk might be deceived, but you'd never deceive her own mother! And now I'll be glad to know what's the meaning of it all."

The tale took a long time to tell, and when she had heard it she had a great deal to say. When she saw the muddy footprints that Biddy and her family had made in the kitchen, she said even more; but Patsy and the cobbler were so glad to see the end of the babies and to have Katie safe and sound that they would have been happy to be scolded for hours together. After all, the cobbler's wife had a right to grumble a little when she thought of all that had happened to Katie and the house while she had been away.

"So that's the end of my fortune!" sighed Patsy, "and I've lost the gold chain as well."

But there he was wrong. He found the chain near the pump when he went to shut the pigs in the sty; and that night as his mother was putting Katie to bed she saw a lump of cobbler's wax clinging to the little red frock.

"Patsy!" she cried, "run with the wax to your father, or he'll have to be wasting time looking for it!" But when Patsy went to the workshop his father had his own piece safe beside him.

"I know what it is!" cried Patsy. "It's the leprechaun's wax! Wasn't Katie sitting under the very foxglove where he'd been at work? And if it's magic wax it will never wear out, and I'll be able to make the best shoes that ever were sewn in Ireland, and so I'll have a fortune after all!"

Whether it was because of the leprechaun's wax, or because Patsy brought a good heart to learn cobbling, no one can say, but for one reason or the other he learnt to make such fine shoes that everyone wanted them. All in good time he had a crockful of gold of his own earning, and he and Katie and the cobbler and his wife lived happily and merrily all the rest of their days.

As for Biddy, if she did not feed on potatoes every day, she had quite as many as were good for her.

ONCE WHEN YOU WERE WALKING*

Annette Wynne

Once when you were walking across the meadow grass,
A little fairy touched you—but you never saw her pass.
One day when you were sitting upon a mossy stone,
A fairy sat beside you, but you thought you were alone.
So no matter what you do, no matter where you go,
A fairy may be near you—but you may never know.

*By permission of the publishers, J. B. Lippincott Company, from *For Days and Days,* by Annette Wynne. Copyright, 1919, by J. B. Lippincott Company.

Isa L. Wright

THE THREE-LEGGED STOOL

ILLUSTRATED BY *Clarence Biers*

ONCE there was a little old man who lived in a little old house with his gentle wife. And most important of all, there lived with them a little three-legged stool. Now there are stools and stools, the world over, little and big; but this stool was not like any other stool in the world, as you will see. It might have been made by the Happy Elves, or blessed by the Fairy of Kind Deeds, or grown in the Forest of Loving Thoughts. I cannot tell you as to that. All I am sure of is this: it was the most wonderful stool I have ever heard of and it dwelt for many a year with the little old man and his gentle wife in the little old house on the hill.

Every morning the little old man carried it to the barn, sat down on it and milked the brindled cow. Then he went back to the little old house with the milking-pail in one hand and the little three-legged stool in the other. One morning as he arose to go to the barn as usual, the little stool stirred on its three legs and said, "Why should I let you carry me to the barn every day when I am able to carry myself?

"What's that?" said the little old man. But before he could say another word, the little stool danced away on its three legs and sat itself down by the brindled cow.

"Now that is very kind of you," said the little old man when he reached the barn.

"Not at all! Not at all!" replied the little stool. "I haven't had so much fun for a long time." So the little old man sat down and milked the brindled cow.

The next morning the stool said to the milking-pail, as they stood side by side in the kitchen, "Why should you let the little old man carry you to the barn? Why not carry yourself?"

"A fine idea!" said the milking-pail.

"What's that?" inquired the little old man. But before he could say another word, off whisked the milking-pail with the little stool, and sat itself down under the brindled cow.

"Now that is very kind of you," said the little old man as he sat down to milk.

"Not at all! Not at all!" laughed the milking-pail. "I haven't had so much fun for a long time."

So the little old man milked the brindled cow and carried the milk to the house.

And the next morning the little stool got to thinking again, as she and the milking-pail waited by the brindled cow for the little old man to come. "Oh, cow," said the little three-legged stool, "why should you make the little old man milk you? He works hard all day long. Why not let down your milk yourself?"

"A fine idea!" smiled the cow as she chewed her cud. "A fine idea!" And when the little old man reached the barn, the pail was full of foamy milk.

"Now that was very kind of you, brindled cow," said the little old man.

"Not at all! Not at all!" answered the cow, switching her tail. "I haven't had so much fun in a long time."

And the little old man reached for the milking-pail to carry it into the house.

"Wait a minute!" called the little stool. "Why should the milking-pail and I let you carry the milk when between us we can take it to the house and not spill a drop?"

"What's that?" asked the little old man. But before he could take hold of the milking-pail, it had jumped up on the stool. Tap! tap! went the three little legs, and in a minute they were safe in the house and not a drop spilled.

The little old man hurried in and told his gentle wife all about it.

"We must do something for them in return for their kindness," said she. "Now do you give the brindled cow of our apples, and I will shine up the milking-pail and cover the little stool with red, red carpet."

"We have but few apples left for winter," said the little old man.

"That matters not," smiled his gentle wife. "We can do without, ourselves."

So the brindled cow ate of the apples and the milking-pail, shining from top to toe, smiled at the little three-legged stool all covered with red, red carpet.

Then the stool leaned over to the pail and said, "Why should the little old man toil day after day and get so little for his labor?"

"Why, indeed?" echoed the milking-pail.

"And why should we sit here in the corner all day while the little old man toils so hard? Let us bestir ourselves!"

"A fine idea!" the milking-pail answered.

"What's that?" asked the little old man.

"We go to seek your fortune!" cried the stool. But before the little old man could speak a word, away they both danced out the door and down the road and on to the village.

By the roadside sat a strong man.

"Why do you sit here?" asked the stool.

"Why, indeed?" echoed the milking-pail.

"The little old man toils hard day after day," the stool continued, "and gets but little for his labor."

"If that be so," answered the strong man, rising, "take me to him! I will gladly work hard, too, in exchange for food and comfort."

"You shall drink your fill of my milk," promised the pail.

"And rest on me when you are weary," agreed the stool.

So they all journeyed back to the little old house.

"We bring you part of your fortune!" they told the little old man. "A strong pair of arms to labor for you in exchange for food and comfort."

"Now that is very kind of you," said the little old man.

"Not at all! Not at all!" rejoined the stranger. "I haven't had so much fun in a long time."

And the little three-legged stool and the milking-pail laughed till they creaked, they were so happy.

"Your face grows shinier every day," whispered the stool to the milking-pail, a few days later.

"And your carpet face grows brighter and brighter," returned the pail. Then they laughed again.

"Why should we sit here in idleness," said the stool after a minute, "when the little old man and the strong man toil hard day after day? They are getting more for their labor, it is true, but yet not half enough. Let us bestir ourselves again."

"A fine idea!" said the milking-pail.

"What's that?" questioned the little old man.

"We go again to seek your fortune," called the little stool, as it ran out the front door and down the road with the milking-pail after it.

On to the village they went, and once more they saw a man sitting by the roadside. A tattered coat covered his thin body, and his face was white and pinched.

The shiny milking-pail and the little stool stopped to talk with him.

"Why do you sit by the roadside?" asked the milking-pail.

"I am weary and hungry," returned the stranger, "and none will give me food."

"Why don't you go to the little old man's house?" suggested the little stool. "He has very little to give, but what he has he will gladly share with you, and his gentle wife will care for you until you are well again."

"It may be," said the stranger, "that the little old man labors hard and has need of all he earns."

"Nevertheless, he will be glad to help you," the little stool assured him.

"You can drink your fill of my milk," said the pail.

"And rest on me when you are weary," added the stool.

So back again they journeyed to the little old man's house.

"We bring you no fortune this time," they called, "but only one who is weary and hungry and needs your help."

"And indeed I am glad to see you," smiled the little old man as he came to meet the stranger. And his gentle wife brought forward the easiest chair.

"Now this is very kind of you," began the stranger.

"Not at all! Not at all!" answered the little old man and his gentle wife together. "We haven't had so much fun for a long time."

And with that they brought the best from the cupboard and set it upon the table. And the stranger ate till he was satisfied, and when night came, he was given the softest bed for sleep and rest.

The morning came and the gentle wife prepared breakfast and put it on a tray and put the tray on the little stool and tap! tap! tap! went the little stool up the stairs and into the stranger's room. And the little old man and his gentle wife followed.

The little stool sat itself down by the bedside. And the little old man and his wife stood by the door. And lo! There upon the bed, they saw, not a weary stranger, but a King with a jeweled crown upon his forehead.

"I was a-hungered and you took me in, sheltered and fed me with the best you had," he said, "and a King does not forget."

Then the little old man and his gentle wife bowed low before the King.

"Nay," he said, "bow not to me, but sit you here by my side and tell me what I can do for you who did so much for me."

But the little old man, sitting by the King's side, shook his head. And the gentle wife, sitting on the other side of the King, shook her head.

"We have done nothing," they said together. "It was the little stool that did it all."

And the King smiled. "Since you will not wish for yourself," he told them, "I shall wish for you." Then he lifted his hands above them.

"I bless you for always," he said, "with peace and happiness. And whatsoever your hands may touch shall prosper. And now, little stool"—the King turned around—"what can I do for you?"

"For me?" The little stool was so surprised he nearly tumbled over.

"For you," said the King, and he smiled again.

"Well, as to that," began the little stool, "if the strong man and the milking-pail and I can live always with the little old man and his gentle wife, we have nothing to wish for."

"Nothing at all?" asked the King. "Think!"

"Well," admitted the little stool with a laugh, "there is one thing we have often talked about, the strong man and the milking-pail and I. We should very much enjoy a little child about the house."

"For me to work for," said the strong man.

"To drink of my white milk," added the shiny pail.

"And to sit upon me," continued the little stool, creaking his legs with joy at the thought.

"Oh! oh! oh!" cried the little old man and his gentle wife.

For there, right before them was a little child with yellow curls and blue eyes and cheeks like roses in June time. And she gave the little old man a kiss on his little left cheek, and his gentle wife a kiss on the right cheek.

Then she sat down on the little three-legged stool with the red, red carpet on it. "May I have it for mine?" she asked.

And the little old man and his gentle wife nodded their heads, and their eyes shone.

"And to think," said the little old man, "it was the little stool that brought it all to us."

"Not at all! Not at all!" cried the little stool, creaking with joy. "I haven't had so much fun for a long time."

THE ELF

Janet Lewis

I wanted a fairy, I wanted an elf,
I wanted a small one all for myself.

I looked for one down at the end of the garden.
I turned up the leaves and I said, "Beg pardon.

Little Mr. Beetle with the gold-spotted shell,
Little Mrs. Ladybug, I know you very well,

But could you by chance be a fairy in disguise,
A small enchanted fairy, strange to human eyes?"

I looked for him away down underneath the grasses
Along the silver track where the slow snail passes.

I looked for him, I wished for him. The more I thought about
 him,
The more extremely difficult it was to do without him.

And the worst of it is, I'm still certain that he's there,
But just as I am coming, he turns himself to air.

Margaret J. Baker

THE FAIRY WHO DIDN'T BELIEVE IN CHILDREN

ILLUSTRATED BY *Clara Ernst*

"WELL, I don't believe in children, so there!" said Tinders and she stamped her foot on the ground. "There could not be such ridiculous creatures. Why, some fairies even say that children's big toes are as long as we are!"

Tinders wasn't a large fairy herself. She was just a little over an inch tall, and she fitted quite easily into the bell of a snapdragon blossom. Her shoes were the smallest possible size, and her stockings often came down to wrinkle round her thin legs. She had yellow, fair hair and a dreadful habit of arguing with everyone, even her mother.

At bedtime all the other fairies listened to stories about some huge wonderful creatures called children, but not Tinders. She lay on her side (because that is the easiest way with wings) and often made up stories for herself, about dragons and witches and hobgoblins. "Of course there aren't any real children. They're just make-believe," she said to her friends at the fairy kindergarten, which was held every morning under a rather gloomy oak tree. "Some silly fairies say children are so clever that they can do sums like Long Division, but everyone knows only our fairy professors possess that secret, and it takes them ages and ages to work it out. Besides, how could children manage to live at all without any wings?"

Tinders flicked her own wings behind her back as she said this, and whisked around the classroom before the fairy teacher came in through the door. Miss Beeswax had filmy, drooping wings and old-fashioned ideas. She wasn't very clever, and she liked to tell long stories about children's adventures instead of teaching arithmetic and other difficult subjects. Tinders was always a great nuisance to Miss Beeswax, asking questions.

"But of course we believe in children, dear," the teacher said one day, as she prepared to tell a story. "All nice little fairies believe in boys and girls."

"But have you ever seen a child?" asked Tinders, fidgeting in her seat. It was the top of an acorn cup, and much too high for her.

"As a matter of fact, I have never seen a child," said Miss Beeswax, "but that is no reason to assume that children are non-existent. Some of our daring fairy explorers have seen boys and girls and have observed their habits, but they have seldom reported the presence of children in these parts."

When talking to Tinders, Miss Beeswax always used the longest words she could think of, hoping that this would keep the obstinate fairy from asking more questions. She went on with her story now, about a park in a big city where children played in charge of larger humans called nursemaids.

Tinders went on fidgeting, but deep in her heart, the little fairy wanted to believe in children. And she suddenly decided to discover a child for herself. And so, when lunchtime came, instead of flying home, she flew straight out of the woods and high in the air, over the trees.

It was a lovely day. Tinders flew on and on. Once she met a swallow who was ten times as large as herself, and she asked him if he had ever seen a child, but the silly bird could not understand a word she said.

Again the fairy flew on, and finally, at dusk, she landed in a large garden. There were flowers everywhere, and best of all, lying on the grass was a creature who must be a child!

Concealing herself behind a birdbath, Tinders looked at the giant-like creature. The child was very long, and yet she did not look grown-up. She had fair hair, just like many of the fairies, and sandals on her feet. Tinders could see the child's toes. "It's really true," the fairy said to herself. "Those toes are almost as big as I am."

Now Tinders noticed that the child was asleep. Deciding it was safe to go closer, the fairy flew round the birdbath and stared at the little girl's face. It was sunburned and freckled. Tinders thought it was very disagreeable. She flew a little nearer and landed on a button of the child's dress. The button was shiny mother-of-pearl, and it made a pleasant seat. But as Tinders sat there, the little girl sneezed! It was like an earthquake. But the fairy hung onto the button with all her might. "For goodness' sake, don't do that again!" she said as soon as she stopped shaking with fright.

The child sat up and looked at Tinders. "You're not really there," she said. "You must be part of a dream. Nurse always reads those silly fairy stories to me when I go to bed, and I suppose that's why I'm dreaming about such a ridiculous little creature. Fairies are only make-believe. Everyone knows that."

Tinders had never been so angry in her life. "I'm not make-believe," she replied, bouncing up and down on the button. "I'm just as real as you are, so there!"

"You're not," said the child.

"I am," said Tinders, "and I wish I hadn't come. You're not a bit clever like the stories say. You're stupid."

It was a dreadful argument, and in the end, because she was so tired, Tinders burst into tears. She sobbed and sobbed. And she had no pocket handkerchief.

"A daisy petal will do," she said, sniffing, as the child began to comfort her. "I'm hungry, too," the fairy added. "I haven't had anything to eat since breakfast. And I've nowhere to sleep. At home I have a lovely bed with rose-petal sheets."

At that moment she stopped speaking and screamed because

she saw an enormous figure hurrying down the path. It was the child's nurse.

"Well now, Janet, you *are* a naughty child leading me this chase," the nurse declared. "I've been searching all over for you. Please come to supper at once now, and no argument."

There was barely time for Tinders to hop into the girl's pocket before the child rose to go with the nurse. In the house Janet popped the fairy into a flower bowl while Nurse began to set a supper table. "You will be quite safe there," the girl whispered to Tinders. "I'll get you something to eat as soon as I can."

Janet had milk and biscuits for supper, and when the nurse wasn't watching she gave the fairy a thimbleful of milk and a doll's plate of crumbs.

After their supper, the nurse came back, and while the fairy lay in the flower bowl giggling, Nurse opened up the nursery windows and said good night to Janet. When the huge grown-up creature had gone away, then, the girl fixed a lovely bed for her fairy guest in among some handkerchiefs. Tinders went to sleep at once and dreamed all night long about children.

In the morning, after breakfast, Tinders decided that it was time to say good-bye. Janet gave the fairy a grain of brown

sugar and half a raisin wrapped to take home, but before Tinders left, Janet showed her all over the house. Tinders was very much excited about the bathroom, with its shower that was like the rain. She liked Janet's own room, too, with its colored pictures of fairies on the walls.

Janet showed the fairy her schoolbooks then, and Tinders was specially impressed with the arithmetic workbook, with numbers that were nearly as large as the fairy herself, and even some long-division problems which Janet had just begun. Janet's papers were somewhat smudged in places, but Tinders admired all of them very much.

By this time, Tinders felt that she really must start home. So Janet stood at the bedroom window waving good-bye till the fairy looked like a speck of dust gleaming in the morning sun. Then the child raced downstairs to play outdoors.

Back in fairyland, Tinders still argued with Miss Beeswax and with her mother. But she no longer denied the existence of children, and she never again refused to listen to a story about them. And when she grew older, Tinders studied to be a teacher of long division in the fairies' school. After that, she even wrote a schoolbook about children.

And to this day, if any clever young fairy tries to tell Tinders that children are only make-believe, she knows exactly what to say to them in reply.

Jacob and Wilhelm Grimm

THE FISHERMAN AND HIS WIFE

RETOLD BY *Jane Beglen*

ILLUSTRATED BY *Frances Eckart*

THERE was once a poor old fisherman. He lived in a small shack with his wife. The shack was on the sand, very near the billowing sea. Every morning the old man went down to the shore and cast his line.

On one particular morning as he sat patiently waiting for a nibble, the fisherman fell asleep. Suddenly he was awakened by a tug on his line. Opening his eyes he saw a gigantic flounder creating a tremendous foam as it thrashed about to free itself of the hook. As the fisherman watched, his eyes grew large with wonder. The fish was *talking* to him!

"Put me back in the water, please!" begged the flounder. "I am an enchanted prince and want only to swim away."

Unbelieving, the old man could only mumble, "All right. I am only too happy to let an enchanted prince swim away."

He gently removed the hook, and the flounder slid back into the water. It swam in a circle several times. Then it stood on its tail and said politely, "Thank you. If you ever want anything, call on me." And it disappeared into the foam.

The fisherman's wife met him at the door that evening. When she saw that he was empty-handed she exclaimed, "No fish?

Out all day and you have caught no fish?"

Quickly the fisherman told her about the flounder and its promise, "If you ever want anything, call on me."

"What did you ask for in return?" asked his wife.

"Why, nothing! I never really thought about it," he said.

"Foolish man!" snapped his wife. "Let me think a minute. . . I know! I would like a cottage with a garden and chickens and ducks. Yes! Hurry, and ask your fish for a nice cottage."

The fisherman sighed, but he saw that he could not argue with her, so he went down to the sea and called:

"Oh man of the sea, come listen to me,
For Alice, my wife, the plague of my life,
Hath sent me to beg a boon of thee!"

As he called, wavy currents and small whirlpools turned the water yellow and green, and *then* the flounder appeared.

"What does your wife want?" he asked.

"She wants a fine cottage for us, with a garden and chickens and ducks," the fisherman replied, hanging his head.

"Go home. Your wife will be waiting in the door." And the flounder dove straight to the bottom of the sea.

As he neared his home, the old man saw at once that things were different, indeed. Where the old shack had been, there now stood a little white cottage with a picket fence and roses around the gate.

"Come in, come in," cried his wife. "See if this is not wonderful!" She beamed with pleasure as she led him through the arched door into the living room, the neat kitchen, and the bright bedroom. "Isn't it nice?"

"Yes, yes. If this will only last," replied her husband.

The old couple spent all the next day in their cottage and garden, more content than they had been in years.

But the following morning, just as the sun came up, the fisherman was awakened by his wife.

"Hurry, get up and go down to the flounder! This cottage is too small and crowded. I want something larger. I think I would like to live in a stone castle," his wife said.

"Put me back . . ." begged the flounder. "I am an enchanted prince."

"My dear wife, I like this cottage. Why would we want a castle?" he asked.

"Never mind why!" she answered. "We just do. Now run down and ask your fish!"

"I don't think we should ask for anything else," the old man said, but the look on his wife's face sent him out the door.

The sea water was purple and dark blue and gray when he reached the shore. He called:

"Oh man of the sea, come listen to me,
For Alice, my wife, the plague of my life,
Hath sent me to beg a boon of thee!"

"What does she want now?" said the fish when he appeared.

"Oh," said the man, more than a little afraid, "she would like to live in a stone castle with a moat and all."

"Go! When you reach home your wife will be in the door."

When the fisherman reached the spot where the cottage had stood he saw in its place a huge stone castle, with a drawbridge over its twenty-foot moat. His wife was waiting for him.

"Come quickly, and see if this isn't nicer than the cottage," she said, as she led him through the magnificent castle.

"Look out the window," the woman ordered. "Just see the beautiful orchards, the rambling stables, and those flower gardens! Isn't it nicer than that old cottage?"

"Yes," said her husband. "If only we can live here always, we shall be content."

It took two weeks for the fisherman's wife to visit and inspect each room in the castle, so it was not until fifteen nights after the appearance of the castle that she drew her husband to a front room and said, "See, see out this window. We can see for miles, and I want to own it all. I want to be king."

"King!" said the man in surprise. "Why king?"

"I must be king, and that is that. Go tell the flounder."

The fisherman went, but he was very troubled.

"Oh man of the sea, come listen to me,
For Alice, my wife, the plague of my life,
Hath sent me to beg a boon of thee!"

As he called, the sea became dark; it rushed over the sand and gave off a terrible odor.

"Now what?" demanded the enchanted prince in a loud voice so close to the old man that he jumped back in fear.

"My wife would like to be king of all the country," he managed to say, although he was very much afraid.

"She is king!" called the fish.

So the fisherman went back to the castle and was not too surprised to see that it had grown larger, with spiral towers, gun turrets, and heralds at the gates. As he entered the hall, the crystal chandeliers shone like diamonds, and his feet sank ankle-deep into the carpets as he walked toward the throne room. There he found his wife seated upon an emerald throne, a silver scepter in her hand, and twelve pages and twenty ladies in waiting attending her.

"Surely you will be happy now?" the fisherman said as he bowed before her.

"Time will tell!" she answered with a wave of her hand which brought all twenty ladies in waiting to wait upon her.

During the banquet that very evening the king sighed, "I am

unhappy here. I only own and rule the land I can see, I want to rule it all. I think that I should be emperor. Go tell your fish!"

"We already have an emperor, and there can only be one to every empire," the fisherman said in dismay.

"You heard my wish. I will be emperor. Go now and be quick. I am your king, and you have my order," she commanded.

The fisherman went, but he feared that the flounder might be angry with his latest request.

When the old man reached the sea he found the water a murky black. Although he was quaking with fright, he called:

"Oh man of the sea, come listen to me,
For Alice, my wife, the plague of my life,
Hath sent me to beg a boon of thee!"

"What now?" bellowed the fish from his perch on the peak of the largest wave.

"My wife . . . my wife wants to be emperor," whispered the old man.

"Go! She is," yelled the flounder.

As he reached the gates the fisherman found imperial troops marching before the palace, imperial guards guarding the bridge, and the imperial band playing "God save her majesty, the emperor!"

"Well, wife, now you are emperor of all the land. At last you will be happy, for you can be nothing else," said the fisherman, as he tiptoed up to his wife seated upon a solid gold throne.

"As a matter of fact, I am not too sure, but we shall see," the woman replied.

For six months the fisherman's wife was happy. Then on a dark and stormy night she rushed to her husband and said, "Seek your fish! If I can't make this storm stop and order the moon and stars to shine, I shall never have a happy minute. I want to control the universe, and I *will* control it!"

"The fish can't give you that power!" cried the fisherman in dismay.

"I will discuss it no longer. Go now!" screamed the emperor, wild with impatience.

The fisherman had no sooner left the palace than the storm grew worse, tearing down trees, houses, and even mountains. Long before he reached the water, he could see it. The crest of each gigantic wave plunged another ship to destruction. The water had turned a blood red around the edge and deathly black in the center. Though he shook all over and his knees trembled, the fisherman called above the roar of the wind:

"Oh man of the sea, come listen to me,
For Alice, my wife, the plague of my life,
Hath sent me to beg a boon of thee!"

"Well?" asked the fish in an unusually calm voice.

"Oh, my wife, dear flounder, would like to rule the sun and the moon and the stars. She says that she will never be happy unless they are in her command," answered the fisherman.

The great fish stared down at him from his peak on the largest wave.

"Go home to your wife. Go home to your *shack*," he boomed.

Then the flounder dove straight to the bottom of the sea. And there he stayed.

THE THREE SILLIES

ADAPTED BY *Joseph Jacobs*

ILLUSTRATED BY *Ruth van Tellingen*

ONCE upon a time there was a farmer and his wife who had one daughter, and she was courted by a gentleman. Every evening he used to come to supper at the farmhouse, and the daughter used to be sent down into the cellar to draw the beer. One evening she had gone to the cellar, and she happened to look up at the ceiling while she was drawing, and she saw a mallet stuck in one of the beams. It must have been there a long, long time, but somehow or other she had never noticed it before, and at the frightful thought which passed through her mind she put down the candle and the jug and sat herself down and began a-crying.

Well, they began to wonder upstairs how it was that she was so long drawing the beer, and her mother went down to see after her, and she found her sitting on the settle crying, and the beer running over the floor. "Why, whatever is the matter?" said her mother.

"Oh, Mother!" says she, "look at that horrid mallet! Suppose we was to be married, and was to have a son, and he was to grow up, and was to come down to the cellar to draw the beer, and the mallet was to fall on his head and kill him, what a dreadful thing it would be!"

"Dear, dear! what a dreadful thing it would be!" said the mother, and she sat her down aside of the daughter and started a-crying too.

In turn came the father, who wept at the sight of daughter and mother a-crying, the beer running on the floor, and his daughter's dreadful thought, then the gentleman, tired of staying in the kitchen by himself. But when the father explained why they wept, the gentleman burst out a-laughing, and reached up and pulled out the mallet, and then he said: "I've traveled many miles, and I never met three such big sillies as you three before; and now I shall start out on my travels again, and when I can find three bigger sillies than you three, then I'll come back and marry your daughter." So he wished them good-bye and left them all crying because the girl had lost her sweetheart.

Well, he set out, and at last he came to a cottage where a woman was trying to get her cow to go up a ladder to the grass on the roof. So the gentleman asked the woman what she was doing. "Why, lookye," she said, "look at all that beautiful grass. I'm going to get the cow on to the roof to eat it. She'll be quite safe, for I shall tie a string round her neck, and pass it down the chimney, and tie it to my wrist as I go about the house, so she can't fall off without my knowing it."

"Oh, you poor silly!" said the gentleman, "you should cut the grass and throw it down to the cow!"

But the woman got the cow up and tied a string round her neck, and passed it down the chimney, and fastened it to her

own wrist, but soon the cow tumbled off the roof, and hung by the string tied round her neck, and it strangled her. And the weight of the cow tied to her wrist pulled the woman up the chimney, and she stuck fast halfway and was smothered in the soot.

Well, that was one big silly.

And the gentleman went on and on, and he went to an inn to stop the night, and they were so full at the inn that they had to put him in a double-bedded room, with a very pleasant fellow. But in the morning, when they were both getting up, the gentleman was surprised to see the other hang his trousers on the knobs of the chest of drawers and run across the room and try to jump into them, and he tried over and over again, and couldn't manage it. At last he said "Oh, dear, I do think trousers are the most awkwardest kind of clothes that ever were. It takes me the best part of an hour to get into mine every morning. How do you manage yours?" So the gentleman burst out a-laughing, and showed him how to put them on.

So that was another big silly.

Then the gentleman went on his travels again; and he came to a village, and outside the village there was a pond, and round the pond was a crowd of people. And they had got rakes, and brooms, and pitchforks, reaching into the pond; and the gentleman asked what was the matter. "Why," they said, "matter enough! Moon's tumbled into the pond, and we can't rake her out anyhow!" So the gentleman burst out a-laughing, and told them to look up into the sky, and that it was only the shadow in the water. But they wouldn't listen to him, and abused him shamefully, and he got away as quick as he could.

So there was a whole lot of sillies bigger than those three sillies at home. So the gentleman turned back home again and married the farmer's daughter, and if they didn't live happily forever after, that's nothing to do with you or me.

Constance Savery

THE LITTLE DRAGON

ILLUSTRATED BY *Robert Lawson*

THERE was once a little dragon, quite nice and tame. His name was Augustus, and he lived with his father and mother in a cave with colored icicles hanging from the roof

As the little dragon could not fly very far, he often had to stay at home in the cave on the hillside, coiled round three times, watching the people who passed in the valley far below. He liked watching the boys and girls and marketfolk; but when the prince rode by in shining armor on his coal-black steed, the poor little dragon nearly cried.

"I wish I were a prince," thought he. "How fine I should look in that flashing armor on that black horse! Oh, I do wish I were a prince!"

"Well, so you are a prince," said the old gypsy woman who had come softly up the hillside to the entrance of the cave.

"But you are under a spell cast by those wicked dragons who are pretending to be your father and mother. They turned their dragon-son into a prince, and they turned you into a dragon and took you to live in their cave."

"But why did they do it?" asked the little dragon.

"Ah, it's a fine thing to have a prince for your son," laughed the gypsy woman. "Mr. and Mrs. Dragon always were ambitious."

"Can't I undo the spell?" said the little dragon.

"You might," said the gypsy. "Take a crystal bowl, fill it with powdered sea shells steeped in elderberry cordial, and drink deep. That should serve you."

Then the gypsy woman hobbled away. She did not mean to tell an untruth, but unfortunately she had made a sad mistake in thinking that Mr. and Mrs. Dragon had cast a spell on their little Augustus. They had done no such thing.

The little dragon felt angry and important. He puffed out his chest at the thought that he was really the prince who owned the white, shining palace down in the valley. "I will undo the spell at once," he said.

So he waddled down to the shore and gathered sea shells and pounded them with his mother's flat iron and steeped them in elderberry cordial. Next he poured the mixture into a crystal bowl, and last of all he drank it. He also swallowed the flatiron quite by mistake, which was perhaps the reason why the spell was not undone.

For he was still a little dragon.

When the gypsy woman came again, he was very cross with her.

"Your spell was worse than useless," said he. "And Mother was dreadfully vexed about her flatiron."

The gypsy woman was sorry for him. "I will tell you other remedies," she said.

And she gave him seven more spells for undoing spells, but none of them were any good. The little dragon slept on young green nettles for nine nights, and ate herbs gathered from thirteen fairy rings and washed in sea foam mixed with

May dew, and drank four potions, each more horrible than the last—but nothing would turn him into a prince.

At last he grew tired of trying spells. One day the prince rode past the cave on his black horse, and at once Augustus pounced on him and dragged him inside.

The prince was not expecting to be pounced on. He was so much taken by surprise that he did not even try to fight the little dragon.

"Now I've got you, wicked creature!" said Augustus. "You're not a prince at all. You're the son of the dragons that live in this cave. I am the real prince under a spell."

"Absurd!" said the prince, as bravely as he could.

"It isn't absurd," said Augustus indignantly. "Take off your armor and your clothes. I am going down to my palace. You must stay here."

The prince struggled hard, but Augustus was the stronger of the two. He tore away all the beautiful shining armor and most of the clothes, and then he dressed himself for his arrival at the palace.

It took him three hours to dress and don his armor. Everything was so small that he had to fasten himself together with pieces of string and many safety pins. The prince sulked in a corner, refusing to help.

As soon as Augustus was dressed, he locked the door of the cave behind him, left the key in the lock, and marched down to the palace. The courtiers and servants were just setting out in search of their gallant prince who had not returned from hunting in the hills.

The sight of the little dragon made them run away screaming.

"Do not be afraid, my friends," said Augustus. "I am your unhappy master under a spell."

So they came timidly up to him, and he was led into the palace.

Meanwhile the prince sat in the cave with colored icicles, wondering what would happen when Mr. and Mrs. Dragon came back from their ride through the air. At midnight he heard the beating of their great wings.

"And pray, who are you?" said Mr. Dragon in surprise.

"I am the prince of this country," answered the young man. "Your son dragged me into this cave and robbed me of my armor and my clothes, saying that he was the true prince. A gypsy woman had told him so. He has gone to my palace to take possession of it."

"So that's what was the matter with Augustus!" said Mrs. Dragon. "I could see that the silly child had something on his mind but I couldn't find out what was troubling him. He thinks he's a prince under a spell, does he? Ha, ha, ha!"

"I should like to go home now," said the prince politely.

"You can't," said Mrs. Dragon. "Not like that! It is beneath your dignity to go to your palace in the few rags Augustus has left you. I would make you some new clothes if I could," she added kindly, "but unluckily I am not very good at sewing. My claws always catch in the stuff."

"You had better stay with us till Augustus returns," said Mr. Dragon. "He'll come home sooner or later. He's not cut out for a prince. He, he, he! Have some supper?"

So they lighted a fire, and cooked a fine supper for the prince,

and lent him Augustus's bed, which was a great deal too large for him. And he lived in the cave on the hill.

As for Augustus, he sat on a tight, uncomfortable golden throne, dressed in glorious robes. All day long tailors were running sharp pins into him as they tried on his new court clothes. At night he slept in the State bed, which was so much too small for him that he often rolled out of it with a terrible bump on the floor. And at mealtimes he never had enough to eat. When he cleared the gold and silver dishes, his courtiers whispered to one another, "What a greedy appetite his Highness has!"

One day he was sitting by himself in the gardens of the palace, a lonely little dragon. His subjects believed that he was their prince, but they were always afraid that a prince under a dragon spell might be tempted to snap. So they left him alone.

He looked up, and there stood the gypsy woman.

"How are you getting on?" she inquired.

"Not very well," said the little dragon.

"The prince is getting on very well indeed," said the gypsy. "He likes his life in the cave. At night your mother and father take him out treasure-hunting. He sits on your father's back, holding his scaly wings. They went to the mountains of the moon last night to gather moonstones. And you should see the emeralds he brought back from the shores of the sea that no man knows!"

"Oh!" said the little dragon.

"Then they come back and make a huge fire of dried ferns and pine cones and sea wood, and your mother cooks the supper. Plum porridge! Great big platefuls!"

"Oh!" said the little dragon. "Oh!"

"And when the dishes are washed and shining dry, your mother and father sing to him—scales and catches and snatches."

"Oh!" said the little dragon. "Oh, oh, oh!"

And he asked anxiously, "Does my mother—Mrs. Dragon, I mean—does she like him better than me?"

The gypsy woman only laughed.

Late that night Mr. and Mrs. Dragon heard a whimpering and sniffling outside the cave. They looked out and saw Augustus. In his claws he held clothes and a suit of armor for the prince.

"Oh, Mother, let me in!" he cried. "I want to come home. I don't believe that gypsy woman spoke the truth. I would rather be a dragon than a prince."

"You are much better fitted to be a dragon than a prince, Augustus," said his mother severely. "Come in at once and don't let me hear any more nonsense."

So Augustus came in and sat down. The prince began to dress himself in his splendid clothes and glittering armor. He looked every inch a prince as he buckled on his sword. Then he drew it from the scabbard and bade Mr. Dragon kneel.

"I wish to reward you for your services," he said.

Mr. Dragon knelt as well as he could for his tail.

The prince struck him lightly on the shoulder and said, "Rise, Sir Dragon."

Then he said good-bye rather coldly to Augustus, climbed onto Sir Dragon's back, and was swiftly borne home to the palace. Lady Dragon went too, carrying the moonstones and emeralds.

Augustus stayed at home and washed the dishes, after he had eaten all that was left of the good supper. Then he crawled into his large bed, saying to himself, "It's better to be a dragon than a prince. There's no place like home."

And the little dragon went happily to sleep.

THE FAIRY SCHOOL

Marjorie Barrows

At goldenrod and aster time
  The fairies near our pool
Put on some freshly laundered wings
  And flutter off to school.

They sit at little toadstool desks
  And do their fairy sums,
And learn to color autumn leaves
  Before the frost king comes.

And then they study very hard
  So they can spin cocoons
And sing the flowers all to sleep
  With little bedtime tunes.

They'd fluttered home for tea today
  When I went past the pool,
But I *almost* saw the fairy dunce
  Staying after school!

Hans Christian Andersen

THE UGLY DUCKLING

RETOLD BY *Nicholas Nirgiotis*

ILLUSTRATED BY *Bianca*

IT WAS summer, and the weather was lovely. The country was beautiful just then, covered with golden corn, green oats, and stacks of hay piled high on the meadows about which the stork tiptoed gingerly on his long red legs, chattering in Egyptian—the language his mother had taught him. The fields and meadows were surrounded by green forests in the midst of which were deep lakes. And in the sunniest spot, close to a river, stood an old farmhouse from whose walls great burdocks grew down to the water's edge, so high that little children could stand under them. In this place, just as wild as the thick woods, sat a duck upon her nest waiting for her eggs to hatch. She was tired of sitting still and alone such a long time, and she so seldom had visitors. The other ducks liked better to swim in the river than to sit under the cool burdocks and cackle with her.

At last one egg after another cracked open, and little heads poked out of them. "Cheep, cheep!" they cried as they climbed out of their shells and looked about them at the large green leaves.

"Quack, quack!" said their mother, and she allowed them to look as much as they liked, since green is good for the eyes.

"How large the world is!" cried the young ducks when they found how much more room they now had than when they were inside their shells.

"Sillies," said their mother. "Do you think this is all the

world? It extends a long way across the other side of the garden up to the parson's field, but I have never been that far. Are you all here now?" she continued, standing up. "No, I have not got you all yet! The largest egg still lies there. Oh, dear! How long is this going to take?" and she sat wearily on the nest again.

"How are you getting on?" asked an old duck who had come to pay her a visit.

"This one egg is taking such a long time!" said the duck. "It will not break open. But just look at the others. Aren't they the prettiest ducklings you have ever seen? They look just like their father—the rascal! He never comes to see me."

"Let me see the egg which won't crack open," said the old visitor. "I was once fooled with a turkey's egg and I had plenty of worry and trouble with it, for turkeys are very much afraid of the water, and you simply cannot get them to go into it. I quacked and clucked but it was no use. Let me see the egg. Yes, that's a turkey's egg. Leave it alone and teach the other children to swim."

"I have sat so long already that I can sit on it a little longer," said the mother duck.

"As you please," said the old duck, and she went away.

At last the large egg burst open. "Cheep, cheep!" said the little duckling as he tumbled out of his shell. The mother duck looked at him. How very big and ugly he was!

"This is an enormous duckling," she said. "Can he be a turkey chick? None of the other ducklings were as large. Well, there is one way to find out. Into the water he must go, even if I have to push him in myself."

The next day the weather was delightful, and the leaves danced in the breeze. The mother duck, followed by her whole family, went down to the river.

"Quack, quack," she said, and splashed into the water first. "Come, children," she cried. One after another, the ducklings plunged into the water, disappeared for an instant, but bobbed up again and began to swim beautifully. They were all in the water; the ugly gray duckling among them.

"No, he is not a turkey," she observed. "Look how well he paddles with his legs, and how erect he holds himself. He must be my own child! I should be proud of him, for, on the whole, he is quite pretty. Now come with me, children, and I will show you the rest of the great world and introduce you to the poultry-yard. But keep close to me so that no one may step on you, and beware of the cat."

When they came into the poultry-yard there was a fearful riot going on, for two families were fighting for the head of an eel, and in the end the cat got it.

"That's how things go in the world," observed the mother duck, and she looked longingly at the delicacy, for she, too, wanted the eel's head. "Now use your legs properly," she added. "Quack properly, and bow your heads to that old duck over there. She is the grandest of us all. She has Spanish blood in her veins—that's why she's so fat. And do you see the red rag around her leg? That is a wonderfully fine thing, and the greatest distinction any duck can have. It shows that one does not want to lose her, and that she is to be recognized by beasts and men. Look smart now, and turn your toes in; a well-brought-up duckling keeps his legs wide apart just like father and mother. That's it. Now bend your necks and say quack!"

The ducklings did as they were told, but the other ducks round about looked at them and said, quite boldly, "Look there! Now we are to have that flock, as if there were not enough of us already. And, oh dear, how ugly that duckling is! We won't stand him!" And immediately a duck flew at him and bit him in the neck.

"Let him alone," said the mother. "He is doing no harm to anyone."

"Yes, but he's too large and ungainly," said the duck who had bitten him, "and therefore he must be whacked."

"Those are handsome children you have," said the old duck with the rag around her leg. "They are all pretty except this one. I wish you could make him over."

"That's impossible, your grace," said the mother duck. "He is not handsome, but he has a very cheerful disposition, and swims as well as any of the others. I may even say that he will improve in time and become smaller. He has lain too long in the egg, and so he has not come out properly shaped." And patting his neck, she said, "Besides, he is a drake, and so it does not matter very much. I think he will be very strong and make his way in the world."

"The other ducklings are pretty enough," said the old duck. "Make yourselves at home now, and if you find the head of an eel, you may bring it to me."

They all felt quite at home now, except for the poor duckling who had been the last to come out of the shell. He was bitten, pushed about, and jeered by both the ducks and the chickens.

"He is too big," they all said. And the turkey cock, who had been born with spurs and thought himself quite an emperor, puffed himself up like a ship in full sail, made straight for him, and gobbled and gobbled till he grew red in the face. The poor duckling, at his wit's end, did not know which way to turn. He was despondent because he was so ugly and the joke of the whole yard.

The first day passed in this manner, and afterwards matters became worse and worse. The poor duckling was chased about by everyone. Even his brothers and sisters abused him, and said, "If only the cat would catch you, you hideous creature!" And his mother said, "I wish you were far away!" The ducks bit him, the chickens chased him, and the girl who fed the poultry kicked him aside with her foot.

Then he ran and flew over the fence, and the little birds on the hedge flew up into the air in a fright.

"That is because I am so ugly!" thought the poor duckling, shutting his eyes, but he ran on farther. Then he came to a great marsh where the wild ducks lived. Weary and miserable, he stayed here the whole night. Early next morning the wild ducks flew up to inspect their new companion.

"What sort of a creature are you?" they asked, as the duckling, turning from side to side and bowing, greeted them as well as he could. "You are dreadfully ugly," said the wild ducks, "but that does not matter to us, so long as you do not marry into our family."

Poor thing! He certainly had not thought of marriage. He only wanted permission to lie among the reeds and drink some of the marsh water.

He stayed there two whole days. Then two wild geese came, or rather two wild ganders. They were not long out of their shell and therefore rather bold.

"Listen, friend," said one. "You are so ugly that we like you. Will you join us and become a bird of passage? Nearby there is another marsh, with some charming wild geese in it. They are sweet young ladies, all unmarried, and all able to say quack! You have a chance to make your fortune among them, ugly as you are."

Just at that moment, *bang! bang!* resounded through the air, and the two ganders fell dead among the reeds, and the water turned blood red. *Bang! bang!* sounded the guns again, and the whole flock of wild geese rose up from the reeds as the shots showered down on them.

There was a great hunting party, and the hunters were lying in wait all round the marsh. Some were even sitting on the branches of the trees which overhung the water. The blue smoke rose up in clouds among the dark-green trees and swept over the pool. The hunting dogs came—*splash, splash!*—into the swamp, and the rushes and reeds bent down beneath their weight on every side. The poor duckling was terribly frightened. He twisted his head round to put it under his wing, and just at that moment a frightful, large dog appeared close behind him. His red tongue hung far out of his mouth, and his eyes glared, horrible and ugly. He thrust his nose close to the duckling, opened his great mouth, showed his sharp teeth, and —*splash, splash!*—went on without touching him.

"Oh, thank Heaven!" sighed the duckling. "I am so ugly that even the dog won't bite me!"

And so he lay quite still while the shots rattled the reeds, and bang after bang split the air. At last, late in the day, the shots ceased, but even then the poor duckling did not dare to get up. He waited several hours before he looked around, and then he hurried away from the marsh as quickly as he could. He ran across fields and meadows, and there was such a storm raging that he had difficulty making his way.

Toward night the duckling came to a little tumble-down cottage. This hut remained standing only because it could not make up its mind which way to fall. The wind continued to blow so fiercely round the duckling that he had to sit down to resist it. The storm grew worse and worse. Then he noticed that the door had fallen off one hinge and hung so crookedly that he could slip through the crack into the house, and in this way he entered the room.

An old woman dwelt in the house with her cat and her hen. The cat, whom she called Sonny, could arch his back, purr, and even give off sparks, though for that you had to stroke his fur the wrong way. The hen's legs were so short that she was called Chickie-low-legs. She laid good eggs, and the old woman loved her as if she had been her own child.

In the morning the strange duckling was discovered at once, and the cat began to purr and the hen to cluck.

"What in the world is that?" said the old woman, looking round, but she could not see well, and she mistook the duckling for a fat duck that had strayed. "This is a wonderful prize!" she said. "Now I shall have duck's eggs—if only it is not a drake. I must wait and see about that."

In this manner, the duckling was admitted on trial for three weeks, but no eggs came. The cat was master of this house, and the hen its mistress. They always said, "We and the world"; for they thought that they represented half of the world, and by far the better half. The duckling thought there might be two opinions about this, but the hen would not permit it.

"Can you lay eggs?" she asked.

"No."

"Be so good as to hold your tongue, then!"

And the cat said, "Can you arch your back, purr, or give off sparks?"

"No."

"Then you better keep your opinions to yourself when sensible people are speaking."

The duckling sat in a corner feeling very melancholy. Then he began to think of the fresh air and the sunshine, and he was seized by a great urge to float on the water. At last, he could not help telling the hen about it.

"What on earth are you thinking of?" asked the hen. "You have nothing to do, that's why you have these strange fancies. Lay some eggs or take to purring, and you will get over it."

"But it is so delightful to swim on the water," said the duckling. "It is so refreshing to feel it rushing over your head when you dive down to the bottom."

"That must be very amusing!" said the hen. "You must have gone mad. Ask the cat about it. He is the cleverest creature I know. Ask him if he likes to float on the water or dive under it. I say nothing about myself. Ask our mistress, the old woman. There is no one in the world wiser than she is. Do you imagine she has any desire to float on the water or to duck underneath it?"

"You do not understand me," said the duckling.

"If we don't understand you, who should? You certainly don't consider yourself cleverer than the cat or the old woman, not to mention me! Don't be foolish, child, and be grateful for all the kindness you have received. Have you not lived in this warm room, and in such company from which you might have learned something? But you are foolish, and there is no pleasure in associating with you. Believe me, I speak for your good. I tell you disagreeable things, and there's no surer way than that of knowing who are one's friends. You just set about laying some eggs, or learn to purr, or to give out sparks!"

"I think I will go out into the wide world," said the duckling.

"Oh, do so by all means," said the hen.

So the duckling went away. He floated on the water and ducked underneath it, but he was slighted by every creature because of his ugliness.

Now came the autumn. The leaves in the woods turned yellow and brown. The wind caught them, and they danced about. The sky looked very cold, and the clouds hung heavy with snow and hail. A raven stood on the fence and cried, "Caw, caw!" from sheer cold. His cry was enough to make one shiver. The poor duckling certainly was in a bad state!

Just as the sun was setting in wintry splendor one evening, a flock of beautiful large birds came out of the bushes. The duckling had never seen anything so beautiful. They were dazzlingly white with long graceful necks. They were swans, and uttering a peculiar cry, they spread out their magnificent broad wings and flew away from the cold regions to warmer lands and open seas. They rose so high, so very high, and the ugly little duckling felt strangely uneasy as he watched them.

He turned round and round in the water like a wheel, stretching his neck up into the air after them. Then he uttered a strange loud cry so piercing that he was quite frightened by it himself. Oh, he could not forget those beautiful, happy birds! And as soon as they were out of sight he ducked right down to the bottom, and when he came up again he was quite beside himself. He did not know what the birds were, or to what place they were flying, but, all the same, he felt closer to them than to any other creature he had ever encountered. He did not envy them in the least. How could he even wish to possess such beauty as they had? He would have been content if even the ducks would have given him their company.

The winter was so bitterly cold that the duckling was forced to swim about in the water to prevent it from freezing entirely, but every night the hole in which he swam became smaller and smaller. Then it froze so hard that the surface ice cracked, and the duckling was obliged to use his legs continually to prevent the hole from freezing up. At last he was so tired that he could move no more, and thus froze fast into the ice.

Early in the morning a peasant came by and saw him. He went out on the ice and hammered a hole in it with his heavy

wooden shoe, and carried the duckling home to his wife. There he soon came to life again. The children wanted to play with him, but the duckling thought they were going to injure him, and in his fright fluttered into the milk pan so that the milk spurted out all over the room. The woman shrieked and clapped her hands, at which the duckling flew down into the butter tub, and then into the meal tub and out again. Imagine how he looked by this time! The woman screamed and tried to hit him with the fire tongs. The children tumbled over one another in their efforts to catch him, and they screamed with laughter. Luckily, the door stood open, and the poor duckling flew out among the bushes into the newly fallen snow. And there he lay, thoroughly exhausted.

It would be too sad to relate all the hardships he had to undergo during that bitter winter. When the sun began to shine warmly again, the duckling was in the marsh. The larks began their songs again. It was a beautiful spring.

Then all at once he could flap his wings with greater strength than before, and they bore him strongly away. Before he knew where he was, he found himself in a large garden where the apple trees were in full blossom and the air smelled with lilacs, whose long branches reached the shores of the lake. The fragrance of spring was everywhere. And from the thicket he saw three beautiful white swans approaching him. With rustling feathers, they swam lightly over the water. The duckling recognized the beautiful birds, and he was overcome by a strange sadness.

"I will fly to them, the royal birds, and they will kill me, because I, who am so ugly, dare to approach them. But it won't matter! Better be killed by them than be chased by ducks, beaten by fowls, pushed about by the hen-wife, or suffer so much hunger and misery in the winter."

So he flew out into the water and swam toward the beautiful swans. They saw him and sailed toward him with ruffled feathers.

"Kill me," said the poor creature, and he bent his head toward the water expecting his death. But what was it that he saw reflected in the clear stream? He saw below him his own image, but he was no longer a clumsy, dark gray bird, ugly and ungainly. He was himself a swan! It does not matter at all if one is born in a duckyard, if only you come out of a swan's egg!

The big swans swam round him and stroked him with their bills. Some little children came into the garden, who threw corn and pieces of bread into the water, and the youngest one cried, "There's a new one!" The other children shouted with joy, "Yes, a new one has come." And they clapped their hands and danced about, running after their father and mother. They tossed more bread into the water, and they all said, "The new one is the most beautiful of all. So young and handsome!" And the old swans bowed their heads before him.

He felt very shy and hid his head under his wings, for he did not know what to do or think. He was very happy, yet not at all proud, for a good heart never becomes proud. He thought how he had been pursued and despised, and now he heard them say that he was the most beautiful of all birds. Even the lilacs bent their boughs down to the water before him, and the bright sun shone warm and cheering. He rustled his feathers and lifted his slender neck, crying with exultation in his heart, "I never dreamed of so much happiness when I was the Ugly Duckling!"

George Webbe Dasent

GUDBRAND ON THE HILLSIDE

ILLUSTRATED BY *Ruth van Tellingen*

ONCE on a time there was a man whose name was Gudbrand; he had a farm which lay far, far away, upon a hillside, and so they called him Gudbrand on the Hillside.

Now, you must know this man and his good wife lived so happily together, and understood one another so well that all the husband did the wife thought so well done there was nothing like it in the world, and she was always glad whatever he turned his hand to. The farm was their own land, and they had a hundred dollars lying at the bottom of their chest, and two cows tethered up in a stall in their farmyard.

So one day his wife said to Gudbrand,—

"Do you know, dear, I think we ought to take one of our cows into town and sell it; that's what I think; for then we shall have some money in hand, and such well-to-do people as we ought to have ready money like the rest of the world. As for the hundred dollars at the bottom of the chest yonder, we can't make a hole in that, and I'm sure I don't know what we want with more than one cow. Besides, we shall gain a little in another way, for then I shall get off with only looking after one cow, instead of having, as now, to feed and litter and water two."

Well, Gudbrand thought his wife talked right good sense, so he set off at once with the cow on his way to town to sell her; but when he got to the town, there was no one who would buy his cow.

"Well, well! never mind," said Gudbrand, "at the worst, I can only go back home again with my cow. I've both stable and tether for her, I should think, and the road is no farther out than in"; and with that he began to toddle home with his cow.

But when he had gone a bit of the way, a man met him who had a horse to sell; so Gudbrand thought 'twas better to have a horse than a cow, so he swapped with the man. A little farther on he met a man walking along and driving a fat pig before him, and he thought it better to have a fat pig than a horse, so he swapped with the man. After that he went a little farther, and a man met him with a goat; so he thought it better to have a goat than a pig, and he swapped with the man that owned the goat. Then he went on a good bit till he met a man who had a sheep, and he swapped with him too, for he thought it always better to have a sheep than a goat. After a while he met a man with a goose, and he swapped away the sheep for the goose; and when he had walked a long, long time, he met a man with a cock, and he swapped with him, for he thought in this wise, " 'Tis surely better to have a cock than a goose." Then he went on till the day was far spent, and he began to get very hungry, so he sold the cock for a shilling, and bought food with the money, for, thought Gudbrand on the Hillside, " 'Tis always better to save one's life than to have a cock."

After that he went on home till he reached his nearest neighbor's house, where he turned in.

"Well," said the owner of the house, "how did things go with you in town?"

"Rather so so," said Gudbrand. "I can't praise my luck, nor

do I blame it, either," and with that he told the whole story from first to last.

"Ah!" said his friend, "you'll get nicely called over the coals, that one can see, when you get home to your wife. Heaven help you, I wouldn't stand in your shoes for something."

"Well," said Gudbrand on the Hillside, "I think things might have gone much worse with me; but now, whether I have done wrong or not, I have so kind a good wife, she never has a word to say against anything that I do."

"Oh!" answered his neighbor, "I hear what you say, but I don't believe it for all that."

"Shall we lay a bet upon it?" asked Gudbrand on the Hillside. "I have a hundred dollars at the bottom of my chest at home; will you lay as many against them?"

Yes, the friend was ready to bet; so Gudbrand stayed there till evening, when it began to get dark, and then they went together to his house, and the neighbor was to stand outside the door and listen, while the man went in to see his wife.

"Good evening!" said Gudbrand on the Hillside.

"Good evening!" said the good wife. "Oh, is that you? now God be praised."

Yes! it was he. So the wife asked how things had gone with him in town.

"Oh! only so so," answered Gudbrand; "not much to brag of. When I got to the town there was no one who would buy the cow, so you must know I swapped it away for a horse."

"For a horse," said his wife; "well, that is good of you; thanks with all my heart. We are so well-to-do that we may drive to church, just as well as other people; and if we choose to keep a horse we have a right to get one, I should think. So run out, child, and put up the horse."

"Ah!" said Gudbrand, "but you see I've not got the horse after all; for when I got a bit farther on the road I swapped it away for a pig."

"Think of that, now!" said the wife; "you did just as I should have done myself; a thousand thanks! Now I can have a bit of bacon in the house to set before people when they come to see me, that I can. What do we want with a horse? People would only say we had got so proud that we couldn't walk to church. Go out, child, and put up the pig in the sty."

"But I've not got the pig, either," said Gudbrand; "for when I got a little farther on I swapped it away for a milch goat."

"Bless us!" cried his wife, "how well you manage everything! Now I think it over, what should I do with a pig? People would only point at us and say, 'Yonder they eat up all they have got.' No! now I have got a goat, and I shall have milk and cheese, and keep the goat, too. Run out, child, and put up the goat."

"Nay, but I haven't got the goat, either," said Gudbrand, "for a little farther on I swapped it away and got a fine sheep instead."

"You don't say so!" cried his wife; "why, you do everything to please me, just as if I had been with you; what do we want with a goat! If I had it I should lose half my time in climbing up the hills to get it down. No! if I have a sheep, I shall have

both wool and clothing, and fresh meat in the house. Run out, child, and put up the sheep."

"But I haven't got the sheep any more than the rest," said Gudbrand; "for when I had gone a bit farther I swapped it away for a goose."

"Thank you! thank you! with all my heart," cried his wife; "what should I do with a sheep? I have no spinning wheel, nor carding comb, nor should I care to worry myself with cutting, and shaping, and sewing clothes. We can buy clothes now, as we have always done; and now I shall have roast goose, which I have longed for so often; and, besides, down to stuff my little pillow with. Run out, child, and put up the goose."

"Ah!" said Gudbrand, "but I haven't the goose, either; for when I had gone a bit farther I swapped it away for a cock."

"Dear me!" cried his wife, "how you think of everything! just as I should have done myself. A cock! think of that! why it's as good as an eight-day clock, for every morning the cock crows at four o'clock, and we shall be able to stir our stumps in good time. What should we do with a goose? I don't know how to cook it; and as for my pillow, I can stuff it with cotton-grass. Run out, child, and put up the cock."

"But after all I haven't got the cock," said Gudbrand; "for when I had gone a bit farther, I got as hungry as a hunter, so I was forced to sell the cock for a shilling, for fear I should starve."

"Now, God be praised that you did so!" cried his wife; "whatever you do, you do it always just after my own heart. What should we do with the cock? We are our own masters, I should think, and can lie abed in the morning as long as we like. Heaven be thanked that I have got you safe back again; you who do everything so well that I want neither cock nor goose, neither pigs nor kine."

Then Gudbrand opened the door and said,—

"Well, what do you say now? Have I won the hundred dollars?" and his neighbor was forced to allow that he had.

CINDERELLA

RETOLD BY *Jane McHenry*

ILLUSTRATED BY *Elise Morton*

MANY years ago in a faraway land lived a lovely maiden named Cinderella. She had a stepmother and two stepsisters who were unkind and disagreeable most of the time. Instead of loving her gentle, winsome ways, they made her work very hard from early morning until the darkness fell. And even then she had no place to call her own, except a corner of the hearth, where she often sat among the cinders—and so was called Cinderella.

"Cinderella, come tidy my room," or "You'd better not feed that stale bread to the birds; it's all you're going to have for supper!" the lazy, wicked sisters would shout. There was never a kind word, but Cinderella did not complain. Strangely enough, she even grew more beautiful with each passing day.

High above the village stood a castle. Here lived a good king with his only son, a handsome young prince. Many of their courtiers were not unlike Cinderella's stepmother and sisters—haughty, vain, and selfish. Not a single maiden could be found among them who was sweet and generous enough to be worthy of a prince and half the kingdom. And so it came to pass that the King, by express command, invited all the maidens throughout his realm to attend a ball at the palace in the hope that thus his son might meet the princess of his choice.

Up and down every street in the village frenzied preparations were being made. Seamstresses had never been so busy! At Cinderella's cottage all were hard at work beautifying the two ugly stepsisters, who had been invited. Poor Cinderella had not, but she scurried about pressing the yards of silk, shirring the bolts of lace, and sitting up very late at night snipping basting threads. When it was almost time for the party, she gazed wistfully at the finished gowns until her stepmother snapped, "Stop dreaming. How they'd laugh to see a cinder girl like you at the ball. Get on with your work!" She frowned and waggled a long finger at Cinderella. The haughty sisters stopped primping long enough to exchange glances and nod their frizzed heads in agreement.

They drove away in their coach without even waving farewell, and Cinderella crept into her chimney corner, hugging the old cat and staring into the fire. Suddenly she heard a *swoosh* and looked up. Out of nowhere appeared a strange little lady. The cat dove behind the coalbox, and Cinderella stared in wonder as a glow filled the room.

"Cinderella, I am your fairy godmother. Why are you so sad?"

"Well, I wish . . . I wish . . ." Cinderella could not go on.

"You wish to go to the ball. Is that not so?"

"Yes, oh, yes I do . . . with all my heart!"

"Well, my child, you have been a good girl and you shall go." Then the fairy godmother leaned close to Cinderella's ear and said, "But first bring from the garden the biggest pumpkin you can find."

Cinderella had no idea how a pumpkin would help her, but she was so happy, she did as she was asked. She staggered up to the door with an enormous, yellow one. Quickly the fairy godmother scooped out its insides, tapped it gently with her wand and—*whing!*—the pumpkin became a glittering, golden coach.

She now requested a mouse trap with six mice; next a rat trap; and then six lizards. All of these things she touched with her wand, and jumping into place were a coachman—a splendid one with green livery,—six trim footmen, and six sleek and spirited horses!

"Now, Cinderella, you have a carriage to take you to the ball."

When Cinderella could speak, she cried, "Oh, but my clothes—these rags—they're all I have in the world."

When it was time for the party, she gazed wistfully at the gowns.

Quick as a wink, the fairy godmother flicked the wand and the girl was transformed, too! Every cinder and bit of soot vanished! Her hair was silken and gleaming. It fell over the shoulders of a fragile gown, which sparkled with jewels. And peeping from under her filmy skirts, were two little slippers of shining glass!

"Now you are quite ready, my child," said the fairy godmother. "But please remember this: unless you return at the first stroke of twelve, your coach will become a pumpkin; your coachman, a big white rat; your horses, frightened mice; your footmen, moist lizards; and your dress nothing but rags!"

Cinderella was almost afraid. But the fairy godmother smiled and led her out into the moonlight to her coach. When the maiden turned with shining eyes to thank this wonderful lady, she was not there at all. In fact, she had completely vanished. At the same instant, the coachman cracked his silver whip, and the horses fairly flew up the hill bearing Cinderella to the ball. Back in the cushiony seats, the girl held tightly to the pillows and tried to repeat her fairy godmother's warning.

In the great hall shimmering with a thousand candles, the Prince caught sight of Cinderella the moment she arrived. Joy danced in her heart as he made his way toward her through the

huge assembly of fine people and bowed low over her hand. She was the loveliest person the Prince had ever seen in his whole life! While everyone whispered excitedly about the enchanting, unknown guest, he stood, bedazzled, by her side. Through the night they danced. Cinderella was as light as a puff of thistledown!

In no time at all the clock in the tower began to strike twelve. With a start, Cinderella slipped out of her partner's arms and raced for the palace gates. She paused hardly at all when one of the little glass slippers flew off and lay twinkling in the dark grass. But the poor Prince, in pursuit, stopped. He picked it up and gently placed it in his velvet pocket. Cinderella was far out of sight as he turned back, vowing to search every inch of the land to find the radiant princess who had so suddenly run away.

When Cinderella reached the courtyard, her coach was gone. Only a big pumpkin stood by the gates surrounded by squealing mice. And she was in rags. No one noticed the little beggar who fled down the hill. Once safe inside her cottage, Cinderella curled up small on the hearth and slept.

After a fanfare of trumpets next day, the King announced that the Prince had already set off to visit each home to find the one maiden who could wear the little glass slipper. All morning the stepsisters wiggled their toes uncertainly in their satin shoes. They did not even trouble to tell Cinderella the exciting news, until a page announced the arrival of the Prince, himself. Shooing Cinderella into the scullery, the three women curtsied nervously.

The mother purred sweetly, "Sire, these are my daughters who attended the ball." To them she added, "Sit down, my dears, and try the slipper."

The page knelt and carefully tried each girl's foot. The first sister's foot was too long and slim and wouldn't do at all. The

second sister's foot was so plump that only her great toe would go in! Flushed and angry, they fled to their room.

"Have you no other daughters, Madame?" the Prince inquired, rising to leave.

"Well, no, not really," stammered the wicked woman, "no one at all, except a grimy little kitchen maid. Certainly she is of no interest to you, Milord."

"I ask that she be seen," commanded the Prince.

Unable to protest, the stepmother shoved Cinderella into the room. She stood with downcast eyes, lest the Prince recognize her in wretched rags and clumsy shoes.

"Be seated, Miss," said the page, while the two sisters, peering around the edge of their door, snickered and sneered.

Timidly, Cinderella thrust a bare foot into the tiny slipper. There was a gasp of surprise, except from Cinderella, for of course it fitted to perfection, just as it had the evening before. Speechless, the Prince looked into Cinderella's eyes, and as she smiled, her tattered rags vanished again. Standing on the hearth was the Princess he truly loved, clad in her sparkling gown and laughing with delight at his astonishment!

With a cry of joy, he carried her out of the humble cottage and lifted her on to his horse. Away they rode, leaving the three cross and ugly women shouting and quarreling among themselves.

Goodness knows *what* happened to them! But gentle Cinderella and her Prince had a long and happy life together.

Padraic Colum

THE MAN WITH THE BAG

ILLUSTRATED BY *Robert Lawson*

ONCE upon a time a man who had a beggar's bag on his back came to the door of a house that was hereabouts. He asked for shelter. "And if you let me take my rest here while I'm begging through the parish I'll ask you for nothing else, ma'am," said he to the woman of the house. "A good beggar doesn't ask for food where he gets shelter and doesn't ask for shelter where he gets food. I know what a good beggar's conduct should be. My father was a beggar, and his father was a beggar before him. I'm no upstart."

The woman of the house told him he could rest by the fire when he finished his round of begging in the evening, and when she told him this the man with the bag on his back turned from the door and went along the crooked lane that went from the house.

The woman's daughter was there, and she looked after him as he went down the laneway. And she thought that only for the grime that was on him and the ragged clothes that he wore he would be good-looking enough. Let the beggarman go on while I tell you about the girl. She was named Liban, and well did she deserve the name which means Beauty of Woman, for her eyes were beaming, her mouth was smiling, her cheeks were like roses, and her hair was brown as a cluster of nuts. But for all her beauty Liban had little chance of being wedded. Young men came to ask for her in marriage, but if they did, her mother told them they were first to climb the tree that overhung the high cliff, and take out of the raven's nest that was there a scissors that the raven had carried off and bring back in addition two of the raven's eggs. One young man and another young man would climb the tree, but when he came to the top branches that overhung the cliff and found them breaking under him, he would get down from the tree and not go to the door of the house again. So Liban stayed and was likely to stay beside her mother's hearth, spinning threads on her spindle while her mother spun them upon her wheel. And this was just what her mother wanted her to be doing, for she got a deal of silver for all the thread that she and Liban spun.

The beggarman came back in the evening, and his bag hung as if there were nothing in it. All the same, he refused the cup of milk and the cut of bread that Liban offered him. "All that I'll take in your house," said he, speaking to her mother, "is the place to rest myself, and leave to put in your charge what I get on my travels." And saying that he put his hand down into the bag, and searched and searched there, and brought up what he found. It was a pea. "I'll leave this in your charge and you'll be accountable for it," said he. "I'll take it back from you when I'm going." She took the pea and put it on the corner of her spinning wheel. Then the beggarman put the bag under his head and went to sleep by the fire.

Liban and her mother came out of the sleeping room at the peep of day, and as they did the beggarman got up from where he was lying, and opened the house door, and went off on his rounds with the crooked lanes of the parish before him. Liban went to get ready the breakfast. The little speckled hen that was her own came in to pick up the crumbs that would be around the table. But when she came as far as the spinning wheel she saw the pea, and when she saw it she picked it and swallowed it.

"Mother," Liban said, "the pea that the beggarman left in your charge, my own little speckled hen has swallowed."

"He'll forget to ask about it," said her mother, "and as for you, take the spindle and get some threads done while the breakfast porridge is cooling."

The first thing the beggarman said when he came in on the

doorway was, "Where is the pea I left in your charge, woman of the house?"

"A hen ate it."

"Which is the hen that ate the pea I left in your charge?"

"The speckled hen that's before you."

"If the speckled hen ate the pea that was mine, the hen herself is mine."

"That cannot be."

"It can be and it is, ma'am. It's the law, and if a beggarman doesn't know the law, who would know it?"

And saying this he took up the hen that was picking from a dish on the floor and put her into his empty bag. And the woman of the house believed what he said, for she had once stood in a court—the Court of Dusty Feet it was—and had heard a sentence passed on a man who had lost something that was left in his charge and that he was accountable for.

When he was going off the next morning he took the speckled hen out of his bag. "I leave her in your charge," he said to Liban's mother.

Then he went off, facing the crooked lanes of the parish, his empty bag hanging on his back. And Liban, so that nothing might happen to her, made a little pen of wattles for the speckled hen and tied her inside of it. Then she took up her spindle, and her mother went to her wheel. "I wish that beggarman had come to ask you in marriage so that I might have made him climb the tree," she said.

Liban was looking out of the door. She saw the pig beside the pen of wattles. The pen was strange to the pig, and she went rooting around it. The speckled hen flew into her mouth. The pig ate her. All that was left of the little speckled hen was the white feathers on the pig's snout.

And the first thing that the beggarman said when he came in on the doorway was, "Where is the speckled hen that I left in your charge?"

"The pig ate her," said Liban's mother.

"Then the pig is mine. That's the law, and if a beggarman doesn't know the law, who'd know it?" He went out to the yard and took the pig by the leg and dragged her into the house. He put her into his bag and tied up the mouth of his bag. Then he went to sleep by the fire.

By the time that the beggarman went out of her door next morning, Liban's mother had lost so much flesh through grief at the loss of her pig that she looked as if the weight of a pig had been taken out of her. And she wasn't able to eat her porridge either. Liban took charge of the pig. She tied her to a bush under a wall of loose stones, thinking no harm could come to her there. Then she went back to her spinning. But before she had more than a few threads spun, the horse galloping towards the house threw the stones of the wall down upon the pig. Then, trying to get up from where he was lying, the horse struck out with his hoofs and killed the pig. When Liban and her mother raised the horse up they found the pig with her head split open. "Every misfortune has come on us since that beggarman came to the house for shelter. He'll want to take our horse now. If he does and rides away on him, I'll be content with my loss—so glad I'll be to see the last of the beggarman."

He came back in the evening with a corner of his bag filled. "Where's my pig?"

"Our horse has killed her."

"Your horse is mine."

"Take him and ride away, and may all my bad luck go with you."

"No. I never stay less than five days in any house. It's due to a promise I made to my father. He feared that I might become a vagabond, one day here and another day there, and he made me promise I'd stay the greater part of the week in any house I had been given shelter in. One day more I'll stay for the sake of the promise I made. Mind the horse for me—I put him in your charge."

He lay by the fire, his head on his bag, and he went to sleep. The next morning he went off, his bag on his back, and his face towards the crooked lanes of the parish. Liban put a halter on the horse, and, so as not to let him get into any danger, went with him everywhere the horse went to graze. Along the cliff he went where the grass was sweetest. When they came to the tree that the raven's nest was in, Liban put her hands before her eyes so that she might look up and see how high the young men had to climb when they had asked for her. Not so high at all, she thought. And there was the raven on the branch above the nest, flapping her wings at her. As she looked, the horse, leaning out to get a mouthful of sweet grass, slipped and slithered down the cliff. And the raven with a croak flew down after him.

So poor Liban went back to her mother's. "Our horse is gone now," she said. "Over the cliff he has fallen, and what will the beggarman take from us now?"

"Nothing at all can he take," said her mother. "Let him take the horse's skin, and come next nor near us no more."

When he came back that evening with only a corner of his bag filled, the beggarman said, "Where's my horse so that I can go riding tomorrow?"

"The horse fell over a cliff and the raven is upon him now."

"Who was minding my horse when he fell over the cliff?"

"My daughter was minding your horse."

"Then your daughter is mine. That's the law, and if you don't think it is the law I'll stand face to face with you about it in the Court of Dusty Feet." And saying this the beggarman lifted up Liban (and, oh, but his arms were strong!) and thrust her into his bag. Then he put the bag on his back and ran from the house with her.

Her mother ran after him. The neighbors ran with the mother. But the beggarman's legs were long and strong and his back was broad and unbending. "Liban's in the bag, Liban's in the bag—stop him! Stop him!" cried her mother and the neighbors. But their cries only made him go faster and faster. When he came to the crossroads he laid the bag upon a bank, and he let Liban come out of it.

"Take me back to my mother," said Liban.

"Indeed, I'll do nothing of the kind," said the man, and now that he had taken off his ragged coat and had washed his face in the stream, he looked a handsome sort of a young man. "Here's a coach," he said. "It's waiting for you and me, and we'll go in it, not to the Court of Dusty Feet, but to the court in my father's castle where there will be one who will marry us. I put on the beggar's garb and carried this bag upon my back only to come to you, Liban, Beauty of Woman. There are many things I can do, but there are a few I can't do, and climbing a tree is one of them." Then he put his arm around her and lifted her into the coach that was waiting there, with two black horses to draw it. They had just got into the coach when

Liban's mother and the neighbors came up. The neighbors stopped to pick up the shower of silver that the coachman threw them, and the footman lifted Liban's mother and left her standing on the board beside him, and the coach went dashing on.

Part II: FOR OLDER READERS

Howard Pyle

THE SWAN MAIDEN

ILLUSTRATED BY *Dorothy Short*

ONCE there was a king who had a pear tree which bore four-and-twenty golden pears. Every day he went into the garden and counted them to see that none were missing.

But, one morning, he found that a pear had been taken during the night, and thereat he was troubled and vexed to the heart, for the pear tree was as dear to him as the apple of his eye. Now, the king had three sons, and so he called the eldest prince to him.

"See," said he, "if you will watch my pear tree tonight and will find me the thief who stole the pear, you shall have half of my kingdom now, and the whole of it when I am gone."

You can guess how the prince was tickled at this: oh, yes, he would watch the tree, and if the thief should come he should not get away again as easily.

Well, that night he sat down beside the tree, with his gun across his knees, to wait for the coming of the thief.

He waited and waited, and still he saw not so much as a thread or a hair. But about the middle of the night there came the very prettiest music that his ears had ever heard, and before he knew what he was about he was asleep and snoring until the little leaves shook upon the tree. When the morning came and he awoke, another pear was gone, and he could tell no more about it than the man in the moon.

The next night the second son set out to watch the pear tree. But he fared no better than the first. About midnight came the music, and in a little while he was snoring till the stones rattled. When the morning came another pear was gone, and he had no more to tell about it than his brother.

The third night it was the turn of the youngest son, and he was more clever than the others, for, when the evening came, he stuffed his ears full of wax, so that he was as deaf as a post. About midnight, when the music came, he heard nothing of it, and so he stayed wide awake. After the music had ended he took the wax out of his ears so that he might listen for the coming of the thief. Presently there was a loud clapping and rattling, and a white swan flew overhead and lit in the pear tree above him. It began picking at one of the pears, and then the prince raised his gun to shoot at it. But when he looked along the barrel it was not a swan that he saw up in the pear tree, but the prettiest girl that he had ever looked upon.

"Don't shoot me, king's son! Don't shoot me!" cried she.

But the prince had no thought of shooting her, for he had never seen such a beautiful maiden in all of his days. "Very well," said he, "I will not shoot, but, if I spare your life, will you promise to be my sweetheart and to marry me?"

"That may be as may be," said the Swan Maiden. "For listen! I serve the witch with three eyes. She lives on the glass hill that lies beyond the seven high mountains, the seven deep valleys, and the seven wide rivers; are you man enough to go that far?"

"Oh, yes," said the prince, "I am man enough for that and more too."

"That is good," said the Swan Maiden, and thereupon she jumped down from the pear tree to the earth. Then she became a swan again, and bade the king's son to mount upon her back at the roots of her wings. When he had done as she had told him, she sprang into the air and flew away, bearing him with her.

On flew the swan, and on and on, until, by and by, she said, "What do you see, king's son?"

"I see the gray sky above me and the dark earth below me, but nothing else," said he.

After that they flew on and on again, until, at last, the Swan Maiden said, "What do you see now, king's son?"

"I see the gray sky above me and the dark earth below me, but nothing else," said he.

So once more they flew on until the Swan Maiden said, for the third time, "And what do you see by now, king's son?"

But this time the prince said, "I see the gray sky above me and the dark earth below me, and over yonder is a glass hill, and on the hill is a house that shines like fire."

"That is where the witch with three eyes lives," said the Swan Maiden; "and now listen: when she asks you what it is that you came for, ask her to give you the one who draws the water and builds the fire; for that is myself."

So, when they had come to the top of the hill of glass, the king's son stepped down to the ground, and the swan flew over the roof.

Rap! tap! tap! he knocked at the door, and the old witch herself came and opened it.

"And what do you want here?" said she.

"I want the one who draws the water and builds the fire," said the prince.

At this the old witch scowled until her eyebrows met.

"Very well," said she, "you shall have what you want if you can clean my stables tomorrow between the rise and the set of the sun. But I tell you plainly, if you fail in the doing, you shall be torn to pieces body and bones."

But the prince was not to be scared away with empty words. So the next morning the old witch came and took him to the stables where he was to do his task. There stood more than a hundred cattle, and the stable had not been cleaned for at least ten long years.

"There is your work," said the old witch, and then she left him.

Well, the king's son set to work with fork and broom and might and main, but—prut!—he might as well have tried to bale out the great ocean with a bucket.

At noontide who should come to the stable but the pretty Swan Maiden herself.

"When one is tired, one should rest for a while," said she; "come and lay your head in my lap."

The prince was glad enough to do as she said, for nothing was to be gained by working at that task. So he laid his head in her lap, and she combed his hair with a golden comb till he fell fast asleep. When he awoke the Swan Maiden was gone, the sun was setting, and the stable was as clean as a plate. Presently he heard the old witch coming, so up he jumped and began clearing away a straw here and a speck there, just as though he were finishing the work.

"You never did this by yourself!" said the old witch, and her brows grew as black as a thunderstorm.

"That may be so, and that may not be so," said the king's son, "but you lent no hand to help; so now may I have the one who builds the fire and draws the water?"

At this the old witch shook her head. "No," said she, "there is more to be done yet before you can have what you ask for. If you can thatch the roof of the stable with bird feathers, no two of which shall be of the same color, and can do it between the rise and the set of sun tomorrow, then you shall have your

sweetheart and welcome. But if you fail your bones shall be ground as fine as malt in the mill."

Very well; that suited the king's son well enough. So at sunrise he arose and went into the fields with his gun; but if there were birds to be shot, it was few of them that he saw; for at noontide he had but two, and they were both of a color. At that time who should come to him but the Swan Maiden.

"One should not tramp and tramp all day with never a bit of rest," said she; "come hither and lay your head in my lap for a while."

The prince did as she bade him, and the maiden again combed his hair with a golden comb until he fell asleep. When he awoke the sun was setting, and his work was done. He heard the old witch coming, so up he jumped to the roof of the stable and began laying a feather here and a feather there, for all the world as though he were just finishing his task.

"You never did that work alone," said the old witch.

"That may be so, and that may not be so," said the prince; "all the same, it was none of your doing. So now may I have the one who draws the water and builds the fire?"

But the witch shook her head. "No," said she, "there is still another task to do before that. Over yonder is a fir tree; on the tree is a crow's nest, and in the nest are three eggs. If you can harry that nest tomorrow between the rising and the setting of the sun, neither breaking nor leaving a single egg, you shall have that for which you ask."

Very well; that suited the prince. The next morning at the rising of the sun he started off to find the fir tree, and there was no trouble in the finding I can tell you, for it was more than a hundred feet high, and as smooth as glass from root to tip. As for climbing it, he might as well have tried to climb a moonbeam, for in spite of all his trying he did nothing but slip and slip. By and by came the Swan Maiden as she had come before.

"Do you climb the fir tree?" said she.

"None too well," said the king's son.

"Then I may help you in a hard task," said she.

She let down the braids of her golden hair, so that it hung down all about her and upon the ground, and then she began singing to the wind. She sang and sang, and by and by the wind began to blow, and, catching up the maiden's hair, carried it to the top of the fir tree, and there tied it to the branches. Then the prince climbed the hair and so reached the nest. There were the three eggs; he gathered them, and then he came down as he had gone up. After that the wind came again and loosed the maiden's hair from the branches, and she bound it up as it was before.

"Now, listen," said she to the prince: "when the old witch asks you for the three crow's eggs which you have gathered, tell her that they belong to the one who found them. She will not be able to take them from you, and they are worth something, I can tell you."

At sunset the old witch came hobbling along, and there sat the prince at the foot of the fir tree. "Have you gathered the crow's eggs?" said she.

"Yes," said the prince, "here they are in my handkerchief. And now may I have the one who draws the water and builds the fire?"

"Yes," said the old witch, "you may have her; only give me my crow's eggs."

"No," said the prince, "the crow's eggs are none of yours, for they belong to him who gathered them."

When the old witch found that she was not to get her crow's eggs in that way, she tried another, and began using words as sweet as honey. Come, come, there should be no hard feeling between them. The prince had served her faithfully, and before he went home with what he had come for he should have a good supper, for it is ill to travel on an empty stomach.

So she brought the prince into the house, and then she left him while she went to put the pot on the fire, and to sharpen the bread knife on the stone doorstep.

While the prince sat waiting for the witch, there came a tap at the door, and whom should it be but the pretty Swan Maiden.

"Come," said she, "and bring the three eggs with you, for the knife that the old witch is sharpening is for you, and so is the great pot on the fire, for she means to pick your bones in the morning."

She led the prince down into the kitchen; there they made a figure out of honey and barleymeal, so that it was all soft and sticky; then the maiden dressed the figure in her own clothes and set it in the chimney corner by the fire.

After that was done, she became a swan again, and, taking the prince upon her back, she flew away, over hill and over dale.

As for the old witch, she sat on the stone doorstep, sharpening

her knife. By and by she came in, and, look as she might, there was no prince to be found.

Then if anybody was ever in a rage it was the old witch; off she went, storming and fuming, until she came to the kitchen. There sat the woman of honey and barleymeal beside the fire, dressed in the maiden's clothes, and the old woman thought that it was the girl herself. "Where is your sweetheart?" said she; but to this the woman of honey and barleymeal answered never a word.

"How now! are you dumb?" cried the old witch; "I will see whether I cannot bring speech to your lips." She raised her hand—*slap!*—she struck, and so hard was the blow that her hand stuck fast to the honey and barleymeal. "What!" cried she, "will you hold me?"—*slap!*—she struck with the other hand, and it too stuck fast. So there she was, and, for all that I know, she is sticking to the woman of honey and barleymeal to this day.

As for the Swan Maiden and the prince, they flew over the seven high mountains, the seven deep valleys, and the seven wide rivers, until they came near to the prince's home again. The Swan Maiden lit in a great wide field, and there she told the prince to break open one of the crow's eggs. The prince did as she bade him, and what should he find but the most beautiful little palace, all of pure gold and silver. He set the palace on the ground, and it grew and grew and grew until it covered as much ground as seven large barns. Then the Swan Maiden told him to break another egg, and he did as she said, and what should come out of it but such great herds of cows and sheep that they covered the meadow far and near. The Swan Maiden told him to break the third egg, and out of it came scores and scores of servants all dressed in gold-and-silver livery.

That morning, when the king looked out of his bedroom window, there stood the splendid castle of silver and gold. Then he called all of his people together, and they rode over to see what it meant. On the way they met such herds of fat sheep and cattle that the king had never seen the like in all of his life before; and when he came to the fine castle, there were two rows of servants dressed in clothes of silver and gold, ready to meet him. But when he came to the door of the castle, there stood the prince himself. Then there was joy and rejoicing, you may be sure! only the two elder brothers looked down in the mouth, for since the young prince had found the thief who stole the golden pears, their father's kingdom was not for them. But the prince soon set their minds at rest on that score, for he had enough and more than enough of his own.

After that the prince and the Swan Maiden were married, and a grand wedding they had of it, with music of fiddles and kettledrums, and plenty to eat and to drink. I, too, was there; but all of the good red wine ran down over my tucker, so that not a drop of it passed my lips, and I had to come away empty.

And that is all.

BLUEBELLS

Walter de la Mare

Where the bluebells and the wind are,
Fairies in a ring I spied,
And I heard a little linnet
Singing near beside.
Where the primrose and the dew are—
Soon were sped the fairies all;
Only now the green turf freshens,
And the linnets call.

Florence Page Jaques

THE PIPING ON CHRISTMAS EVE

ILLUSTRATED BY *Robert Lawson*

ONCE, on an island near a little old town, there lived a small boy called Timothy Piper. He was all alone except for a flock of goats, and so he made willow pipes to pipe on. He lived in an old grass-grown fort at the end of the island; the goats lived just outside.

It was lucky that he liked his pipes and his goats, for no one ever came to see him, except to buy goats' milk and cheese,—and even then they stayed in their boats and shouted, "I want goats' milk!" or "I want cheese!" For Timothy's grandfather, who had brought him up, had been a fierce old hermit, and forbade anyone to step foot on his island. And so fierce had he been that even after he died, people kept on not stepping.

One blustering winter day, Timothy was sitting high up in the ramparts of the fort, in a corner sheltered from the cold wind, piping to himself. But at last he put his pipes away and looked out over the rough gray water to the town. The air was stormy with dark clouds, and the red roofs of the village looked dimly beautiful through the chill mist.

"But how busy everyone is!" Timothy thought. "How fast they scurry about and how many bundles they all carry! And everything seems scarlet and green and sparkly—" He leaned far out over the wall. "Why, it must be Christmastime!"

Timothy liked Christmas. He liked the sound of Christmas bells across the water. He liked to see candles shining like little stars from the windows at night. And the year before a fisherman had given him a handful of walnuts and raisins—a year before that he had found a holly wreath washed up on the rocks and had put it carefully away till he could ask someone what it was for. Before that, Timothy couldn't remember. But he knew he liked Christmas.

Now he ran down the stone steps as fast as he could go, out to the flock of goats.

"Look here," he said to the Gray Goat. "What day is it?"

"It's the day before Christmas," said Gray Goat immediately, for he always knew the answer to everything. He was a large and shaggy goat, with a long beard and very bright yellow eyes, and he was older than anyone knew.

"Well, look here," said Timothy breathlessly. He had thought of something so reckless and exciting that he could hardly bring himself to say it out loud. "Do you know what I want to do? I want to go over to the village and see Christmas!"

"Why not?" said Gray Goat calmly.

Timothy looked at him in despair. Timothy had never been across the water to the village in his life, and now he was thinking of doing it, and Gray Goat only stood and chewed. What a goat!

"Perhaps you have some idea as to how I could possibly get over there?" Timothy said politely.

"I'll take you over on my back if you like," said Gray Goat. "I often swim across at night and stroll about."

Timothy looked at Gray Goat in awe. You never knew what he was doing. You certainly never knew. But Timothy was not going to give him the satisfaction of acting surprised, so he

only said, "Thank you, Gray Goat." And off he started on Gray Goat's back.

The waves tumbled about them, gray and icy-white, and spray blew across Timothy's face. Timothy had never in his life had a ride of any kind, and this ride on a goat's back across stormy water was such fun he could not keep from shouting. He held tight to Gray Goat's curling horns and kicked his heels with joy until Gray Goat said, "Stop! You tickle."

Nearer and nearer to the little town they came, and Timothy could see bright lights and gay shops, and he could hear rattles and clatters and laughter. He felt terrifically excited. He looked up to the tower which loomed above the town, and at one of its windows a little girl with dark curls waved gaily at him!

"She waved at *me,*" Timothy told Gray Goat proudly.

"She waves at everyone," Gray Goat said carelessly. "That's the Major General's daughter. She never has anyone to play with up there, so she waves. She even waves at me, when she catches sight of me on bright moonlight nights."

"Oh!" said Timothy, quite crestfallen.

Just then they reached the stone steps of the wharf, and Timothy jumped off Gray Goat's back. "Stroll around an hour or so, if you like," said Gray Goat. "I'm going to curl up in the dried grass under this wall and get warm."

Timothy ran up the steps to the crowded streets. He was more breathless than ever. There were so many wonders to see that he simply couldn't help bumping into people as he whirled around. Shopwindows, for instance. He had never seen a shop-window of any kind, and here were the gayest ones of all the year.

He forgot all about the cold wind nipping his ears as he gazed into warm lighted shops full of shining toys! Shops full of candy canes and chocolates and taffy! Shops full of oranges and apples and Christmas cakes and spicy smells! And then Timothy saw a window with tracks and toy trains dashing around on them, and he stayed there till he almost turned into an icicle!

For two whole hours Timothy wandered, seeing holiday sights he had never dreamed of. He even saw a Christmas tree all hung with silver,—and when they turned its rainbow-colored lights on, Timothy turned somersaults in his joy.

At last he came to the square by the tower, and there he saw an enormous paper nailed to the wall. For this town had one queer custom; no one ever bought presents till the day before Christmas. This made shopping into the wildest scramble and people got all mixed up in their minds about presents.

So to make things easier, the Major General wrote a list with everyone's name on it and hung it against the tower wall. And whoever wanted to give a certain person a present made a cross after that person's name. Then the person, on the day before Christmas, looked to see how many people were giving him presents and bought that many to give back. It *was* a queer custom, I must admit.

So Timothy, strolling by, saw this list. "Whee! How many presents for the Major General's daughter," he said, seeing the rows and rows of crosses after her name. Then he looked down the list for his own. It was there, down at the very bottom, and there was not a single cross after it. Timothy couldn't believe his eyes. Not a single present for him, when there were so many in the shops! He stood and stared.

Now it was only that people quite forgot about Timothy; they didn't mean to leave him out. But it *was* selfish of them not to take the trouble to remember. Timothy certainly thought so. He stood there in the foggy afternoon, and his anger grew fiercer and fiercer. No one was giving him a single gift! He turned on his heel and stalked back to the wharf.

Gray Goat was waiting, and when he saw Timothy's grim face, he simply walked into the water. "Nobody in this whole town thought of giving me a present," Timothy said bitterly.

He leaped on Gray Goat's back, and they sped back across the tossing waves to the island. Timothy went straight into the fort and began to stride up and down, kicking at the stone floor.

"I'm glad you are mad instead of sad," said Gray Goat behind him. "Your grandfather always said that when you first got angry at the village it was time for me to show you your great-grandfather's pipe. Did you know he was the Pied Piper?"

"No! You mean the one who could make anything follow him by piping? Who piped away the rats and the children from Hamelin Town?" asked Timothy, quite round-eyed.

"His pipe is there on the high shelf," said Gray Goat, and then he went softly away.

Timothy sat and looked at the shelf. It was twilight now, and sleet was falling outside, rattling against the dim windows. Timothy lifted the pipe of the Pied Piper of Hamelin down from the shelf. It made him feel quite queer to hold it in his hands.

"But—but how can you know who you are calling?" he wondered, and blew a few notes. He found he was making a little tune, all his own. He played it over and over and all at once he heard a pattering. The whole flock of goats came rushing into the room.

"No, no!" said Timothy. "I certainly didn't mean to bring you here! My goodness, I can see you any time."

The goats turned around and went pattering out to their pasture again. Timothy tried another tune. This time, flap, flap, outside the window he saw big silver fish jump from the water and come bouncing up his steps. "*No!* I don't want you at all!" he called, and stopped playing that tune at once. The fish hopped back into the water with sighs of relief.

"I'll have to play a sort of a faraway tune, to reach the town," Timothy thought. "And I know what I'll do. I'll try to play the kind of a tune that will bring all the Christmas presents over. *That* will surprise the village!"

He waited by his window till he saw the candles in the town go out, one by one. Then when everything was quite dark and still, he picked up his pipe and began to play once more, a queer little, bright little tune. He made it as queer as he could, for he didn't want to pipe the children over, as his great-grandfather had once done. That was far too cruel a joke.

Soon he was sure he could hear faint noises over in the town, shuffles and slides and doors that were opening. What *was* astir? The storm clouds had passed, there was a faint moon, and he thought he could see movement, down by the wharf. Then he actually saw boats putting off,—yes, boat after boat!

"Oh, I hope I have piped the Christmas presents over," Timothy said. "And if not, what *is* coming?"

He piped on and on. After a while he could hear the bumping of boats against the rocks below. And Gray Goat's voice said, "Ho, ho! Well, fancy seeing *you* here!" (Then it isn't the Christmas presents, Timothy thought with sharp disappointment.) "Come along; this way!"

Timothy rushed to throw open the door of the fort, piping all the while.

Then into the big hall came the strangest procession you ever saw. Turkeys and oysters and round plum puddings, thin celery, fat cabbages, round potatoes, sacks of sugar, pumpkin pies, mince pies, apple pies, roast beef, sausages, cranberries, in fact, every single thing to eat that there was in the whole town came marching into Timothy's hall.

Timothy gasped. What would happen in the town? Then he caught Gray Goat's eye, and they both began to laugh.

"You have certainly played a joke this time!" said Gray Goat. "Not bad. Not bad at all. Just wait until they find out tomorrow!"

Timothy looked helpless. "What shall we do with them?" he said.

"I'll see to that," said Gray Goat. "You've had almost too many adventures today, my lad, what with a ride, a Christmas town, your great-grandfather's pipe and all. Better hop off to bed."

Timothy was still asleep the next morning when Gray Goat prodded him.

"Wake up, Timothy," Gray Goat said. "There are more visitors below. Everyone in town has come over, even the Major General himself. It seems his daughter was looking at the moon last night and saw the Christmas dinners start off. Ho, ho!"

"Shall I go down?" said Timothy.

"I took the liberty," said Gray Goat, "of telling the Major General that we couldn't possibly send the dinners back, when they had come here of their own accord. But that you would be delighted to have everyone in the village dine with us. Only, of course, to be polite, they would each bring along a Christmas present for you."

"Gray Goat," said Timothy, with his hair standing up stiff with delight, "what a goat you are!"

And what a frolic everyone had, eating Christmas dinner all together, in Timothy's hall! Even the Major General and his daughter came, with their presents tied up in gold paper. And after dinner everyone sang and Timothy opened his presents, three hundred and thirty-three of them, and the Major General's daughter helped him, and so did all the other children.

After that, the children often came to the island to play with Timothy and his presents and his goats. The Major General's daughter came especially often, and Timothy went to visit her in her tower, so she no longer had to sit waving at her window.

But Timothy put his great-grandfather's pipe back on its high shelf again. It was exciting to pipe on a pipe like that, but you could never be sure what *might* happen!

James Thurber

THE GREAT QUILLOW

ILLUSTRATED BY *Hardie Gramatky*

ONCE upon a time, in a far country, there lived a giant named Hunder. He was so enormous in height and girth and weight that little waves were set in motion in distant lakes when he walked. His great fingers could wrench a clock from its steeple as easily as a child might remove a peanut from its shell. Every morning he devoured three sheep, a pie made of a thousand apples, and a chocolate as high and as wide as a spinning wheel. It would have taken six ordinary men to lift the great brass key to his front door, and four to carry one of the candles with which he lighted his house.

It was Hunder's way to strip a town of its sheep and apples and chocolate, its leather and cloth, its lumber and tallow and brass, and then move on to a new far village and begin his depredations again. There had been no men strong enough to thwart his evil ways in any of the towns he had set upon and impoverished. He had broken their most formidable weapons between his thumb and forefinger, laughing like the hurricane. And there had been no men cunning enough in any of the towns to bring about his destruction. He had crushed their most ingenious traps with the toe of his mammoth boot, guffawing like a volcano.

One day Hunder strode hundreds and hundreds of leagues and came to a little town in a green valley. It was a staunch little town and a firm little valley, but they quaked with the sound of his coming. The houses were narrow and two stories high; the streets were narrow and cobbled. There were not many people in the town: a hundred men, a hundred women, a hundred children.

Every Tuesday night at seven o'clock a town council met to administer the simple affairs of the community. The councilors were the most important tradesmen and artisans of New Moon Street, a short, narrow, cobbled street that ran east and west. These men were the tailor, the butcher, the candymaker, the blacksmith, the baker, the candlemaker, the lamplighter, the cobbler, the carpenter, and the locksmith. After the small business of the tranquil town had been taken care of, the council members sat around and speculated as to the number of stars in the sky, discussed the wonderful transparency of glass, and praised the blueness of violets and the whiteness of snow. Then they made a little fun of Quillow, the toymaker (whose work they considered a rather pretty waste of time), and went home.

Quillow, the toymaker, did not belong to the council but he attended all its meetings. The councilmen were fond of Quillow because of the remarkable toys he made, and because he was a droll and gentle fellow. Quillow made all kinds of familiar playthings on his long and littered workbench: music boxes, jumping jacks, building blocks; but he was famous for a number of little masterpieces of his own invention: a clown who juggled three marbles, a woodman who could actually chop wood, a trumpeter who could play seven notes of a song on a tiny horn, a paperweight in which roses burst into bloom in falling snow.

Quillow was as amusing to look at as any of his toys. He was the shortest man in town, being only five feet tall. His ears were large, his nose was long, his mouth was small, and he had a shock of white hair that stood straight up like a dandelion clock. The lapels of his jacket were wide. He wore a gay tie in a deep-pointed collar, and his pantaloons were baggy and unpressed. At Christmastime each year Quillow made little hearts of gold for the girls of the town and hearts of oak for the boys. He considered himself something of a civic figure, since he had designed the spouting dolphins in the town fountain, the wooden animals on the town merry-go-round, and the twelve scarlet men who emerged from the dial of the town clock on the stroke of every hour and played a melody on little silver bells with little silver hammers.

It was the custom of Quillow's colleagues to shout merrily, "Why, here comes the Great Quillow!" when the toymaker appeared. The lamplighter or the tailor or the locksmith would sometimes creep up behind him and pretend to wind a key in his back as if he were a mechanical figure of his own devising. Quillow took all this in good part, and always, when the imaginary key in his back was turned, he would walk about stiff-legged, with jerky movements of his arms, joining in the fun and increasing the laughter.

It was different on the day the giant arrived. Laughter was hushed, and the people hid in their houses and talked in frightened whispers when Hunder's great bulk appeared like a cyclone in the sky and the earth shook beneath him. Panting a little after his thousand-league walk, Hunder pulled up four trees from a hillside to make room for his great hulk and sat down. Hunder surveyed the town and grunted. There was no one to be seen in the streets. Not even a cat crept over the cobblestones.

"Ho, town!" bawled Hunder. The doors shook and the windows rattled. "Ho, town! Send me your clerk that you may hear Hunder's will!"

The town clerk gathered up quill and ink and parchment. "There are ninety-nine other men in town," he grumbled, "but it's the town clerk this, and the town clerk that, and the town clerk everything." He walked out of his house, still grumbling, and trudged across the valley to hear the giant's will.

An hour later the town clerk sat at the head of a long table in the council room and began to call the roll. "We're all here," snapped the blacksmith. "You can see that."

The clerk continued with the roll call.

"Baker," he called. "Here," said the baker. "Blacksmith," he droned. "Here," said the blacksmith sourly.

The clerk finished calling the roll and looked over his spectacles. "We have a visitor tonight, as usual," he said, "Quillow, the toymaker. I will make the proper entry in the minutes."

"Never mind the minutes," said the blacksmith. "Read us the demands of Hunder the giant."

The clerk entered Quillow's name in the minutes. "Now," he said, "I will read the minutes of the last meeting."

The candymaker stood up. "Let's dispense with the minutes of the last meeting," he said.

The clerk looked over his spectacles. "It must be properly moved and duly seconded," he said. It was properly moved and duly seconded. "Now read the demands of Hunder the giant!" shouted the blacksmith.

The clerk rapped on the table with his gavel. "Next," he

The black scowl cleared from the giant's brow, and he laughed . . .

said, "comes unfinished business. We have before us a resolution to regulate the speed of merry-go-rounds."

"Dispense with it!" bawled the blacksmith.

"It must be properly moved and duly seconded," said the clerk. It was properly moved and duly seconded and the clerk at last unrolled a long scroll of parchment. "We come now," he said, "to the business of the day. I have here the demands of Hunder the giant. The document is most irregular. It does not contain a single 'greeting' or 'whereas' or 'be it known by these presents'!"

Everyone sat motionless as the clerk began to read the scroll. "I, Hunder, must have three sheep every morning," he read.

"That would use up all the sheep in the valley in a week and a fortnight," said the butcher, "and there would be no mutton for our own people."

"I, Hunder, must have a chocolate a day as high and as wide as a spinning wheel," read the town clerk.

"Why, that would exhaust all the chocolate in my storeroom in three days!" cried the candymaker.

The town clerk read from the parchment again. "I, Hunder, must have a new jerkin made for me in a week and a fortnight."

"Why, I would have to work night and day to make a jerkin in a week and a fortnight for so large a giant," gasped the tailor, "and it would use up all the cloth on my shelves and in my basement."

"I, Hunder," went on the town clerk, "must have a new pair of boots within a week and a fortnight."

The cobbler moaned as he heard this. "Why, I would have to work night and day to make a pair of boots for so large a giant in a week and a fortnight," he said. "And it would use up all the leather in my workshop and in my back room."

The council members shook their heads sadly as each demand was read off by the town clerk. Quillow had folded his arms and crossed his legs and shut his eyes. He was thinking, but he looked like a sleeping toy.

"I, Hunder," droned the town clerk, "must have an apple pie each morning made of a thousand apples."

The baker jumped from his chair. "Why, that would use up all the apples and flour and shortening in town in a week and a fortnight," he cried. "And it would take me night and day to make such a pie, so that I could bake no more pies or cakes or cookies, or blueberry muffins or cinnamon buns or cherry boats or strawberry tarts or plum puddings for the people of the town."

All of the councilmen moaned sadly because they loved the list of good things the baker had recited. Quillow still sat with his eyes closed.

"I, Hunder," went on the town clerk, "must have a house to live in by the time a week and a fortnight have passed."

The carpenter wept openly. "Why, I would have to work night and day to build a house for so large a giant in a week and a fortnight," sobbed the carpenter. "All my nephews and uncles and cousins would have to help me, and it would use up all the wood and pegs and hinges and glass in my shop and in the countryside."

The locksmith stood up and shook his fist in the direction of the hillside on which the giant lay snoring. "I will have to work night and day to make a brass key large enough to fit the keyhole in the front door of the house of so large a giant," he said. "It will use up all the brass in my shop and in the community."

"And I will have to make a candle for his bedside so large it will use up all the wick and tallow in my shop and the world!" said the candlemaker.

"This is the final item," said the town clerk. "I, Hunder, must be told a tale each day to keep me amused."

Quillow opened his eyes and raised his hand. "I will be the teller of tales," he said. "I will keep the giant amused."

The town clerk put away his scroll.

"Does anyone have any idea of how to destroy the giant Hunder?" asked the candymaker.

"I could creep up on him in the dark and set fire to him with my lighter," said the lamplighter.

Quillow looked at him. "The fire of your lighter would not

harm him any more than a spark struck by a colt-shoe in a meadow," said Quillow.

"Quillow is right," said the blacksmith. "But I could build secretly at night an enormous catapult which would cast a gigantic stone and crush Hunder."

Quillow shook his head. "He would catch the stone as a child catches a ball," said Quillow, "and he would cast it back at the town and squash all our houses."

"I could put needles in his suit," said the tailor.

"I could put nails in his boots," said the cobbler.

"I could put oil in his chocolates," said the candymaker.

"I could put stones in his mutton," said the butcher.

"I could put tacks in his pies," said the baker.

"I could put gunpowder in his candles," said the candlemaker.

"I could make the handle of his brass key as sharp as a sword," said the locksmith.

"I could build the roof of his house insecurely so that it would fall on him," said the carpenter.

"The plans you suggest," said Quillow, "would merely annoy Hunder as the gadfly annoys the horse and the flea annoys the dog."

"Perhaps the Great Quillow has a plan of his own," said the blacksmith with a scornful laugh.

"Has the Great Quillow a plan?" asked the candymaker, with a faint sneer.

The little toymaker did not answer. The councilors got up and filed slowly and sadly from the council room. That night none of them wound the imaginary key in Quillow's back.

Quillow did not leave the council chamber for a long time, and when he walked through New Moon Street, all the shops of the councilmen were brightly lighted and noisily busy. There was a great ringing and scraping and thumping and rustling. The blacksmith was helping the locksmith make the great brass key for Hunder's house. The carpenter was sawing and planing enormous boards. The baker was shaping the crust for a gigantic pie, and his wife and apprentice were peeling a thousand apples. The butcher was dressing the first of the three sheep. The tailor was cutting the cloth for Hunder's jerkin. The cobbler was fitting together mammoth pieces of leather for Hunder's boots. The candymaker was piling all his chocolate upon his largest table, while his wife and his daughter made soft filling in great kettles. The candlemaker had begun to build the monumental candle for Hunder's bedside.

As Quillow reached the door of his shop, the town clock in its steeple began to strike, the moon broke out of a patch of cloud, and the toymaker stood with his hand on the door latch to watch the twelve little men in scarlet hats and jackets and pantaloons emerge, each from his own numeral, to make the night melodious with the sound of their silver hammers on the silver bells of the round white dial.

Inside his shop, Quillow lighted the green-shaded lamp over his workbench, which was littered with odds and ends and beginnings and middles of all kinds of toys. Working swiftly with his shining tools, Quillow began to make a figure eight inches high out of wire and cloth and leather and wood. When it was finished it looked like a creature you might come upon hiding behind a tulip or playing with toads. It had round eyes, a round nose and a wide mouth, and no hair. It was blue from head to foot. Its face was blue, its jacket was blue, its pantaloons were blue, and its feet were blue.

As Quillow stood examining the toy, the lamplighter stuck his head in the door without knocking, stared for a moment, and went away. Quillow smiled with satisfaction and began to make another blue man. By the time the first cock crowed he had made ten blue men and put them away in a long wooden chest with a heavy iron clasp.

The lamplighter turned out the last street light, the sun rose, the crickets stopped calling and the clock struck five. Disturbed by the changing pattern of light and sound, the giant on the hillside turned in his sleep. Around a corner into New Moon Street tiptoed the town crier. "Sh!" he said to the lamplighter. "Don't wake the giant."

"Sh!" said the lamplighter. "His food may not be ready."

The town crier stood in the cobbled street and called softly, "Five o'clock, and all's well!"

All the doors in New Moon Street except Quillow's flew open.

"The pie is baked," said the baker.

"The chocolate is made," said the candymaker.

"The sheep are dressed," said the butcher.

"I worked all night on the great brass key," said the locksmith, "and the blacksmith helped me with his hammer and anvil."

"I have scarcely begun the enormous candle," said the candlemaker.

"I am weary of sawing and planing," said the carpenter.

"My fingers are already stiff," said the tailor, "and I have just started the giant's jerkin."

"My eyes are tired," said the cobbler, "and I have hardly begun to make his boots."

The sun shone full on the giant's face, and he woke up and yawned loudly. The councilors jumped, and a hundred children hid in a hundred closets.

"Ho!" roared Hunder. It was the sign the blacksmith had waited for. He drove his wagon drawn by four horses into New Moon Street and climbed down.

"Ho!" roared the giant.

"Heave," grunted the councilors as they lifted the sheep onto the wagon.

"Ho!" roared the giant.

"Heave," grunted the councilors, and up went the pie.

"Ho!" roared the giant.

"Heave," grunted the councilors, and they set the great chocolate in place.

Hunder watched the loading of the wagon, licking his lips and growling like a cave full of bulldogs.

The councilors climbed up on the wagon and the blacksmith yelled "Giddap!", and then "Whoa!" He glared about him. "Where is Quillow?" he demanded. "Where is that foolish little fellow?"

"He was in his shop at midnight," said the lamplighter, "making toys."

The nine other councilors snorted.

"He could have helped with the key," said the locksmith.

"The pie," said the baker.

"The sheep," said the butcher.

"The boots," said the cobbler.

At this, Quillow bounced out of his shop like a bird from a clock, bowing and smiling.

"Well!" snarled the blacksmith.

"Ho!" roared Hunder.

"Good morning," said Quillow. He climbed up on the wagon, and the blacksmith spoke to each horse in turn. (Their names were Lobo, Bolo, Olob, and Obol.)

"I worked all night with my hammer and anvil," said the blacksmith as the horses lurched ahead, "helping the locksmith with the great brass key." He scowled at Quillow. "The lamplighter tells us *you* spent the night making toys."

"Making toys," said Quillow cheerily, "and thinking up a tale to amuse the giant Hunder."

The blacksmith snorted. "And a hard night you must have spent hammering out your tale."

"And twisting it," said the locksmith.

"And leveling it," said the carpenter.

"And rolling it out," said the baker.

"And stitching it up," said the tailor.

"And fitting it together," said the cobbler.

"And building it around a central thread," said the candlemaker.

"And dressing it up," said the butcher.

"And making it not too bitter and not too sweet," said the candymaker.

When the wagon came to a stop at Hunder's feet, the giant clapped his hands, and Quillow and the councilors were blown to the ground. Hunder roared with laughter and unloaded the wagon in half a trice.

"Tell me your silly names," said Hunder, "and what you do."

The new slaves of Hunder, all except Quillow, bowed in turn and told the giant who they were and what they did. Quillow remained silent.

"You, smallest of men, you with the white hair, who are you?" demanded Hunder.

"I am Quillow, the teller of tales," said the toymaker, but unlike the others he did not bow to the giant.

"Bow!" roared Hunder.

"Wow!" shouted Quillow.

The councilors started back in dismay at the toymaker's impertinence, their widening eyes on Hunder's mighty hands, which closed and then slowly opened. The black scowl cleared from the giant's brow, and he laughed suddenly.

"You are a fairly droll fellow," he said. "Perhaps your tales will amuse me. If they do not, I will put you in the palm of my hand and blow you so far it will take men five days to find you. Now be off to your work, the rest of you!"

As the wagon carried the frightened councilors back to town, Quillow sat on the ground and watched the giant eat a sheep as an ordinary man might eat a lark. "Now," said Hunder, "tell me a tale."

"Once upon a time," began Quillow, crossing his legs and tickling a cricket with a blade of grass, "a giant came to our town from a thousand leagues away, stepping over the hills and rivers. He was so mighty a giant that he could stamp upon the ground with his foot and cause the cows in the fields to turn flip-flops in the air and land on their feet again."

"Garf," growled Hunder, "I can stamp upon the ground with my foot and empty a lake of its water."

"I have no doubt of that, O Hunder," said Quillow, "for the thunder is your plaything and the mountains are your stool. But the giant who came over the hills and rivers many and many a year ago was a lesser giant than Hunder. He was weak. He fell ill of a curious malady. He was forced to run to the ocean and bathe in the yellow waters, for only the yellow waters in the middle of the sea could cure the giant."

"Rowf," snarled Hunder, picking up another sheep. "That giant was a goose, that giant was a grasshopper. *Hunder* is never sick." The giant smote his chest and then his stomach mighty blows without flinching, to show how strong he was.

"This other giant," said Quillow, "had no ailment of the chest or the stomach or the mouth or the ears or the eyes or the arms or the legs."

"Where else can a giant have an ailment?" demanded Hunder.

Quillow looked dreamily across the green valley toward the town, which was bright in the sun. "In the mind," said Quillow, "for the mind is a strange and intricate thing. In lesser men than Hunder, it is subject to mysterious maladies."

"Wumf," said the giant, beginning his third sheep. "Hunder's mind is strong like the rock." He smote himself heavily across the forehead without wincing.

"No one to this day knows what brought on this dreadful disease in the mind of the other giant," said Quillow. "Perhaps he killed a turtle after sundown, or ran clockwise thrice around a church in the dark of the moon, or slept too close to a field of asphodel."

Hunder picked up the pie and began to devour it. "Did this goose, this grasshopper, have pains in his head?" he asked. "Look, teller of tales!" Hunder banged his head savagely against a tree, and the trunk of the tree snapped in two. The giant grinned, showing his jagged teeth.

"This other giant," said Quillow, "suffered no pain. His symptoms were marvelous and dismaying. First he heard the word. For fifteen minutes one morning, beginning at a quarter of six, he heard the word."

"Harumph!" said Hunder, finishing his pie and reaching for his chocolate. "What was the word the giant heard for fifteen minutes one day?"

"The word was 'woddly,'" said Quillow. "All words were one word to him. All words were 'woddly.'"

"All words are different to Hunder," said the giant. "And do you call this a tale you have told me? A blithering goose of a giant hears a word and you call that a tale to amuse Hunder?"

Quillow arose as the clock in the steeple struck six and the scarlet figures came out to play the silver bells.

"I hear all words," said Hunder. "This is a good chocolate; otherwise I should put you in the palm of my hand and blow you over the housetops."

"I shall bring you a better tale tomorrow," said Quillow. "Meanwhile, be sure to see the first star over your left shoulder, do not drink facing downstream, and always sleep with your heart to the east."

"Why should Hunder practice this foolish rigmarole?" asked the giant.

"No one knows to this day," said Quillow, "what caused the weird illness in the mind of the other giant." But Hunder gave only a murmurous growl in reply, for he had lain down again on the hillside and closed his eyes. Quillow smiled as he saw that the giant lay with his heart to the east.

The toymaker spent the day making twenty more little blue men and when the first owl hooted he stood in the doorway of his shop and whistled. The hundred children collected in the cobbled street before the toyshop from every nook and corner and cranny and niche of the town. "Go to your homes," said Quillow, "each Sue and John of you, each Nora and Joe, and tell your fathers and mothers to come to the merry-go-round in the carnival grounds one quarter-hour before the moon comes over the hill. Say that Quillow has a plan to destroy the giant Hunder."

The group of children broke like the opening of a rose and the cobbled streets rang with the sound of their running.

Even the scowling blacksmith, the scornful lamplighter, the mumbling town crier, and the fussy town clerk (who had spent the day searching for an ancient treaty the people of the town had once signed with a giant) came at the appointed hour to hear what Quillow had to say.

"What is this clown's whim that brings us here like sheep?" demanded the blacksmith.

Quillow climbed up on the merry-go-round, sat on a swan, and spoke. At first there was a restless stir like wind in the grass, but as Quillow explained his plan, even the chattering wives fell silent. Quillow finished speaking as the moon peeped over the hill, and the hundred men and the hundred women and the hundred children straggled away from the carnival grounds.

"It will never work," said the lamplighter.

"It is worth trying," said the candymaker.

"I have a better plan," said the town crier. "Let all the women and all the children stand in the streets and gaze sorrowfully at the giant, and perhaps he will go away."

His wife took him by the arm and led him home. "We will try Quillow's plan," she said. "He has a magic, the little man."

The next morning, just as the clock in the steeple struck five, the weary blacksmith, with Quillow sitting beside him, drove the wagon loaded with three sheep and a fresh apple pie and another monster chocolate to where the giant sat on the hillside. Hunder unloaded the wagon in a third of a trice, placed the food beside him on the hill, and began to gnaw at a sheep. "Tell me a tale, smallest of men," he said, "and see to it that I do not nod, or I shall put you in the palm of my hand and blow you through yonder cloud."

"Once upon a time," began Quillow, "there was a king named Anderblusdaferafan, and he had three sons named Ufabrodoborobe, Quamdelrodolanderay, and Tristolcomofarasee."

"Those names are hard names," said Hunder. "Tell me those names again that I may remember them." So Quillow started over slowly with "Once upon a time," and again the giant made him repeat the names.

"Why did this king and his sons have such long and difficult names?" demanded Hunder, eating his second sheep.

"Ah," said Quillow, "it was because of the king's mother, whose name was Isoldasadelofandaloo."

"Tell me her name once more," said Hunder, "that I may remember it." So Quillow told him the name again slowly.

Thus the wily Quillow, who really had thought of no tale to tell, wasted the long minutes as the hands of the clock in the steeple crept around the dial. As they neared a quarter of six o'clock, Quillow went on. "One day as the king and his sons were riding through the magical forest," he said, "they came upon a woddly. Woddly woddly woddly. Woddly woddly woddly."

The giant's eyes grew narrow, then wide.

"Woddly woddly woddly," said Quillow, "woddly woddly woddly woddly."

The giant dropped the chocolate he was eating. "Say it with words!" he bellowed. "You say naught but 'woddly.' "

Quillow looked surprised. "Woddly woddly woddly woddly woddly woddly woddly woddly," he said. "Woddly woddly woddly."

"Can this be the malady come upon me?" cried the giant. He caught the toymaker up in his hand. "Or do you seek to frighten Hunder?" he roared.

"Woddly woddly woddly," said Quillow, trembling in spite of himself, as he pointed to a farmer in a field and to a child gathering cowslips and to the town crier making his rounds. "Woddly woddly woddly," repeated Quillow.

The giant dropped Quillow and arose. He strode to where the farmer stood and picked him up. "Say words!" bawled Hunder. "Say many words!"

"Woddly," said the farmer, and Hunder dropped him in the field and turned to the child.

"What is your name?" roared Hunder.

"Woddly woddly," said the child.

Hunder stepped over to the town crier. "What is the time of day?" he bellowed.

"Woddly woddly," said the town crier.

Then Hunder shouted questions at men and women and children who came running into the streets. He asked them how old they were, and what day it was, and where they were going, and how they were feeling. And they said "Woddly" and "Woddly woddly" and "Woddly woddly woddly."

Hunder strode back across the green valley to where Quillow sat brushing flies off the half-eaten chocolate. "It is the malady! I have heard the word! It is the malady!" cried Hunder. "What am I to do to cure the malady?"

Just then the clock in the steeple struck six, and as the scarlet men came out to play the bells, Quillow spoke reproachfully. "I was telling you how the king and his three sons rode through the magical forest," he said, "when you picked me up and flung me to the earth and ran away, leaving your chocolate uneaten."

The giant sat on the ground, panting heavily, his lower teeth showing. "I heard the word," he said. "All men said the word."

"What word?" asked Quillow.

"Woddly," said the giant.

"That is but the first symptom," said Quillow reassuringly, "and it has passed. Look at the chimneys of the town. Are they not red?"

Hunder looked. "Yes, the chimneys are red," said Hunder. "Why do you ask if the chimneys are red?"

"So long as the chimneys are red," said Quillow, "you have no need to worry, for when the second symptom is upon you, the chimneys of the town turn black."

"I see only red chimneys," said the giant. "But what could have caused Hunder to hear the word?" he asked as he hurled the half-eaten chocolate far away over the roofs of the town.

"Perhaps," said Quillow, "you stepped on a centaur's grave, or waked the sleeping unicorn, or whistled on Saint Nillin's Day."

Hunder the giant rested badly on the hillside that night, twisting and turning in his sleep, tormented by ominous dreams. While he slept, the youngest and most agile men of the town, in black smocks and slippered feet, climbed to the roofs of the houses and shops, each carrying a full pail and a brush, and painted all the chimneys black.

Quillow, the toymaker, worked busily all night, and by the dark hour before the dawn, had made twenty more blue men, so that he now had fifty blue men in all. He put the new ones with the others he had made, in the large chest with the iron clasp.

As the first birds twittered in the trees, the lamplighter and the town crier came into the toyshop. Quillow was repairing a doll for a little girl who was ill. He smiled and bowed to his friends confidently, but the palms of their hands were moist, and the roofs of their mouths were dry.

"Perhaps he will detect your trick," said the lamplighter.

"Perhaps he will smash all our houses," said the town crier.

As the three men talked, they heard the giant stirring on the hillside. He rubbed his eyes with his great knuckles, yawned with the sound of a sinking ship, and stretched his powerful arms. The toymaker and the lamplighter and the town crier watched through a window and held their breath.

Hunder sat up, staring at the ground and running his fingers through his hair. Then slowly he lifted his head and looked at the town. He closed his eyes tightly and opened them again and stared. His mouth dropped open, and he lurched to his feet. "The chimneys!" he bellowed. "The chimneys are black! The malady is upon me again!"

Quillow began to scamper through the cobbled streets and across the green valley as the giant's eyes rolled and his knees trembled. "Teller of tales, smallest of men!" bellowed Hunder. "Tell me what I must do. The chimneys are black!" Quillow reached the feet of the giant, panting and flushed. "Look, teller of tales," said the giant, "name me fairly the color of yonder chimneys."

Quillow turned and looked toward the town. "The chimneys are red, O Hunder," he said. "The chimneys are red. See how they outdo the red rays of the sun."

"The rays of the sun are red," said Hunder, "but the chimneys of the town are black."

"You tremble," said Quillow, "and your tongue hangs out, and these are indeed the signs of the second symptom. But still there is no real danger, for you do not see the blue men. Or do you see the blue men, O Hunder?" he asked.

"I see the men of the town standing in the streets and staring at me," said Hunder. "But their faces are white, and they wear clothes of many colors. Why do you ask me if I see blue men?"

Quillow put on a look of grave concern. "When you see the blue men," he said, "it is the third and last symptom of the malady. If that should happen, you must rush to the sea and bathe in the yellow waters or your strength will become the strength of a kitten." The giant groaned. "Perhaps if you fast for a day and a night," said Quillow, "the peril will pass."

"I will do as you say, teller of tales," said the giant, "for you are wise beyond the manner of men. Bring me no food today, tell me no tale." And with a moan Hunder sat back upon the hillside and covered his eyes with his hands.

When Quillow returned to the town, the people cheered him softly, and the children flung flowers at his feet. But the blacksmith was skeptical. "The giant is still there on the hillside," he said. "I shall save my cheers and my flowers until the day he is gone, if that day shall ever come." And he stalked back to his smithy to help the locksmith make the great brass key for Hunder's front door.

That noon there was enough mutton and pie and chocolate for all the people of the town, and they ate merrily and well.

Hunder the giant fretted and worried so profoundly during the day that he fell quickly to sleep as the night came. It was a night without moon or stars, as Quillow had hoped. A town owl who lived on the roof of the tavern—at the Sign of the Clock and Soldier—was surprised at the soft and shadowy activities of the toymaker. The bat and the firefly hovered about him in wonder as he worked secretly and swiftly in the green valley at the feet of the snoring giant. The squirrel and the nightingale watched like figures in a tapestry as he dug and planted in the woods at the giant's head. If the giant thrashed suddenly in his sleep or groaned, the cricket and the frog fell silent in high anxiety. When Quillow's work was finished and he returned to his shop, the bat and the firefly moved in dreamy circles, the squirrel and the nightingale stirred freely again, and the cricket and the frog began to sing. The owl on the roof of the Clock and Soldier nodded and slept. Quillow lay down on his workbench and closed his eyes.

When the scarlet men played the bells of five o'clock, and the first birds twittered in the trees and the gray light came, Quillow awoke and opened his door. The town crier stood in the cobbled street in front of the shop. "Cry the hour," said Quillow. "Cry all's well."

"Five o'clock!" cried the town crier. "Five o'clock and all's well!"

The people crept out of their houses and on the hillside across the green valley, Hunder the giant stirred and yawned and stretched and rubbed his eyes and sat up. He saw that the chimneys were still black, but he grinned at them and winked. "The malady passes," said Hunder. "I see men with white faces wearing clothes of many colors, but I see no blue men." He flexed the muscles of his powerful arms and he smote himself mighty blows upon his brow and chest and stomach. "Ho, councilors!" roared Hunder, "bring me my sheep and my pie and my chocolate, for I have a vast hunger."

The people fled from the streets, and behind the barred doors and shuttered windows of their houses they listened and trembled. The baker, the butcher, and the candymaker hid under their beds. They had prepared no meal for the giant and they were afraid for their lives. But the brave little toymaker, his white hair flowing like the dandelion clock in the morning wind, ran through the cobbled streets and across the green valley and stood at the giant's feet.

"Behold, I am still a whole man!" bellowed the giant, thumping his brow. "I have heard the word and I have seen the black chimneys, but I have not beheld the blue men."

"That is well," said Quillow, "for he who beholds the blue men must bathe in the yellow waters in the middle of the sea, or else he will dwindle, first to the height of the pussy willow, then to the height of the daffodil, then to the height of the violet, until finally he becomes a small voice in the grass, lost in the thundering of the crickets."

"But *I* shall remain stronger than the rock and taller than the oak," said Hunder, and he clapped his hands together.

"If you are stronger than the rock and taller than the oak," said Quillow, "then stamp on the ground and make yonder cow in the field turn a flip-flop."

Hunder stood up and chortled with glee. "Behold, smallest of men," he said, "I will make the cow turn twice in the air." He brought his right foot down upon the earth sharply and heavily. The cow turned a double flip-flop in the field, Quillow bounced as high as the giant's belt, and great boughs fell from

trees. But the giant had no eyes for these familiar wonders. He stared at something new under the sun, new and small and terrible. The blue men had come. The blue men were popping high into the air. They popped up in the valley and they popped up in the woods. They popped up from behind stones and they popped up from behind cowslips. They popped up in front of Hunder and they popped up behind him and under him and all around him.

"The blue men!" cried Hunder. "The blue men have come! The world is filled with little blue men!"

"I see no blue men," said Quillow, "but you have begun to shrink like the brook in dry weather, and that is the sign of the third symptom."

"The sea! The sea! Point me the sea!" bellowed Hunder, who now stood shivering and shaking.

"It is many leagues to the east," said Quillow. "Run quickly toward the rising sun and bathe in the yellow waters in the middle of the sea."

Hunder the giant ran toward the rising sun, and the town trembled as he ran. Pictures fell from walls and plates from plate rails and bricks from chimneys. The birds flew and the rabbits scampered. The cows turned flip-flops in the fields, and the brook jumped out of its bed.

A fortnight later a traveler from afar, stopping at the Sign of the Clock and Soldier, told the innkeeper a marvelous tale of how a giant, panting and moaning like a forest on fire, had stumbled down out of the mountains and plunged into the sea, flailing and threshing, and babbling of yellow waters and black chimneys and little blue men; and of how he had floundered farther and farther out to sea until at last he sank beneath the waves, starting a mighty tide rolling to the shore and sending up water spouts as high as the heavens. Then the giant was seen no more, and the troubled waters quieted as the sea resumed its inscrutable cycle of tides under the sun and the moon.

The innkeeper told this tale to the blacksmith, and the blacksmith told it to the locksmith, and the locksmith told it to the baker, and the baker told it to the butcher, and the butcher told it to the tailor, and the tailor told it to the cobbler, and the cobbler told it to the candymaker, and the candymaker told it to the candlemaker, and the candlemaker told it to the town crier, and the town crier told it to the lamplighter, and the lamplighter told it to the toymaker.

As the lamplighter spoke, Quillow put the finishing touches on a new toy, whistling softly, his eyes sparkling. The lamplighter saw that the toy was a tiny replica of Quillow himself.

"What do you do with that?" he asked.

"You put it in the palm of your hand, like this," said Quillow, and he put the figure in the palm of his hand. "And then you blow, like this." He blew, and the miniature Quillow floated slowly through the air and drifted gently to the floor. "I think it will amuse the children," said the little toymaker. "I got the idea from a giant."

Ray St. Clair

THE FOX FERRY

ILLUSTRATED BY *Esther Friend*

BY THE time the giant got home from the grocery store it was dark, and the foxes across the river had begun their barking at the moon. The barking made him feel even lonesomer than usual; besides, he was hungry and cross. He threw his empty shopping bag on the floor and jumped on it with both feet.

"Ninety cents for a can of ham!" he shouted. "It is an outrage!" Finnigan was his name, and his red hair stood out in all directions.

"I shall never trade there again," Finnigan boomed wrathfully. "I shall live on vegetables from my own garden."

"Yap yap yap yap yap," barked the foxes across the river, and the giant shook his fist at them.

"Be quiet!" he thundered, but they paid no attention to him.

The foxes barked all night, so that it was broad daylight before the giant could get to sleep. Then, first thing in the morning, the mailman woke him up by ringing his doorbell. By the time Finnigan had found his club and opened the door, the mailman had gone, leaving a package.

It was a cookbook the giant had sent for. His anger faded as he read the title with his sleep-blurred eyes, *Simple Recipes for Hard Times.* Clutching the cookbook, he stumbled into the garden to gather his breakfast. Soon he had collected a basket of radishes. They were not very good radishes, but they were all he could raise.

He set the basket of radishes on the kitchen floor and put his feet on the table, since there was nothing else to put there. He opened up his cookbook and popped a radish into his mouth.

Then his eyes widened, and he gulped down the radish without even noticing its strong, unpleasant taste. Right there, on page thirty-eight, was exactly the recipe he had been looking for. It was called "Baked Fox Pie with Radishes." Finnigan slapped his thigh with glee as he read, "Take six young foxes—."

"So, those foxes are good for something after all!" he exclaimed.

Baked fox pie with radishes—it sounded delicious. Thick, rich gravy, tender foxes, melting young radishes; yum, yum, thought the giant.

But how to catch the foxes? Foxes are clever—you can't just hold out the pie tin and expect them to jump into it. You have to be cleverer than a fox. So Finnigan plotted and planned, until he had a perfect scheme.

Right after breakfast he bought an old barge and cleaned it up. Then he painted grapevines all over the inside and hung several artificial chickens about to make it attractive for foxes.

After this was done, he built a fox bin to hold the foxes until the pie crust was ready. It was dark by now, but before he went to bed he salted down his whole crop of radishes.

The next morning, after a refreshing sleep, Finnigan waded across the river pushing his ferryboat and whistling as he splashed. On the other shore he built a pier and painted a pretty sign which read:

FOX FERRY
OPEN FOR BUSINESS
FOXES: SEE THE WORLD! TRAVEL!
SPECIAL RATES FOR YOUNG TENDER FOXES

He looked at his sign, then crossed out the word "Tender." No use giving them ideas, he thought. Now it was a good sign, and he sat down on his pier to wait for customers. "From pier to pie," he thought. "Yum, yum!"

Soon three foxes strolled by, their eyes bright, their tails bushy and neatly combed. They were young (and tender), and the giant offered them special rates at once.

"And what are your names, my little beauties?" beamed Finnigan, patting their heads.

"This is Biter," answered one of the foxes, "and that is Fighter. My name is Brighter, and I think you are up to no good!"

The giant drew himself up proudly. "That is not true," he

protested. "I am a legitimately enfranchised transportation corporation, under the jurisdiction of the Interstate Commerce Commission. There will be no funny business."

"That only means they let him run a ferryboat," said Brighter doubtfully.

Then Finnigan, seeing that they half believed in him, told them that they would be cleverer and more intelligent foxes if they traveled. He told them of the strange and romantic people who lived on the other side of the river. He painted a glowing picture of the climate and the scenery and the good hunting. "The land cries out for foxes!" he finished. "The land *hungers* for foxes!"

Biter, Fighter, and Brighter looked at each other and nodded. Then Finnigan remembered that the recipe for baked fox pie with radishes called for six foxes, so he asked them if they didn't have three little friends who would also like to come. "Three's a crowd," he smiled falsely, "but six is a party—and *everybody* likes a party!"

The foxes scampered off, wagging their bushy tails, to find three friends. The giant could almost hear the pie bubbling as it baked.

Soon Biter, Fighter, and Brighter trotted back, followed by Darker, Larker, and Barker. Barker yapped as he trotted, and Finnigan recognized his voice. "After I have had my pie," he thought, grinning to himself, "maybe I can sleep nights. There'll be no more yapping at the moon."

The six foxes were still a little timid, especially Brighter, but Finnigan playfully herded them all on to the ferryboat and showed them the painted grapes and the artificial chickens. "See," he pointed out. "Lunch!" Then he tied their tails together, explaining that this was necessary to keep them from being swept overboard in case of storm. Finally, he gave each of them a chocolate-flavored rubber bone to gnaw.

The giant stepped into the river and began to push the ferry ahead of him toward the other bank.

Brighter raised his nose and sniffed. "Those chickens," he said, "are fakes. And those grapes are probably sour. And I

don't like the way this bone bounces." The others gnawed contentedly, except Barker, who sometimes yapped a little.

As Finnigan waded through the river pushing his ferry he thought about his pie, how flaky the crust, how tender the young foxes, how tasty, and a wide smile spread over his face.

Brighter saw the smile. "Look at that grin!" he whispered. "He's too happy about something. He's up to no good!"

His uneasiness spread to the others. Barker stopped yapping and whimpered instead. "He's too happy," they muttered to each other. So they set to work and gnawed through the rope that tied their tails together. "When we land," said Brighter, "we'll all run in different directions. Then he can't catch us."

But when they reached the shore, the giant simply picked up the whole fox ferry. Before the foxes could do any running, he shot them all into his fox bin and locked the door.

They were neatly trapped.

But foxes are clever. Barker and Larker yapped with all their might, while Biter and Darker gnawed at the sides of the fox bin, and Brighter and Fighter sat and planned. The whole house shook from the gnawing, and the yapping nearly deafened Finnigan because it was so close to him.

He threw down his cookbook and ran up to see what was going on. They had gnawed a board almost through. While

Finnigan was hunting for another board, the foxes changed about. Biter and Darker now rested, Barker and Larker gnawed, and Brighter and Fighter yapped.

So it went. The foxes worked in shifts, gnawing, yapping, and resting, but there was no rest for the giant. They kept him so busy hunting new boards and nailing them that he had no time to sift flour for pie crust, or to open the cookbook.

Then Finnigan happened to think. All this exercise that his foxes were getting would be likely to make them lean and tough unless they got something to eat. So now he had to feed them.

Besides repairing the fox bin, he caught mice, rats, bats, gophers, moles, and rabbits to keep his foxes fat. The radishes he had salted down for the pie began to spoil. His red hair hung sadly over his eyes. He was a tired and hungry giant.

The foxes wagged their bushy tails gratefully at whatever food he gave them, but as soon as they had gulped it down they began to yap, gnaw, and rest again.

A bitter week passed. The foxes grew fat, their voices became stronger than ever, their teeth remained as sharp as razors. The giant was in despair. His radishes were by now entirely spoiled, he had not been able to leave the foxes long enough to open the sack of flour—and besides, the gas company had turned off the gas because he had been too busy to pay the bill.

At last Finnigan admitted he was beaten. There would be no baked fox pie with radishes for him. "I'll saw no more boards," he sighed in relief. "I'll let those foxes gnaw their way out. I'm through with foxes!"

He threw the cookbook as far as he could out into the river. Then he wrote an insulting letter to the people he had bought it from, while his six foxes gnawed, yapped, and rested.

He shook his fist at the fox bin, and set off down the road to the grocery store. He hated having to go back there for canned ham but there was nothing else he could do. He ground his teeth in helpless rage.

"Ninety cents a can," said the grocer. "Take it or leave it."

"It's an outrage!" Finnigan shouted, pounding the counter with his club.

"Take it or leave it," the grocer repeated, yawning. Then his eyes widened, as six bushy-tailed foxes trotted in the door.

"GRRRRRRRRRRRRRRRRRRR!" said the foxes, eyeing the grocer, their jaws wide open.

The grocer paled. "Sixty cents then," he quavered.

"GRRRRRRRRRRRR!" said the foxes. Their teeth were sharp and white.

"Listen," said the grocer, "I've got a wife and family to support. Forty cents."

"GRRR!" the foxes said. They advanced toward the grocer.

He backed away. "Rock bottom!" he said. "Not a penny less! All right, thirty cents then."

"I'll take two cases of ham," the giant said. The foxes watched the grocer tie up the cases. Barker yapped a little.

On the way home, the giant dropped the cases on the ground and sat on them to rest. He mopped his forehead, and looked at the six foxes who sat around him in a circle, bushy tails

straight behind them. "Why don't you run away?" he asked. "I let you escape."

"We like you," said Larker.

"You tamed us," said Darker.

"You fed us," said Biter. "Gophers! Yum, yum!"

"Yap yap yap yap yap yap," said Barker.

"Be quiet!" said Fighter. "Our boss doesn't like your yapping."

"You promised us a boat ride and adventure," said Brighter. "You told us how nice it is on this side of the river. We didn't believe you for a while, but now we see that you were telling us the truth. We are your foxes now, and we shall live with you always."

Finnigan looked them over and sighed. "No baked fox pie with radishes," he thought. Instead, there would be mice, rats, bats, gophers, moles, and rabbits to catch. Still—they *were* pretty little foxes, bright-eyed and bushy-tailed. They would be company for him; he needn't ever be lonesome again. He patted their heads and tickled behind their sharp, pointed ears.

Then he hoisted the two cases of ham onto his back and started home again. "It isn't every giant," he thought contentedly, "who has six foxes. Six-Fox-Finnigan," he grinned, "that's me!"

CITY FAIRIES

Mildred Bowers Armstrong

Fairies live in forests
And have tremendous larks,
But there are city fairies, too,
Who much prefer the parks.
Merry-go-rounds are their rings—
Why dance when they can ride?
They think the forest fairies
Are slow and countrified.

James Barrie

PETER PAN AND CAPTAIN HOOK

ILLUSTRATED BY

Margaret W. Tarrant

PETER PAN, the fairy boy who never wanted to grow up, flew away to Never Never Land with Wendy and her brothers John and Michael. Here lived mermaids, Indians, pirates, and fairies. Here in their underground home Wendy mothered Peter and all his lost boy friends. Everyone loved her except Peter's special fairy friend Tinker Bell. She was jealous.

Captain Hook, the one-armed pirate, also was on the island, fighting Peter every chance he got, and fleeing from the large crocodile that had bit off his arm and now wanted another bite. He could always hear the crocodile coming, for it had swallowed an alarm clock and ticked loudly.

At last one day in their underground home the children could hear the Indians and the pirates fighting. When they heard the Indian tom-tom they decided their friends the Indians had won. Joyously they ran outside and fell right into the arms of the pirates who had beaten the tom-tom to fool them.

And this is what happened next!

THE first to emerge from his tree was Curly. He rose out of it into the arms of Cecco, who flung him to Smee, who flung him to Starkey, who flung him to Bill Jukes, who flung him to Noodler, and so he was tossed from one to another till he fell at the feet of the black pirate. All the boys were plucked from their trees in this ruthless manner; and several of them were in the air at a time, like bales of goods flung from hand to hand.

A different treatment was accorded to Wendy, who came

last. With ironical politeness Hook raised his hat to her, and, offering her his arm, escorted her to the spot where the others were being gagged. He did it with such an air, he was so frightfully *distingué*, that she was too fascinated to cry out. She was only a little girl.

Perhaps it is telltale to divulge that for a moment Hook entranced her, and we tell on her only because her slip led to strange results. Had she haughtily unhanded him (and we should have loved to write it of her), she would have been hurled through the air like the others, and then Hook would probably not have been present at the tying of the children; and had he not been at the tying he would not have discovered Slightly's secret, and without the secret he could not presently have made his foul attempt on Peter's life.

They were tied to prevent their flying away, doubled up with their knees close to their ears; and for the trussing of them the black pirate had cut a rope into nine equal pieces. All went well until Slightly's turn came, when he was found to be like those irritating parcels that use up all the string in going round and leave no tags with which to tie a knot. The pirates kicked him in their rage, just as you kick the parcel (though in fairness you should kick the string); and strange to say it was Hook who told them to belay their violence. His lip was curled with malicious triumph. While his dogs were merely sweating because every time they tried to pack the unhappy lad tight in one part he bulged out in another, Hook's master mind had gone far beneath Slightly's surface, probing not for effects but for causes; and his exultation showed that he had found them. Slightly, white to the gills, knew that Hook had surprised his secret, which was this, that no boy so blown out could use a tree wherein an average man could stand. Poor Slightly, most wretched of all the children now, for he was in a panic about Peter, bitterly regretted what he had done. Madly addicted to the drinking of water when he was hot, he had swelled in consequence to his present girth, and instead of reducing himself to fit his tree he had, unknown to the others, whittled his tree to make it fit him.

Sufficient of this Hook guessed to persuade him that Peter at last lay at his mercy; but no word of the dark design that now formed in the subterranean caverns of his mind crossed his lips; he merely signed that the captives were to be conveyed to the ship, and that he would be alone.

How to convey him? Hunched up in their ropes they might indeed be rolled downhill like barrels, but most of the way lay through a morass. Again Hook's genius surmounted difficulties He indicated that the little house must be used as a conveyance. The children were flung into it, four stout pirates raised it on their shoulders, the others fell in behind, and singing the hateful pirate chorus the strange procession set off through the wood. I don't know whether any of the children were crying; if so, the singing drowned the sound; but as the little house disappeared in the forest, a brave though tiny jet of smoke issued from its chimney as if defying Hook.

Hook saw it, and it did Peter a bad service. It dried up any trickle of pity for him that may have remained in the pirate's infuriated breast.

The first thing he did on finding himself alone in the fast falling night was to tiptoe to Slightly's tree and make sure that it provided him with a passage. Then for long he remained brooding; his hat of ill omen on the sward, so that a gentle breeze which had arisen might play refreshingly through his hair. Dark as were his thoughts his blue eyes were as soft as the periwinkle. Intently he listened for any sound from the nether world, but all was as silent below as above; the house under the ground seemed to be but one more empty tenement in the void. Was that boy asleep, or did he stand waiting at the foot of Slightly's tree, with his dagger in his hand?

There was no way of knowing, save by going down. Hook let his cloak slip softly to the ground, and then biting his lips till . . . blood stood on them, he stepped into the tree. Hook was a brave man; but for a moment he had to stop there and wipe his brow, which was dripping like a candle. Then silently he let himself go into the unknown.

He arrived unmolested at the foot of the shaft, and stood still again, biting at his breath, which had almost left him. As his eyes became accustomed to the dim light various objects in the home under the trees took shape; but the only one on which his greedy gaze rested, long sought for and found at last, was the great bed. On the bed lay Peter fast asleep.

Unaware of the tragedy being enacted above, Peter had continued, for a little time after the children left, to play gaily on his pipes: no doubt rather a forlorn attempt to prove to himself that he did not care. Then he decided not to take his medicine, so as to grieve Wendy. Then he lay down on the bed outside the coverlet, to vex her still more; for she had always tucked them inside it, because you never know that you may not grow chilly at the turn of the night. Then he nearly cried; but it struck him how indignant she would be if he laughed instead; so he laughed a haughty laugh and fell asleep in the middle of it.

Sometimes, though not often, he had dreams, and they were more painful than the dreams of other boys. For hours he could not be separated from these dreams, though he wailed piteously in them. They had to do, I think, with the riddle of his existence. At such times it had been Wendy's custom to take him out of bed and sit with him on her lap, soothing him in dear ways of her own invention, and when he grew calmer to put him back to bed before he quite woke up, so that he should not know of the indignity to which she had subjected him. But on this occasion he had fallen at once into a dreamless sleep. One arm dropped over the edge of the bed, one leg was arched, and the unfinished part of his laugh was stranded on his mouth, which was open, showing the little pearls.

Thus defenceless Hook found him. He stood silent at the foot of the tree looking across the chamber at his enemy. Did no feeling of compassion disturb his somber breast? The man was not wholly evil; he loved flowers (I have been told) and sweet music (he was himself no mean performer on the harpsichord); and, let it be frankly admitted, the idyllic nature of the scene stirred him profoundly. Mastered by his better self he would have returned reluctantly up the tree, but for one thing.

What stayed him was Peter's impertinent appearance as he slept. The open mouth, the drooping arm, the arched knee: they were such a personification of cockiness as, taken together, will never again one may hope be presented to eyes so sensitive to their offensiveness. They steeled Hook's heart. If his rage had broken him into a hundred pieces every one of them would have disregarded the incident, and leapt at the sleeper.

Though a light from the one lamp shone dimly on the bed Hook stood in darkness himself, and at the first stealthy step forward he discovered an obstacle, the door of Slightly's tree. It did not entirely fill the aperture, and he had been looking over it. Feeling for the catch, he found to his fury that it was low down, beyond his reach. To his disordered brain it seemed then that the irritating quality in Peter's face and figure visibly increased, and he rattled the door and flung himself against it. Was his enemy to escape him after all?

But what was that? The red in his eye had caught sight of Peter's medicine standing on a ledge within easy reach. He fathomed what it was straightway, and immediately he knew that the sleeper was in his power.

Lest he should be taken alive, Hook always carried about his person a dreadful drug, blended by himself of all the death-dealing rings that had come into his possession. These he had boiled down into a yellow liquid quite unknown to science, which was probably the most virulent poison in existence.

Five drops of this he now added to Peter's cup. His hand shook, but it was in exultation rather than in shame. As he did it he avoided glancing at the sleeper, but not lest pity should unnerve him; merely to avoid spilling. Then one long gloating look he cast upon his victim, and turning, wormed his way with difficulty up the tree. As he emerged at the top he looked the very spirit of evil breaking from its hole. Donning his hat at its most rakish angle, he wound his cloak around him, holding one end in front as if to conceal his person from the night, of

It was Tink. She flew in excitedly.

which it was the blackest part, and muttering strangely to himself stole away through the trees.

Peter slept on. The light guttered and went out, leaving the tenement in darkness; but still he slept. It must have been not less than ten o'clock by the crocodile, when he suddenly sat up in his bed, wakened by he knew not what. It was a soft cautious tapping on the door of his tree.

Soft and cautious, but in that stillness it was sinister. Peter felt for his dagger till his hand gripped it. Then he spoke.

"Who is that?"

For long there was no answer: then again the knock.

"Who are you?"

No answer.

He was thrilled, and he loved being thrilled. In two strides he reached his door. Unlike Slightly's door it filled the aperture, so that he could not see beyond it, nor could the one knocking see him.

"I won't open unless you speak," Peter cried.

Then at last the visitor spoke, in a lovely bell-like voice.

"Let me in, Peter."

It was Tink, and quickly he unbarred to her. She flew in excitedly, her face flushed and her dress stained with mud.

"What is it?"

"Oh, you could never guess," she cried, and offered him three guesses. "Out with it!" he shouted; and in one ungrammatical sentence, as long as the ribbons conjurers pull from their mouths, she told of the capture of Wendy and the boys.

Peter's heart bobbed up and down as he listened. Wendy bound, and on the pirate ship; she who loved everything to be just so!

"I'll rescue her," he cried, leaping at his weapons. As he leapt he thought of something he could do to please her. He could take his medicine.

His hand closed on the fatal draught.

"No!" shrieked Tinker Bell, who had heard Hook muttering about his deed as he sped through the forest.

"Why not?"

"It is poisoned."

"Poisoned? Who could have poisoned it?"

"Hook."

"Don't be silly. How could Hook have got down here?"

Alas, Tinker Bell could not explain this, for even she did not know the dark secret of Slightly's tree. Nevertheless Hook's words had left no room for doubt. The cup was poisoned.

"Besides," said Peter, quite believing himself, "I never fell asleep."

He raised the cup. No time for words now; time for deeds; and with one of her lightning movements Tink got between his lips and the draught, and drained it to the dregs.

"Why, Tink, how dare you drink my medicine?"

But she did not answer. Already she was reeling in the air.

"What is the matter with you?" cried Peter, suddenly afraid.

"It was poisoned, Peter," she told him softly; "and now I am going to be dead."

"O Tink, did you drink it to save me?"

"Yes."

"But why, Tink?"

Her wings would scarcely carry her now, but in reply she alighted on his shoulder and gave his chin a loving bite. She whispered in his ear, "You silly ass"; and then, tottering to her chamber, lay down on the bed.

His head almost filled the fourth wall of her little room as he knelt near her in distress. Every moment her light was growing fainter; and he knew that if it went out she would be no more. She liked his tears so much that she put out her beautiful finger and let them run over it.

Her voice was so low that at first he could not make out what she said. Then he made it out. She was saying that she thought she could get well again if children believed in fairies.

Peter flung out his arms. There were no children there, and it was nighttime; but he addressed all who might be dreaming of the Never Never Land, and who were therefore nearer to him than you think: boys and girls in their nighties, and naked papooses in their baskets hung from trees.

"Do you believe?" he cried.

Tink sat up in bed almost briskly to listen to her fate.

She fancied she heard answers in the affirmative, and then again she wasn't sure.

"What do you think?" she asked Peter.

"If you believe," he shouted to them, "clap your hands; don't let Tink die."

Many clapped.

Some didn't.

A few little beasts hissed.

The clapping stopped suddenly; as if countless mothers had rushed to their nurseries to see what on earth was happening; but already Tink was saved. First her voice grew strong; then she popped out of bed; then she was flashing through the room more merry and impudent than ever. She never thought of thanking those who believed, but she would have liked to get at the ones who had hissed.

"And now to rescue Wendy."

The moon was riding in a cloudy heaven when Peter rose from his tree, begirt with weapons and wearing little else, to set out upon his perilous quest. It was not such a night as he would have chosen. He had hoped to fly, keeping not far from the ground so that nothing unwonted should escape his eyes;

but in that fitful light to have flown low would have meant trailing his shadow through the trees, thus disturbing the birds and acquainting a watchful foe that he was astir.

He regretted now that he had given the birds of the island such strange names that they are very wild and difficult of approach.

There was no other course but to press forward in redskin fashion, at which happily he was an adept. But in what direction, for he could not be sure that the children had been taken to the ship? A slight fall of snow had obliterated all footmarks; and a deathly silence pervaded the island, as if for a space Nature stood still in horror of the recent carnage. He had taught the children something of the forest lore that he had himself learned from Tiger Lily and Tinker Bell, and knew that in their dire hour they were not likely to forget it. Slightly, if he had an opportunity, would blaze the trees, for instance, Curly would drop seeds, and Wendy would leave her handkerchief at some important place. But morning was needed to search for such guidance, and he could not wait. The upper world had called him, but would give no help.

The crocodile passed him, but not another living thing, not a sound, not a movement; and yet he knew well that sudden death might be at the next tree, or stalking him from behind.

He swore this terrible oath: "Hook or me this time."

Now he crawled forward like a snake, and again, erect, he darted across a space on which the moonlight played: one finger on his lip and his dagger at the ready. He was frightfully happy.

One green light squinting over Kidd's Creek, which is near the mouth of the pirate river, marked where the brig, the *Jolly Roger*, lay, low in the water; a rakish-looking craft foul to the hull, every beam in her detestable, like ground strewn with mangled feathers. She was the cannibal of the seas and scarce needed that watchful eye, for she floated immune in the horror of her name.

She was wrapped in the blanket of night, through which no sound from her could have reached the shore. There was little sound, and none agreeable save the whir of the ship's sewing

machine at which Smee sat, ever industrious and obliging, the essence of the commonplace, pathetic Smee. I know not why he was so infinitely pathetic, unless it were because he was so pathetically unaware of it; but even strong men had to turn hastily from looking at him, and more than once on summer evenings he had touched the fount of Hook's tears and made it flow. Of this, as of almost everything else, Smee was quite unconscious.

A few of the pirates leant over the bulwarks drinking in the miasma of the night; others sprawled by barrels over games of dice and cards; and the exhausted four who had carried the little house lay prone on the deck, where even in their sleep they rolled skillfully to this side or that out of Hook's reach, lest he should claw them mechanically in passing.

Hook trod the deck in thought. O man unfathomable! It was his hour of triumph. Peter had been removed forever from his path, and all the other boys were on the brig, about to walk the plank. It was his grimmest deed since the days when he had brought Barbecue to heel; and knowing as we do how vain a tabernacle is man, could we be surprised had he now paced the deck unsteadily, bellied out by the winds of his success?

But there was no elation in his gait, which kept pace with the action of his somber mind. Hook was profoundly dejected.

He was often thus when communing with himself on board ship in the quietude of the night. It was because he was so terribly alone. This inscrutable man never felt more alone than when surrounded by his dogs. They were socially so inferior to him.

Hook was not his true name. To reveal who he really was would even at this date set the country in a blaze; but as those who read between the lines must already have guessed, he had been at a famous public school; and its traditions still clung to him like garments, with which indeed they are largely concerned. Thus it was offensive to him even now to board a ship in the same dress in which he grappled her; and he still adhered in his walk to the school's distinguished slouch. But above all he retained the passion for good form.

. . . .

He cried, "Are all the children chained, so that they cannot fly away?"

"Ay, ay."

"Then hoist them up."

The wretched prisoners were dragged from the hold, all except Wendy, and ranged in line in front of him. For a time he seemed unconscious of their presence. He lolled at his ease, humming, not unmelodiously, snatches of a rude song, and fingering a pack of cards. Ever and anon the light from his cigar gave a touch of color to his face.

"Now then, bullies," he said briskly, "six of you walk the plank tonight, but I have room for two cabin boys. Which of you is it to be?"

"Don't irritate him unnecessarily," had been Wendy's instructions in the hold; so Tootles stepped forward politely. Tootles hated the idea of signing under such a man, but an instinct told him that it would be prudent to lay the responsibility on an absent person; and though a somewhat silly boy, he knew that mothers alone are always willing to be the buffer. All children know this about mothers and despise them for it, but make constant use of it.

So Tootles explained prudently, "You see, sir, I don't think my mother would like me to be a pirate. Would your mother like you to be a pirate, Slightly?"

He winked at Slightly, who said mournfully, "I don't think so," as if he wished things had been otherwise. "Would your mother like you to be a pirate, Twin?"

"I don't think so," said the first twin, as clever as the others. "Nibs, would—"

"Stow this gab," roared Hook, and the spokesmen were dragged back. "You, boy," he said, addressing John, "you look as if you had a little pluck in you. Didst never want to be a pirate, my hearty?"

Now John had sometimes experienced this hankering at school while preparing his mathematics lesson, and he was struck by Hook's picking him out.

"I once thought of calling myself Red-handed Jack," he said.

"And a good name too. We'll call you that here, bully, if you join."

"What do you think, Michael?" asked John.

"What would you call me if I join?" Michael demanded.

"Blackbeard Joe."

Michael was naturally impressed. "What do you think, John?" He wanted John to decide, and John wanted him to decide.

"Shall we still be respectful subjects of the King?" John inquired.

Through Hook's teeth came the answer: "You would have to swear, 'Down with the King.' "

Perhaps John had not behaved very well so far, but he shone out now.

"Then I refuse," he cried, banging the barrel in front of Hook.

"And I refuse," cried Michael.

"Rule Britannia!" squeaked Curly.

The infuriated pirates buffeted them in the mouth; and Hook

roared out, "That seals your doom. Bring up their mother. Get the plank ready."

They were only boys, and they went white as they saw Jukes and Cecco preparing the fatal plank. But they tried to look brave when Wendy was brought up.

No words of mine can tell you how Wendy despised those pirates. To the boys there was at least some glamour in the pirate calling; but all that she saw was that the ship had not been scrubbed for years. There was not a porthole on the grimy glass of which you might not have written with your finger "Dirty pig"; and she had already written it on several. But as the boys gathered round her she had no thought, of course, save for them.

"So, my beauty," said Hook, as if he spoke in syrup, "you are to see your children walk the plank."

Fine gentleman though he was, he had soiled his ruff, and suddenly he knew that she was gazing at it. With a hasty gesture he tried to hide it but he was too late.

"Are they to die?" asked Wendy, with a look of such frightful contempt that he nearly fainted.

"They are," he snarled. "Silence all," he called gloatingly, "for a mother's last words to her children."

At this moment Wendy was grand. "These are my last words, dear boys," she said firmly. "I feel that I have a message to you from your real mothers, and it is this: 'We hope our sons will die like English gentlemen.' "

Even the pirates were awed; and Tootles cried out hysterically, "I am going to do what my mother hopes. What are you to do, Nibs?"

"What my mother hopes. What are you to do, Twin?"

"What my mother hopes. John, what are—"

But Hook had found his voice again.

"Tie her up," he shouted.

It was Smee who tied her to the mast. "See here, honey," he whispered, "I'll save you if you promise to be my mother."

But not even for Smee would she make such a promise. "I would almost rather have no children at all," she said.

It is sad to know that not a boy was looking at her as Smee tied her to the mast; the eyes of all were on the plank: that last little walk they were about to take. They were no longer able to hope that they would walk it manfully, for the capacity to think had gone from them; they could stare and shiver only.

Hook smiled on them with his teeth closed and took a step toward Wendy. His intention was to turn her face so that she should see the boys walking the plank one by one. But he never reached her, he never heard the cry of anguish he hoped to wring from her. He heard something else instead.

It was the terrible tick-tick of the crocodile.

They all heard it—pirates, boys, Wendy; and immediately every head was blown in one direction; not to the water whence the sound proceeded, but toward Hook. All knew that what was about to happen concerned him alone, and that from being actors they were suddenly become spectators.

Very frightful was it to see the change that came over him. It was as if he had been clipped at every joint. He fell in a little heap.

The sound came steadily nearer; and in advance of it came this ghastly thought, "The crocodile is about to board the ship."

Even the iron claw hung inactive; as if knowing that it was no intrinsic part of what the attacking force wanted. Left so fearfully alone, any other man would have lain with his eyes shut where he fell: but the gigantic brain of Hook was still working, and under its guidance he crawled on his knees along the deck as far from the sound as he could go. The pirates respectfully cleared a passage for him, and it was only when he brought up against the bulwarks that he spoke.

"Hide me," he cried hoarsely.

They gathered round him; all eyes averted from the thing that was coming aboard. They had no thought of fighting it. It was Fate.

Only when Hook was hidden from them did curiosity loosen the limbs of the boys so that they could rush to the ship's side to see the crocodile climbing it. Then they got the strangest surprise of this Night of Nights; for it was no crocodile that was coming to their aid. It was Peter.

He signed to them not to give vent to any cry of admiration that might rouse suspicion. Then he went on ticking.

Odd things happen to all of us on our way through life without our noticing for a time that they have happened. Thus, to take an instance, we suddenly discover that we have been deaf in one ear for we don't know how long, but, say, half an hour. Now such an experience had come that night to Peter. When last we saw him he was stealing across the island with one finger to his lips and with his dagger ready. He had seen the crocodile pass by without noticing anything peculiar about it, but by and by he remembered that it had not been ticking. At first he thought this eerie, but soon he concluded rightly that the clock had run down.

Without giving a thought to what might be the feelings of a fellow-creature thus abruptly deprived of its closest companion, Peter at once considered how he could turn the catastrophe to his own use; and he decided to tick, so that wild beasts should believe he was the crocodile and let him pass unmolested. He ticked superbly, but with one unforeseen result. The crocodile was among those who heard the sound, and it followed him, though whether with the purpose of regaining what it had lost, or merely as a friend under the belief that it was again ticking itself, will never be certainly known, for, like all slaves to a fixed idea, it was a stupid beast.

Peter reached the shore without mishap and went straight on; his legs encountering the water as if quite unaware that they had entered a new element. Thus many animals pass from land to water, but no other human of whom I know. As he swam he had but one thought: "Hook or me this time." He had ticked so long that he now went on ticking without knowing that he was doing it. Had he known he would have stopped, for to board the brig by the help of the tick, though an ingenious idea, had not occurred to him.

On the contrary, he thought he had scaled her side as noiseless as a mouse; and he was amazed to see the pirates cowering from him, with Hook in their midst as abject as if he had heard the crocodile.

The crocodile! No sooner did Peter remember it than he heard the ticking. At first he thought the sound did come from the crocodile, and he looked behind him swiftly. Then he realized that he was doing it himself, and in a flash he understood the situation. "How clever of me," he thought at once, and signed to the boys not to burst into applause.

It was at this moment that Ed Teynte, the quartermaster, emerged from the forecastle and came along the deck. Now, reader, time what happened by your watch. Peter struck true and deep. John clapped his hands on the ill-fated pirate's mouth to stifle the dying groan. He fell forward. Four boys caught him to prevent the thud. Peter gave the signal, and the carrion was cast overboard. There was a splash, and then silence. How long has it taken?

"One!" (Slightly had begun to count.)

None too soon, Peter, every inch of him on tiptoe, vanished into the cabin; for more than one pirate was screwing up his courage to look round. They could hear each other's distressed breathing now, which showed them that the more terrible sound had passed.

"It's gone, captain," Smee said, wiping his spectacles. "All's still again."

Slowly Hook let his head emerge from his ruff, and listened so intently that he could have caught the echo of the tick. There was not a sound, and he drew himself up firmly to his full height.

"Then here's to Johnny Plank," he cried brazenly, hating the boys more than ever because they had seen him unbend. He broke into the villainous ditty:

"Yo ho, yo ho, the frisky plank,
  You walks along it so,
Till it goes down and you goes down
  To Davy Jones below!"

To terrorize the prisoners the more, though with a certain loss of dignity, he danced along an imaginary plank, grimacing at them as he sang; and when he finished he cried, "Do you want a touch of the cat before you walk the plank?"

At that they fell on their knees. "No, no," they cried so piteously that every pirate smiled.

"Fetch the cat, Jukes," said Hook; "it's in the cabin."

The cabin! Peter was in the cabin! The children gazed at each other.

"Ay, ay," said Jukes blithely, and he strode into the cabin. They followed him with their eyes; they scarce knew that Hook had resumed his song, his dogs joining in with him:

"Yo ho, yo ho, the scratching cat,
  Its tails are nine, you know,
And when they're writ upon your back—"

What was the last line will never be known, for of a sudden the song was stayed by a dreadful screech from the cabin. It wailed through the ship and died away. Then was heard a crowing sound which was well understood by the boys, but to

the pirates was almost more eerie than the screech.

"What was that?" cried Hook.

"Two," said Slightly solemnly.

The Italian Cecco hesitated for a moment and then swung into the cabin. He tottered out, haggard.

"What's the matter with Bill Jukes, you dog?" hissed Hook, towering over him.

"The matter wi' him is he's dead, stabbed," replied Cecco in a hollow voice.

"Bill Jukes dead!" cried the startled pirates.

"The cabin's as black as a pit," Cecco said, almost gibbering, "but there is something terrible in there: the thing you heard crowing."

The exultation of the boys, the lowering looks of the pirates, both were seen by Hook.

"Cecco," he said in his most steely voice, "go back and fetch me out that doodle-doo."

Cecco, bravest of the brave, cowered before his captain, crying "No, no"; but Hook was purring to his claw.

"Did you say you would go, Cecco?" he said musingly.

Cecco went, first flinging up his arms despairingly. There was no more singing, all listened now; and again came a death-screech and again a crow.

No one spoke except Slightly. "Three," he said.

Hook rallied his dogs with a gesture. " 'Sdeath and odds fish," he thundered, "who is to bring me that doodle-doo?"

"Wait till Cecco comes out," growled Starkey, and the others took up the cry.

"I think I heard you volunteer, Starkey," said Hook, purring again.

"No, by thunder!" Starkey cried.

"My hook thinks you did," said Hook, crossing to him. "I wonder if it would not be advisable, Starkey, to humor the hook?"

"I'll swing before I go in there," replied Starkey doggedly, and again he had the support of the crew.

"Is it mutiny?" asked Hook more pleasantly than ever. "Starkey's ringleader."

"Captain, mercy," Starkey whimpered, all of a tremble now.

"Shake hands, Starkey," said Hook, proffering his claw.

Starkey looked round for help, but all deserted him. As he backed, Hook advanced, and now the red spark was in his eye. With a despairing scream the pirate leapt upon a big gun and precipitated himself into the sea.

"Four," said Slightly.

"And now," Hook asked courteously, "did any other gentleman say mutiny?" Seizing a lantern and raising his claw with a menacing gesture, "I'll bring out that doodle-doo myself," he said, and sped into the cabin.

"Five." How Slightly longed to say it. He wetted his lips to be ready, but Hook came staggering out, without his lantern.

"Something blew out the light," he said a little unsteadily.

"Something!" echoed Mullins.

"What of Cecco?" demanded Noodler.

"He's as dead as Jukes," said Hook shortly.

His reluctance to return to the cabin impressed them all

unfavorably, and the mutinous sounds again broke forth. All pirates are superstitious; and Cookson cried, "They do say the surest sign a ship's accurst is when there's one on board more than can be accounted for."

"I've heard," muttered Mullins, "he always boards the pirate craft at last. Had he a tail, captain?"

"They say," said another, looking viciously at Hook, "that when he comes it's in the likeness of the wickedest man aboard."

"Had he a hook, captain?" asked Cookson insolently; and one after another took up the cry, "The ship's doomed." At this the children could not resist raising a cheer. Hook had well-nigh forgotten his prisoners, but as he swung round on them now his face lit up again.

"Lads," he cried to his crew, "here's a notion. Open the cabin door and drive them in. Let them fight the doodle-doo for their lives. If they kill him, we're so much the better; if he kills them, we're none the worse."

For the last time his dogs admired Hook, and devotedly they did his bidding. The boys, pretending to struggle, were pushed into the cabin and the door was closed on them.

"Now, listen," cried Hook, and all listened. But not one dared to face the door. Yes, one, Wendy, who all this time had been bound to the mast. It was for neither a scream nor a crow that she was watching; it was for the reappearance of Peter.

She had not long to wait. In the cabin he had found the thing for which he had gone in search: the key that would free the children of their manacles; and now they all stole forth, armed with such weapons as they could find. First signing to them to hide, Peter cut Wendy's bonds, and then nothing could have been easier than for them all to fly off together; but one thing barred the way, an oath, "Hook or me this time." So when he had freed Wendy, he whispered to her to conceal herself with the others, and himself took her place by the mast, her cloak around him so that he should pass for her. Then he took a great breath and crowed.

To the pirates it was a voice crying that all the boys lay slain in the cabin; and they were panic-stricken. Hook tried to hearten them; but like the dogs he had made them they showed him their fangs, and he knew that if he took his eyes off them now they would leap at him.

"Lads," he said, ready to cajole or strike as need be, but never quailing for an instant, "I've thought it out. There's a Jonah aboard."

"Ay," they snarled, "a man wi' a hook."

"No, lads, no, it's the girl. Never was luck on a pirate ship wi' a woman on board. We'll right the ship when she's gone."

Some of them remembered that this had been a saying of Flint's. "It's worth trying," they said doubtfully.

"Fling the girl overboard," cried Hook; and they made a rush at the figure in the cloak.

"There's none can save you now, missy," Mullins hissed jeeringly.

"There's one," replied the figure.

"Who's that?"

"Peter Pan the avenger!" came the terrible answer; and as he spoke Peter flung off his cloak. Then they all knew who 'twas that had been undoing them in the cabin, and twice Hook essayed to speak and twice he failed. In that frightful moment I think his fierce heart broke.

At last he cried, "Cleave him to the brisket," but without conviction.

"Down, boys, and at them," Peter's voice rang out; and in another moment the clash of arms was resounding through the ship. Had the pirates kept together it is certain that they would have won; but the onset came when they were all unstrung, and they ran hither and thither, striking wildly, each thinking himself the last survivor of the crew. Man to man they were the stronger; but they fought on the defensive only, which enabled the boys to hunt in pairs and choose their quarry. Some of the miscreants leapt into the sea; others hid in dark recesses, where they were found by Slightly, who did not fight, but ran about with a lantern which he flashed in their faces, so that they were half blinded and fell an easy prey to the reeking swords of the other boys. There was little sound to be heard but the clang of weapons, an occasional screech or splash, and Slightly monotonously counting—five—six—seven—eight—nine—ten—eleven.

I think all were gone when a group of savage boys surrounded Hook, who seemed to have a charmed life, as he kept them at bay in that circle of fire. They had done for his dogs, but this man alone seemed to be a match for them all. Again and again they closed upon him, and again and again he hewed a clear space. He had lifted up one boy with his hook, and was using him as a buckler, when another, who had just passed his sword through Mullins, sprang into the fray.

"Put up your swords, boys," cried the newcomer, "this man is mine."

Thus suddenly Hook found himself face to face with Peter. The others drew back and formed a ring round them.

For long the two enemies looked at one another; Hook shuddering slightly, and Peter with the strange smile upon his face.

"So, Pan," said Hook at last, "this is all your doing."

"Ay, James Hook," came the stern answer, "it is all my doing."

"Proud and insolent youth," said Hook, "prepare to meet thy doom."

"Dark and sinister man," Peter answered, "have at thee."

Without more words they fell to and for a space there was no advantage to either blade. Peter was a superb swordsman and parried with dazzling rapidity; ever and anon he followed up a feint with a lunge that got past his foe's defence, but his shorter reach stood him in ill stead, and he could not drive the steel home. Hook, scarcely his inferior in brilliancy, but not quite so nimble in wrist play, forced him back by the weight of his onset, hoping suddenly to end all with a favorite thrust, taught him long ago by Barbecue at Rio; but to his astonishment he found this thrust turned aside again and again. Then he sought to close and give the quietus with his iron hook, which all this time had been pawing the air; but Peter doubled under it and, lunging fiercely, pierced him in the ribs. At sight of his own blood, whose peculiar color, you remember, was

offensive to him, the sword fell from Hook's hand, and he was at Peter's mercy.

"Now!" cried all the boys, but with a magnificent gesture Peter invited his opponent to pick up his sword. Hook did so instantly, but with a tragic feeling that Peter was showing good form.

Hitherto he had thought it was some fiend fighting him, but darker suspicions assailed him now.

"Pan, who and what art thou?" he cried huskily.

"I'm youth, I'm joy," Peter answered at a venture, "I'm a little bird that has broken out of the egg."

This, of course, was nonsense; but it was proof to the unhappy Hook that Peter did not know in the least who or what he was, which is the very pinnacle of good form.

"To 't again," he cried despairingly.

He fought now like a human flail, and every sweep of that terrible sword would have severed in twain any man or boy who obstructed it; but Peter fluttered round him as if the very wind it made blew him out of the danger zone. And again and again he darted in and pricked.

Hook was fighting now without hope. That passionate breast no longer asked for life; but for one boon it craved: to see Peter bad form before it was cold forever.

Abandoning the fight he rushed into the powder magazine and fired it.

"In two minutes," he cried, "the ship will be blown to pieces."

Now, now, he thought, true form will show.

But Peter issued from the powder magazine with the shell in his hands and calmly flung it overboard.

What sort of form was Hook himself showing? Misguided man though he was, we may be glad, without sympathizing with him, that in the end he was true to the traditions of his race. The other boys were flying around him now, flouting, scornful; and as he staggered about the deck striking up at them impotently, his mind was no longer with them; it was slouching in the playing fields of long ago, or being sent up for good, or watching the wall-game from a famous wall. And his shoes were right, and his waistcoat was right, and his tie was right, and his socks were right.

James Hook, thou not wholly unheroic figure, farewell.

For we have come to his last moment.

Seeing Peter slowly advancing upon him through the air with dagger poised, he sprang upon the bulwarks to cast himself into the sea. He did not know that the crocodile was waiting for him; for we purposely stopped the clock that this knowledge might be spared him: a little mark of respect from us at the end.

He had one last triumph, which I think we need not grudge him. As he stood on the bulwark looking over his shoulder at Peter gliding through the air, he invited him with a gesture to use his foot. It made Peter kick instead of stab.

At last Hook had got the boon for which he craved.

"Bad form," he cried jeeringly, and went content to the crocodile.

Thus perished James Hook.

"Seventeen," Slightly sang out; but he was not quite correct in his figures. Fifteen paid the penalty for their crimes that night; but two reached the shore: Starkey to be captured by the redskins, who made him nurse for all their papooses, a melancholy comedown for a pirate; and Smee, who henceforth wandered about the world in his spectacles, making a precarious living by saying he was the only man that Jas. Hook had feared.

Wendy, of course, had stood by taking no part in the fight, though watching Peter with glistening eyes; but now that all was over she became prominent again. She praised them

equally, and shuddered delightfully when Michael showed her the place where he had killed one; and then she took them into Hook's cabin and pointed to his watch which was hanging on a nail. It said "half-past one!"

The lateness of the hour was almost the biggest thing of all. She got them to bed in the pirates' bunks pretty quickly, you may be sure; all but Peter, who strutted up and down on deck, until at last he fell asleep by the side of the big gun. He had one of his dreams that night, and cried in his sleep for a long time, and Wendy held him tight.*

SEA-SHELL

Ivy O. Eastwick

It is so smooth,
and pale, and pink—
it is a magic
shell, I think.
I'll hold it up
against my ear,
and learn its magic
spell, my dear. . . .
. . . I hear the sound
of sea and spray,
the splash of boats
across the bay,
the tinkle of
a far-off bell
that marks a rock
(and warns us well!)
and then—a song
so clear! so wild!

I think it is
a Merman's child!

*Permission granted for slight adaptations.

Jacob and Wilhelm Grimm

RUMPELSTILTSKIN

ADAPTED BY *Pauline Rosenberg*

ILLUSTRATED BY *Marie Lawson*

THERE was once a miller who was poor, but who had a beautiful daughter. Now it happened that he came to speak to the King, and in order to seem important, he said, "I have a daughter who can spin straw into gold."

The King said to the miller, "That is an art which pleases me well! If your daughter is as clever as you say, bring her to my castle tomorrow, and I will put her to the test."

When the girl was brought to the King, he led her into a room which was all full of straw, gave her a spinning wheel and winder, and said, "Now set to work, and if by tomorrow morning you have not spun this straw into gold, you must die." So saying, he locked the room, and she remained alone.

There sat the poor miller's daughter, and for the life of her she did not know what to do. She had not the least idea how to spin straw into gold, and she became more and more worried, and at last she began to weep.

All at once the door sprang open, and in stepped a tiny little man and said, "Good evening, miller's daughter, why are you weeping so?"

"Ah," answered the girl, "I have to spin straw into gold and I do not know how."

Then said the little man, "What will you give me, if I spin it for you?"

"My necklace," said the maiden.

The little man took the necklace, seated himself at the spinning wheel, and *whir, whir, whir*—three times around—and the reel was full. Then he put on another reel, and *whir, whir, whir*—three times around—and the second reel also was full. So he went on till morning, when all the straw was spun and all the reels were full of gold.

At sunrise the king came, and when he saw the gold he was surprised and pleased, but he became all the more greedy for gold. He had the miller's daughter brought to another, much larger, room full of straw.

"If life is dear to you," he said, "you must spin all this straw into gold before morning."

The maiden did not know what to do and she began to weep. Then again the door sprang open and the little man appeared and said, "What will you give me if I spin the straw into gold?"

"The ring from my finger," answered the girl.

The little man took the ring, began to *whir* again at the spinning wheel, and by morning had spun all the straw into shining gold.

The King was delighted when he saw the masses of gold, but still he didn't have enough. He had the miller's daughter taken to a still larger room full of straw and said, "All this you must spin tonight, but if you succeed you shall be my wife." "Even if she is only a miller's daughter," he thought, "I shall not find a richer wife in the whole world."

When the girl was alone, the little man came a third time and said, "What will you give me this time if I spin the straw for you?"

"I have nothing more that I can give," answered the girl.

"Then promise, if you become queen, to give me your first child."

"Who knows what may happen by that time?" thought the maiden. And not knowing what else to do in her trouble, she promised the little man what he demanded. And in return once more he spun the straw into gold.

When the King came in the morning and found everything as he had wished, he married the miller's daughter and she became queen.

A year later she brought a beautiful child into the world. She had forgotten all about the little man, when suddenly he

entered her room and said, "Now give me what you promised."

The Queen was terrified and offered the little man all the riches of the kingdom if he would let her keep the child, but he said, "No, something living is dearer to me than all the treasures of the world."

Then the Queen began to weep so bitterly that the little man had pity on her and said, "I will give you three days' time, and if within that time you can find out my name, you shall keep your child."

Then all night long the Queen thought of every name she had ever heard, and she sent a messenger over the whole country to inquire what other names there were. When the little man came the next day, she began with Caspar, Melchior, Balzer, and named all the names she knew, one after the other; but each time the little man said, "That is not my name."

The second day she found out the names of all the people living near the castle. Then she repeated the strangest and most unusual names to the little man.

"Is your name perhaps Ribsteer or Sheepshanks or Stringbone?"

But each time he answered, "That is not my name."

The third day the messenger returned and said, "I haven't been able to find a single new name, but as I came to the corner of the wood on the side of a high mountain, where the fox and the hare bid each other good night, I saw a little house, and in front of the house a fire was burning, and around the fire the funniest little man was jumping and hopping on one leg and crying out:

"Today I bake, tomorrow brew;
Next day I'll have the queen's child too;
I've kept my secret just the same,
That *Rumpelstiltskin* is my name."

You can imagine how happy the Queen was when she heard the name. Soon after the little man came again and asked, "Well, Your Majesty, what is my name?"

The Queen asked, "Is your name Conrad?"

"No."

"Is it Henry?"

"No."

"Are you perhaps called Rumpelstiltskin?"

"A witch has told you that—a witch has told you that!" shrieked the little man, and in rage he stamped his right foot so deep into the ground that it sank up to his waist. Then in fury he seized his left foot with both hands and brought it down so hard that he sank deep into the earth and was never seen again.

Hans Christian Andersen

THE EMPEROR'S NEW CLOTHES

RETOLD BY *Marjorie Gordon*

FULL PAGE ILLUSTRATION BY *Arthur Rackham*

OTHER ILLUSTRATIONS BY *Frances Eckart*

MANY years ago there lived an emperor who was so fond of new clothes that he spent all his money on them. He was not interested in his soldiers, or in the theater, or in driving in the park unless there was an opportunity to show off his new costumes. He had a different outfit for every hour in the day, and so, instead of saying, as one usually does about an emperor, "He is in his council hall," here one said, "The emperor is in his dressing room."

The great city in which the emperor lived was a busy one. Many strangers visited it. Among the many who came one day were two swindlers. They told everyone that they were weavers and that they knew how to weave the most beautiful cloth that could ever be imagined. And the colors and patterns of this cloth, they said, were most delicate. Indeed, they added, clothes made of this material would seem invisible to those who were either unsuited to the office they held, or were very, very stupid.

"These must be wonderful clothes," thought the emperor. "If I wear them I will be able to tell which men in my realm are unfitted for their office. And I shall know who is wise and who is stupid. Yes, I must order some cloth to be woven immediately!"

And so he gave the two swindlers great sums of money, as he wished them to begin to work for him at once.

The weavers put up two looms and pretended to be very busy; but there was nothing on the looms.

They asked for the very finest silk and the most expensive

gold, and these they kept themselves; but they sat at the empty looms far into the night.

"I would like to know," thought the emperor, "how much work has been completed on my clothes." But he felt a little uncomfortable when he remembered that anyone who was unsuited for his position, or was very foolish, would not be able to see the material. He felt that he himself had no need to fear. However, he decided to send someone else for the first inspection.

Everyone in the city knew of the cloth's magical powers. All were eager to see who was evil, or who was stupid.

"I think I will send my loyal old cabinet-minister to the weavers," thought the emperor. "He should be able to see the cloth better than anyone for he is clever. No one else is as capable as he."

So the kindly old minister went into the room where the two impostors were busily working at their empty looms.

"Merciful Heavens!" thought the good man, beginning to stare, "can I be so stupid? I can't see anything!" But he said nothing at all.

The two swindlers urged him to tell them if he were satisfied with their progress, and if he didn't think the colors and design were beautiful. And they pointed to the empty looms.

"Don't you have anything to say?" asked one of the weavers.

"Oh, it is most exquisite!" said the poor old man, adjusting his spectacles. "The colors and design are unusual. I shall tell the emperor that I am quite satisfied."

"We are happy to know that you are pleased," said the swindlers, and they pointed out the subtle patterns and colors again. The minister listened with care. He wished to report everything to the emperor.

Then the swindlers asked for more money, and more silk, and more gold. This again they put aside for themselves and went on weaving, as before, on the empty looms.

Soon the emperor sent another official to see how the weavers were progressing and how soon the cloth would be finished. But this official, too, could see nothing at all on the looms.

"Isn't this material magnificent?" asked the swindlers, pointing to colors and designs which were not there.

"I am sure I am not a stupid man," thought the official, "therefore I must be unsuited to my office. It is very strange, but I surely cannot let anyone know." So he admired the cloth, which he could not see, and praised the brilliance of the colors, and the intricacy of the design. "It is very beautiful," he told the emperor.

Now everyone in the city was talking about the wonderful material, and the emperor decided to see it while it was still being woven. Accompanied by a group of special courtiers, among whom were the two who had already seen the imaginary cloth, he went to call upon the two weavers, whose hands were busily at work in the empty air above the looms.

"Isn't it magnificent?" cried the loyal officials who had been there before. "Look at the amazing pattern, Your Majesty, and the colors!" And they pointed to the empty looms, for they believed that the others could see the material.

"What can this mean?" thought the emperor. "I see nothing at all! How terrible! Am I a fool? Am I unfit to be emperor? Oh, nothing more dreadful could happen to me!"

But aloud he said, "It is handsome, indeed. We approve." And he gazed at the empty looms. He too would not admit that no cloth was there.

One by one the courtiers looked at the looms. One by one they could see nothing on the looms at all. But they all said "Handsome; indeed!" and suggested that he wear the new clothes in a great procession which was soon to take place. The emperor agreed and, before leaving, decorated each of the swindlers with special orders which were to be hung in their buttonholes and gave them the title of "Knights of the Cloth."

On the night before the procession the weavers stayed up late, burning sixteen candles, so that everyone could see how hard they were working on the emperor's new clothes. They pretended to take the material down from the looms. They made great cuts in the air with their huge scissors. They even made stitches with needles which held no thread. Finally they announced: "The emperor's new clothes are ready!"

The great day had arrived.

The emperor himself went to the weavers with his highest officials; and the two impostors lifted their arms as if they were holding something, and said: "Look, here are the trousers, here is the coat, and here is the mantle!" So they went on. "It is as light as a spider's web. One might think when donning it that one had nothing on, but that is the beauty of it!"

"Oh, yes," said all the courtiers, but they could see nothing —for there was nothing to see.

"Will Your Imperial Majesty graciously allow himself to be disrobed?" asked one of the swindlers. "Then we may put on the new clothes in front of this great mirror."

And so the emperor took off all his clothes, and the swindlers pretended to put on the new costume, one article after another. Finally, they seemed to fasten something around his waist, which was the train; and the emperor turned round and round before the mirror.

"How wonderful the emperor looks! What a beautiful fit!" everyone exclaimed. "Look at the pattern and colors!"

"The canopy which is to be carried above Your Majesty in the procession is now outside," announced the master of ceremonies.

"I am ready," said the emperor, and he turned around again and again in front of the great mirror.

Then the chamberlains, who had been appointed to carry the train, groped along the ground with their hands, and pretended to lift the train in the air. They did not dare to let anyone know that they held nothing at all.

And so the emperor walked forth under the splendid canopy, and all the people cried from the streets and from the windows, "Behold the emperor! How beautiful are his new clothes! See the royal train!" No one would say that he could not see the new clothes, for that would have meant that he was unfit for his office or that he was stupid. Never before had the emperor's clothes made such a sensation!

Suddenly a little child cried out, "But he has nothing on!"

"Ah, listen to the innocent," said the father, and the people began to repeat in whispers what the child had said.

"But he has nothing on—a child says he has nothing on at all!" they said. And at last everyone cried, "The emperor has nothing on!"

And the emperor trembled, for he knew that they spoke the truth. But he told himself, "The procession cannot stop now." And so he walked on more proudly than before, and the chamberlains followed, holding on high the train which was not there.

George Webbe Dasent

THE LAD WHO WENT TO THE NORTH WIND

ADAPTED BY *Pauline Rosenberg*

ILLUSTRATED BY *Marie Lawson*

ONCE upon a time there was an old widow who had one son, and as she was feeble and weak, she sent her son up into the storehouse to fetch meal for cooking. But when he got outside the storehouse and was just going down the steps, along came the North Wind puffing and blowing, caught up the meal, and so away with it through the air.

Then the lad went back into the storehouse for more, but when he came out again on the steps, if the North Wind didn't come again and carry off the meal with a puff! And more than that—when the boy went back again, the North Wind carried off the meal for the third time. At this the lad got very angry. He thought it hard that the North Wind should behave so, and he decided to visit him and ask him to give up the meal.

So off the lad went. The way was long, and he walked and walked, but at last he came to the North Wind's house.

"Good day!" said the lad, "and thank you for coming to see us yesterday."

"GOOD DAY!" answered the North Wind, for his voice was loud and gruff, "AND THANK YOU FOR COMING TO SEE ME. WHAT DO YOU WANT?"

"Oh!" answered the lad, "I only wished to ask you to be so good as to let me have back the meal you took from me on the storehouse steps, for we haven't much to live on, and if you're to go on snapping up the little we have, there'll be nothing left for us but to starve."

"I haven't got your meal," said the North Wind, "but if you are in such need, I'll give you a cloth which will get you everything you want, if you only say,—

"Cloth, spread yourself, and serve up all kinds of good dishes!"

With this the lad was well content. But, as the way was so long that he couldn't get home in one day, he turned into an inn on the way. When suppertime came he laid the cloth on a table which stood in the corner and said,—

"Cloth, spread yourself, and serve up all kinds of good dishes."

He had scarce said so before the cloth did as it was bid, and the table was covered with all kinds of good things to eat. All who stood by thought it a fine thing, but most of all the landlord. So, when all were fast asleep, at dead of night, he took the lad's cloth and put another in its place. It looked just like

the one he had got from the North Wind, but it couldn't so much as serve up dry bread.

When the lad awoke, he took the cloth and went off with it, and that day he got home to his mother.

"Now," said he, "I've been to the North Wind's house, and a good fellow he is, for he gave me this cloth, and when I only say to it,—

" 'Cloth, spread yourself, and serve up all kinds of good dishes,' I get any sort of food I please."

"All very true, I dare say," said his mother, "but seeing is believing, and I shan't believe it till I see it."

So the lad made haste, drew out a table, and laid the cloth on it and said,—

"Cloth, spread yourself, and serve up all kinds of good dishes." But never a bit of dry bread did the cloth serve up.

"Well!" said the lad, "there's no help for it but to go to the North Wind again," and away he went.

Late in the afternoon he came to where the North Wind lived.

"Good evening!" said the lad.

"Good evening!" said the North Wind.

"I want my rights for the meal of ours which you took," said the lad, "for, as for that cloth I got, it isn't worth a penny."

"I've got no meal," said the North Wind, "but yonder you have a ram which coins nothing but golden ducats as soon as you say to it,—

" 'Ram, ram! make money!' "

The lad thought this a fine thing. But as it was too far to get home that day, he turned in for the night to the same inn where he had slept before.

Before he called for anything, he tried what the North Wind had said of the ram and found it all right. But when the landlord saw that, he thought it was a famous ram, and when the lad had fallen asleep, he took another which couldn't coin a penny and changed the two.

Next morning off went the lad, and when he got home to his mother, he said,—

"After all, the North Wind is a jolly fellow, for now he has given me a ram which can coin golden ducats, if I only say,—

" 'Ram, ram! make money.' "

"All very true, I dare say," said his mother, "but I shan't believe any such stuff until I see the ducats made."

"Ram, ram! make money!" said the lad, but the ram didn't make a penny.

So the lad went back again to the North Wind and said the ram was worth nothing, and he must have his rights for the meal.

"Well!" said the North Wind, "I've nothing else to give you but that old stick in the corner yonder, but it's a stick of that kind that if you say,—

" 'Stick, stick! lay on!' it lays on till you give the command, 'Stick, stick! now stop!' "

As the way was long, the lad turned in this night, too, to the landlord; but as he could pretty well guess how things stood as to the cloth and the ram, he lay down at once on the bench and began to snore as if he were asleep.

Now the landlord saw that the stick must be worth something, and he hunted up one like it. When he heard the lad snore, he was going to change the two, but just then the lad cried out,—

"Stick, stick! lay on!"

So the stick began to beat the landlord, till he jumped over chairs and tables and benches, and yelled and roared,—

"Oh my! oh my! bid the stick be still, and you shall have back both your cloth and your ram."

When the lad thought the landlord had got enough, he said,—

"Stick, stick! now stop!"

Then he took his cloth and put it in his pocket, and went home with his stick in his hand, leading the ram by a cord round its horns, and so he got his rights for the meal he had lost.

Jacob and Wilhelm Grimm

LITTLE SNOW-WHITE

ILLUSTRATED BY *Wanda Gág*

ONCE upon a time it was the middle of winter; the flakes of snow were falling like feathers from the sky; a queen sat at a window sewing, and the frame of the window was made of black ebony. As she was sewing and looking out of the window at the snow, she pricked her finger with the needle, and three drops of blood fell upon the snow. And the red looked pretty upon the white snow, and she thought to herself,—

"Would that I had a child as white as snow, as red as blood, and as black as the wood of the windowframe!" Soon after that she had a little daughter, who was as white as snow, and as red as blood, and her hair was as black as ebony; so she was called Little Snow-white. And when the child was born, the queen died.

A year after, the king took to himself another wife. She was beautiful but proud and she could not bear to have any one else more beautiful. She had a wonderful Looking-glass, and when she stood in front of it, and looked at herself in it, and said,—

"Looking-glass, Looking-glass, on the wall,
Who in this land is the fairest of all?"

the Looking-glass answered,—

"Thou, O Queen, art the fairest of all!"

At that she was well pleased, for she knew the Looking-glass spoke the truth.

Now Snow-white grew up and became more and more beautiful; and when she was seven years old she was as beautiful as the day and more beautiful than the queen herself. And once when the queen asked her Looking-glass,—

"Looking-glass, Looking-glass, on the wall,
Who in this land is the fairest of all?"

it answered,—

"Thou art fairer than all who are here, Lady Queen,
But more beautiful by far is Snow-white, I ween."

Then the queen was angry, and turned green with envy. From that hour, whenever she looked at Snow-white, her breath came and went, she hated the girl so much.

And envy grew higher and higher in her heart like a weed, so that she had no peace day or night. She called a huntsman, and said,—

"Take the child away into the wood; I will no longer have her in my sight. Kill her, and bring me back her heart as a token." The huntsman did as he was told, and took her away; but when he had drawn his knife and was about to pierce Snow-white's little heart, she began to weep, and said,—

"Ah, dear huntsman, leave me my life! I will run away into the wild wood and never come home again."

And as she was so beautiful the huntsman had pity on her and said,—

"Run away, then, you poor child.—The wild beasts will soon kill you," thought he; and yet it seemed as if a stone had been rolled from his heart, since it was no longer needful for him to kill her. As a young boar just then came running by, he stabbed it, and cut out its heart, and took it to the queen as a proof that the child was dead.

But now the poor child was all alone in the great wood, and so afraid that she started at every bush and did not know what to do. Then she began to run and ran over sharp stones and through thorns, and the wild beasts ran past her but did her no harm.

She ran as long as her feet would go, until it was almost evening; then she saw a little cottage and went into it to rest herself. Everything in the cottage was small, but neater and cleaner than can be told. There was a table on which was a white cover, and seven little plates, and by each plate was a little spoon;

there were seven little knives and forks, and seven little mugs. Against the wall stood seven little beds side by side, covered with snow-white coverlets.

Little Snow-white was so hungry and thirsty that she ate some fruit and bread from each plate and drank a drop of milk out of each mug, for she did not wish to take all from one only. Then, as she was so tired, she lay down on one of the little beds, but none of them suited her; one was too long, another too short; but at last she found the seventh one was just right and so she stayed in it, said her prayers, and went to sleep.

When it was quite dark the owners of the cottage came back; they were seven dwarfs who dug in the hills for gold. They lit their seven candles, and as it was now light within the cottage they could see that someone had been there, for everything was not in the same order in which they had left it.

The first said, "Who has been sitting on my chair?"

The second, "Who has been eating off my plate?"

The third, "Who has been taking some of my bread?"

The fourth, "Who has been eating my fruit?"

The fifth, "Who has been using my fork?"

The sixth, "Who has been cutting with my knife?"

The seventh, "Who has been drinking out of my mug?"

Then the first looked round and saw that there was a little hole in his bed, and he said,—

"Who has been getting into my bed?" The others came up and each called out,—

"Somebody has been lying in my bed too." But the seventh, when he looked at his bed, saw little Snow-white, who was lying asleep there. And he called the others, who came running up, and they cried out with wonder and brought their seven little candles and let the light fall on little Snow-white.

"Oh, heavens! oh, heavens!" cried they, "what a lovely child!" and they were so glad that they did not wake her but let her sleep on in the bed. And the seventh dwarf slept with the others, one hour with each, and so got through the night.

When it was morning little Snow-white awoke and was afraid when she saw the seven dwarfs. But they were friendly and asked her what her name was.

"My name is Snow-white," she answered.

"How have you come to our house?" said the dwarfs. Then she told them that the queen had wished to have her killed, but that the huntsman had spared her life; she had run for the whole day, until at last she had found their house. The dwarfs said,—

"If you will take care of our house, cook, make the beds, wash, sew, and knit; and if you will keep everything neat and clean, you can stay with us, and you shall want for nothing."

"Yes," said Snow-white, "with all my heart," and she stayed with them. She kept the house in order for them; in the mornings they went to the hills and looked for gold; in the evenings they came back, and then their supper had to be ready. The girl was alone the whole day, so the good dwarfs warned her and said,—

"Beware of the queen; she will soon know that you are here; be sure to let no one come in."

But the queen, thinking Snow-white to be dead, began to suppose she was again the first and most beautiful person in the world; and she went to her Looking-glass and said,—

"Looking-glass, Looking-glass, on the wall,
Who in this land is the fairest of all?"

And the Glass answered,—

"O Queen, thou art fairest of all I see,
But over the hills, where the seven dwarfs dwell,
Snow-white is still alive and well,
And no one else is so fair as she."

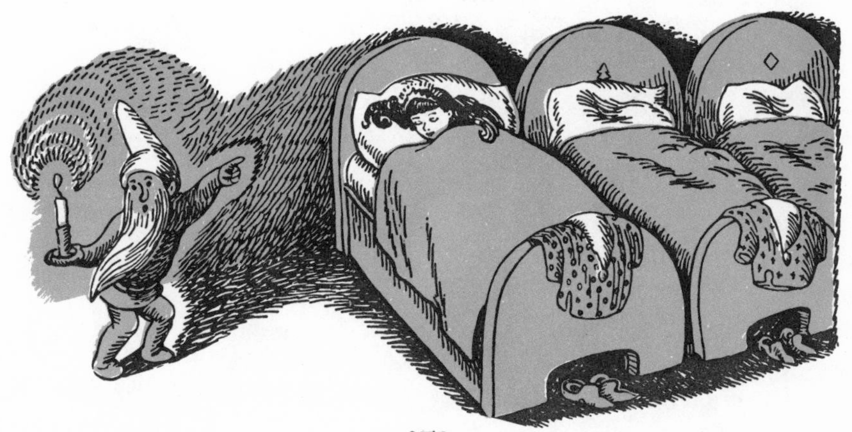

And so she thought and thought again how she might kill Snow-white, for so long as she was not the fairest in the whole land, envy let her have no rest. And when she had at last thought of something to do, she painted her face and dressed herself like an old peddler-woman, and no one could have known her. Then she went over the seven hills to the seven dwarfs, and knocked at the door and cried,—

"Pretty things to sell, very cheap, very cheap." Little Snow-white looked out of the window and called out,—

"Good day, my good woman, what have you to sell?"

"Good things, pretty things," she answered; "staylaces of all colors," and she pulled out one which was woven of bright silk.

"I may let the good old woman in," thought Snow-white, and she unbolted the door and bought the pretty laces.

"Child," said the old woman, "what a fright you look! Come, I will lace you properly for once."

Snow-white stood before her, and let herself be laced with the new laces. But the old woman laced so quickly and laced so tightly that Snow-white lost her breath and fell down as if dead. "Now I am the most beautiful," said the queen to herself, and ran away.

Not long after, in the evening, the seven dwarfs came home, but how shocked they were when they saw their dear little Snow-white lying on the ground! She did not stir or move and seemed to be dead. They lifted her up, and, as they saw that she was laced too tightly, they cut the laces; then she began to breathe a little and after a while came to life again. When the dwarfs heard what had happened they said,—

"The old peddler-woman was no one else than the wicked queen; take care and let no one come in when we are not with you."

But the wicked woman, when she was at home again, went in front of the Glass and asked,—

"Looking-glass, Looking-glass, on the wall,
Who in this land is the fairest of all?"

And it answered as before,—

"O Queen, thou art fairest of all I see,
But over the hills, where the seven dwarfs dwell,
Snow-white is still alive and well,
And no one else is so fair as she."

When she heard that, all her blood rushed to her heart with fear, for she saw plainly that little Snow-white was again alive.

"But now," she said, "I will think of something that shall put an end to you," and so she made a comb that was full of poison. Then she took the shape of another old woman. So she went over the seven hills to the seven dwarfs, knocked at the door, and cried, "Good things to sell, cheap, cheap!" Little Snow-white looked out and said,—

"Go away; I cannot let any one come in."

"I suppose you can look," said the old woman, and pulled the comb out and held it up. It pleased the girl so well that she let herself be coaxed and opened the door. When they had made a bargain the old woman said, "Now I will comb you properly for once." Poor little Snow-white had no fear and let the old woman do as she pleased, but hardly had she put the comb in her hair than the poison worked, and the girl fell down senseless.

"You piece of beauty," said the wicked woman, "you are done for now," and she went away.

But as good luck would have it, it was almost evening, and the seven dwarfs soon came home. When they saw Snow-white lying as if dead upon the ground, they knew at once the queen had been there, and they looked and found the comb. Scarcely had they taken it out when Snow-white came to herself and told them what had happened. Then they warned her once more to be upon her guard and to open the door to no one.

The queen, at home, went in front of the Glass, and said,—

"Looking-glass, Looking-glass, on the wall,
Who in this land is the fairest of all?"

Then it answered as before,—

"O Queen, thou art fairest of all I see,
But over the hills, where the seven dwarfs dwell,
Snow-white is still alive and well,
And no one else is so fair as she."

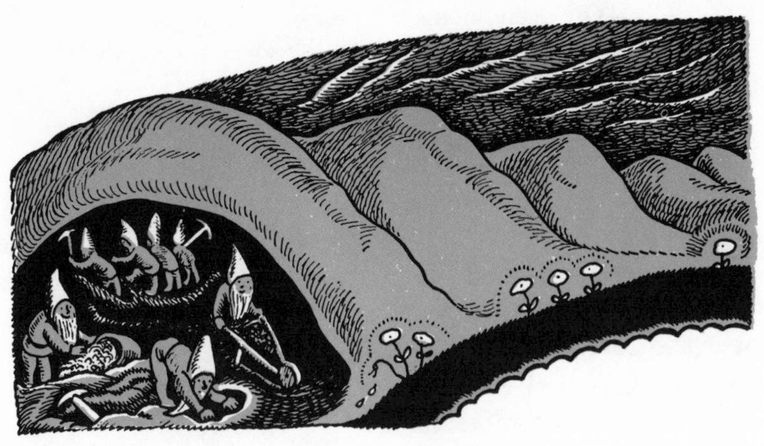

When she heard the Glass speak thus she trembled and shook with rage.

"Snow-white shall die," she cried, "even if it costs me my life!"

She went into a quiet, secret, lonely room, where no one ever came, and there she made an apple full of poison. It was white with a red cheek, so that everyone who saw it longed for it; but whoever ate a piece of it must surely die.

When the apple was ready she painted her face and dressed herself up as a countrywoman, and so she went over the seven hills to the seven dwarfs. She knocked at the door. Snow-white put her head out of the window and said,—

"I cannot let any one in; the seven dwarfs have told me not to."

"It is all the same to me," said the woman. "I shall soon get rid of my apples. There, I will give you one."

"No," said Snow-white, "I dare not take anything."

"Are you afraid of poison?" said the old woman. "Look, I will cut the apple in two pieces; you eat the red cheek, and I will eat the white." The apple was so cunningly made that only the red cheek was poisoned. Snow-white longed for the fine apple, and when she saw that the woman ate part of it she could stand it no longer, and stretched out her hand and took the other half. But hardly had she a bit of it in her mouth when she fell down

dead. Then the queen looked at her with a dreadful look, and laughed aloud and said,—

"White as snow, red as blood, black as ebony-wood! This time the dwarfs cannot wake you up again."

And when she asked of the Looking-glass at home,—

> "Looking-glass, Looking-glass, on the wall,
> Who in this land is the fairest of all?"

it answered at last,—

> "O Queen, in this land thou art fairest of all."

Then her envious heart had rest, so far as an envious heart can have rest.

When the dwarfs came home in the evening, they found Snow-white lying upon the ground; she breathed no longer and was dead. They lifted her up, unlaced her, combed her hair, washed her with water and wine, but it was all of no use; the poor child was dead and stayed dead. They laid her upon a bier, and all seven of them sat round it and wept for her, and wept three whole days.

Then they were going to bury her, but she still looked as if she were living, and still had her pretty red cheeks. They said,—

"We could not bury her in the dark ground," and they had a coffin of glass made, so that she could be seen from all sides, and they laid her in it, and wrote her name upon it in golden letters,

and that she was a king's daughter. Then they put the coffin out upon the hill, and one of them always stayed by it and watched it. And birds came too and wept for Snow-white; first an owl, then a raven, and last a dove.

And now Snow-white lay a long, long time in the coffin, and she did not change, but looked as if she were asleep; for she was as white as snow, as red as blood, and her hair was as black as ebony.

It happened that a king's son came into the wood and went to the dwarfs' house to spend the night. He saw the coffin on the hill, and the beautiful Snow-white within it, and read what was written upon it in golden letters. He said to the dwarfs,—

"Let me have the coffin. I will give you whatever you want for it." But the dwarfs answered,—

"We will not part with it for all the gold in the world." Then he said,—

"Let me have it as a gift, for I cannot live without seeing

Snow-white. I will honor and prize her as the dearest thing I have." As he spoke in this way the good dwarfs took pity upon him and gave him the coffin.

And now the king's son had it carried away by his servants on their shoulders. And it happened that they stumbled over a tree-stump, and with the shock the piece of apple which Snow-white had bitten off came out of her throat. And before long she opened her eyes, lifted up the lid of the coffin, sat up, and was once more alive.

"Oh, heavens, where am I?" she cried. The king's son, full of joy, said,—

"You are with me," and told her what had happened, and said, "I love you more than everything in the world; come with me to my father's palace; you shall be my wife."

Snow-white was willing and went with him, and their wedding was held with great show and splendor. The wicked queen was also bidden to the feast. When she had put on her beautiful clothes, she went before the Looking-glass, and said,—

> "Looking-glass, Looking-glass, on the wall,
> Who in this land is the fairest of all?"

The Glass answered,—

> "O Queen, of all here the fairest art thou,
> But the young Queen is fairer by far I trow."

Then the wicked woman gave a scream and was so wretched, so utterly wretched, that she knew not what to do. At first she would not go to the wedding at all, but she had no peace and must go to see the young queen. And when she went in she knew Snow-white; and she was filled with rage and fear, and fell down and died.

Ella Young

BALLOR'S SON GOES RIDING

ILLUSTRATED BY *Alexander Key*

"BALLOR'S Son," said Flame of Joy, as they sat together in the Wood of Pomegranates, "I have a plot in mind. We'll go into your country, catch a couple of Kyelins, and ride them. I daresay you could stick on a Kyelin."

"Kyelins are not ridden," said Ballor's Son. "They are Sacred Beasts. Kyelins would bite large pieces out of us."

"Not if we were invisible," said Flame of Joy, "and had the courage to bridle them. I know where to get two Cloaks of Invisibility. I'll borrow them, and we'll hunt up the Kyelins."

"You can bridle Kyelins if you want to," said Ballor's Son. "I don't want to ride a Kyelin."

"O yes, you will when I give you a Cloak," said Flame of Joy. "Just lean against a tree and count leaf-shadows on the moss till I come back."

Flame of Joy was scarcely gone till he was back. He carried two cloaks fine as cobwebs and glittering with every color of day and night. He put one on himself, wrapped the other round Ballor's Son, and said,—

"Now reach your hand to me, shut your eyes, think steadily of those Kyelins, and I'll take you wind-running."

Ballor's Son reached a hand, shut his eyes, and felt himself running, or rather floating, light as a wind-borne leaf. Presently he was aware of a many-throated murmur and a stir of people below him. Flame of Joy gripped him tighter, jerked him slightly, and said,—

"Here we are."

Ballor's Son opened his eyes. They were in the great plaza of Ballor's City, invisible in their Cloaks. Ballor's palanquin was there with lords and slaves round it. Magicians were leading out a procession of Sacred Animals to honor the Cat of Cruachan. Very great and much to be honored was the Cat of Cruachan. His temple of jacinth and chalcedony filled one whole side of the plaza, flaunting the pallid sky.

Led by black, slant-eyed magicians, the beasts passed. Marocots, bulky and slow-moving, with ears that swept the ground; double-headed Llanitos, white as snow; Gryphons; fire-breathing Dragons; scaled Chimeras; Kyelins walking two and two, a blue Kyelin beside a green Kyelin. Midmost of the plaza was Ballor's palanquin crusted with gems and gold. Ballor sat there, blind—for he dared not open the one terrible eye that he had in the center of his forehead. It killed more swiftly than a lightning stroke. The beasts were led before Ballor two by two. He stretched his hands over them and said,—

"My benison to you: strength and pride and length of days.
Make glad, make glad the festival of the Cat of Cruachan!"

"Ballor's Son," said Flame of Joy, "do you see those two Kyelins with gilded tails and tusks and black manes that are coming up now? We will ride those Kyelins. When they come abreast of us, be ready! You take the green Kyelin. I'll catch the blue one."

"Look at their claws," said Ballor's Son. "Look at their teeth! They will just make one bite of us."

"No, they won't," said Flame of Joy. "I have got something that I did not tell you about. I brought a hazel rod for each of us out of the hazel wood that is near the Garden of Delight that Angus has. If we strike the Kyelins with those rods they will be tame."

"I'll strike my Kyelin at the beginning," said Ballor's Son.

"If you do it at the beginning you'll lose a lot of fun," said Flame of Joy.

"I'll have fun enough watching your Kyelin," said Ballor's Son.

By this the Kyelins were well abreast. Ballor's Son reached out and struck the green Kyelin with his hazel rod. The beast

stood stock-still, so astonished was he, and Ballor's Son climbed carefully on his back, gripped his black mane, and began to swathe his head and eyes in a fold of the Cloak. Flame of Joy thrust the hazel rod in his girdle and leaped on the back of the blue Kyelin.

With a scream the beast stood upright. His scythed paws tore the air, he leaped and writhed as though he had sustained a mortal hurt.

"Strike him with the rod," said Ballor's Son.

"No," cried Flame of Joy. "I am going to bridle him," and bridle him he did with a fold of the Cloak thrust between his gaping jaws.

Round and round in maddened, dizzying circles swung the blue Kyelin, screaming and striking at everybody and everything. His priest-custodians dropped the golden chains and ran. Everywhere people shouted and ran. The crowded plaza swayed like a sea-wave that topples over on itself.

Llanitos and Gryphons broke loose, tearing and clawing. Marocots trampled and trumpeted, Chimeras writhed and struck. And all the while the blue Kyelin screamed and gyrated, till of a sudden the fold of Cloak that bridled him slipped from his screeching mouth and completely covered his face and head. Rage held him motionless and dumb. The folk nearest him had time to rally.

"The Kyelin is headless!" they cried. "The Sacred Kyelins are headless both, yet they live! Sorcerers have done this! Sorcerers and warlocks are amongst us! Those that walk invisible are come to destroy us! We are stricken! We are doomed. Destruction is come to the City of Ballor!"

"Let Ballor open his eye and smite his enemies!" cried some.

"No, no," shrieked others, "that is the worst destruction, the consuming fire! We are but ashes and fire dust before the Eye of Ballor. Call on the Cat of Cruachan; let him succor us, the mighty one!"

"Call on the Cat of Cruachan, invoke the Cat of Cruachan," cried voices everywhere. "Prostrate yourselves, rend your garments. Call on the Cat of Cruachan!"

A gong sounded above the crying of men and beasts, smiting the confusion and tumult.

Boum—Boum—Boum—Boum—

The Arch-Priest was striking it in the Temple of the Cat. At the sound of that gong priests everywhere lifted their voices in a chant:

"O Mighty Cat of Cruachan,
Hear us,
Succor us,
Protect us,
Protect the Sacred Beasts,
Hear us, Cat of Cruachan!"

"Hear us!" cried the people. "Hear us, Cat of Cruachan! Succor us! Protect us! Hear us! Hear us! Hear us!"

Boum—Boum—Boum—Boum—

Suddenly the air trembled. The sky bulged and shook like a tent-flap. There was a roar that loosened the very roots of the hills; and out of that roar, out of nothingness the Cat of Cruachan flashed into being. He was immense. The brightness of him was terrible. He glittered amongst the broken standards and overturned palanquins with a blinding magnificence.

"The Cat of Cruachan! The Cat of Cruachan!" cried the people, throwing themselves on their faces.

"We are lost!" whispered Flame of Joy, crouching low on his Kyelin. "The Cat of Cruachan can see us! He belongs to the world of Faery!"

Ballor's Son huddled further into his Cloak and crouched low as Flame of Joy was crouching.

Meteor-swift the Cat approached. With a turn of the head he flung Flame of Joy across his shoulders. A second turn, and Ballor's Son was on his shoulders, too!

Then he stretched his mighty flanks and bounded into the air in a great arching leap. That leap took him over the arid, saber-sharp mountains and poisonous waters that encircle Ballor's Country.

A second time he stretched his mighty flanks and bounded into the air in a great arching leap. That leap took him over Harmotrasan, the mountain of black obsidian that shuts out half the world and draws to itself the dark light of the moon.

A third time he stretched his mighty flanks and bounded into the air in a great arching leap. That leap took him over Gormidon, the mountain of chalcedony that blossoms against the stars and draws to itself the bright light of the moon.

The fourth leap that he made took him over Frondisande, the mountain of the Silver Unicorns, where the moon walks with lingering footsteps, where she loiters on nights that she does not show herself in the sky.

When the Cat had crossed that mountain he was in Cruachan, his own country. He widened his padded feet joyously and dug his sickle-sharp claws into the earth, the way a cat does—a caress to his own country. Then he lowered his great head and Flame of Joy and Ballor's Son came foot to ground, falling with clutched hands in a huddled, shame-faced heap.

"It is small and innocent ye look," said the Cat, "to have stirred up such a turmoil."

"I wish the ground would open," said Ballor's Son, "and swallow up every Kyelin in the world. I wish it would!"

"You have affronted the Sacred Beasts," said the Cat, "and they are under my protection. It is a cause of offense."

"I wish I hadn't 'fronted them," said Ballor's Son. "I wish I'd never been born. I do!"

"I made him ride the Kyelin," said Flame of Joy. "He didn't want to. I thought of it."

The Cat considered Flame of Joy with grave attention for a few moments. Then he said,—

"You have my permission, you and Ballor's Son, to find your own way home from Cruachan."

Flame of Joy flung himself forehead to the earth and cried out,

"O Jewel of Two Worlds, O Mighty Lord beloved of the Sun, O Splendor of the Forest, O Darling of every star in heaven, do not destroy us! We could not live and cross the mountain of the Silver Unicorns."

"Have you it in mind that you could cross Harmotrasan and Gormidon?" asked the Cat.

"I have it in mind that we could try."

"O no," sobbed Ballor's Son, who had also prostrated himself forehead to earth, "O no, we could not try. Great Cat of Cruachan, we could not cross the mountains. O, I want to go home!"

"Which of you two," said the Cat, "has the greater spark of intelligence?"

Ballor's Son sat up and stared at the Cat of Cruachan. So did Flame of Joy.

"What's intelligence?" asked Ballor's Son.

"If you were not here," said the Cat, "where would you be?"

"At home," said Ballor's Son.

"I am not so sure of that," said the Cat. "You might be trampled out of semblance to yourself by the crowd in the plaza, or clawed to pieces by a Kyelin, or tossed halfway to the moon by one of the horned Chimeras!"

"Try me with a question," said Flame of Joy.

"I will," said the Cat. "*What is that you find without seeking, seek without finding, and carry about with you because you cannot be rid of it?*"

"Let me think," said Flame of Joy.

"I know," said Ballor's Son, "it's a riddle like what the First Lord asks when I'm lonesome in the evenings. There is only one true answer to a riddle!"

"It is a riddle," said the Cat, "and if one or other of you can answer it, I will take you across the mountain of the Silver Unicorns."

"I have it," shouted Ballor's Son. "I know the answer. It's like a riddle the First Lord gave me once:

'He went to the wood and got it,
He sat him down and sought it,
And because he could not find it
He brought it home with him.'

I know the answer to that riddle. The one true answer is: *'A thorn in the foot.'* "

"Luck favors you," said the Cat. "The First Lord may chance to lay eyes on you again. You have answered my riddle. Climb, both of you, on my shoulders, take a good grip, and we will set out."

They did not need to be told a second time. Joyfully they climbed those mischance-defying shoulders.

"Hold tight now," said the Cat, and with one splendid bound he rose in the air, cleared the mountain of the Unicorns and landed on the topmost ridge of the mountain of chalcedony.

"What plan commends itself to you," said the Cat, "for the crossing of this mountain?"

"I can wind-run," said Flame of Joy, "and so can Ballor's Son when I hold his hand. We will wind-run till we come to an end of the mountain."

"It is a long way to the end of it," said the Cat, "but wind-running is good exercise. Stand on my back and take off."

They climbed to their feet in the space between his broad shoulders.

"We thank you, noble Cat of Cruachan, Jewel of Two Worlds," said Flame of Joy, "for the help that you have given to us. May your shadow—golden in one World, ebon in the other—never grow less!"

"May the wind bear you lightly," said the Cat of Cruachan.

"Now," said Flame of Joy, "reach me your hand. Draw a deep breath and shut your eyes—and we start!"

Ballor's Son took a firm grip of the hand that Flame of Joy stretched out to him, drew a deep breath, shut his eyes, and they leaped clear of the Cat's shoulders.

They were wind-running. They were wind-running on the mountain of chalcedony.

Swiftly they ran—swiftly, swiftly, swiftly, and more swiftly still.

It was good wind-running. Flame of Joy stretched himself in his stride, and Ballor's Son put strength and heart into it.

Good wind-runners they! Swift and swifter yet. Wind-running on the mountain of chalcedony!

It seemed to Ballor's Son that hours—and days—and years spent themselves in that running. At first he was proud to vaunting. He joyed in the adventure. But too many hours and years went by! He snatched a look. Beneath him the mountain of chalcedony flowed endlessly: like a stream, like a torrent, like a cataract, like a sea. Terror gripped Ballor's Son. His heart twisted within him.

"I am falling," he cried. "The mountain is sucking me down. O Flame of Joy, hold me, hold fast to me!"

Flame of Joy held fast, and they came down together. It was a hard bump, but they had no chance to finger their bruises. In the place where they fell, the mountain-slant was smooth as polished ice. They slid, and slid, and slid—and slid, holding to each other. At length something halted them. Something warm and soft and furry. It was the great padded foot of the Cat of Cruachan!

Pure gold against the crystal and amethyst of the mountain, the Cat sprawled at full length on the crevassed slope. His scimitar-sharp claws, translucent as agate, were curved idly in a nonchalant claw-caress. Between his claws Ballor's Son and Flame of Joy were buttressed.

"What is it," said the Cat, *"that goes with equal swiftness over land and sea, carries no rider, and leaves no track of its running?"*

"The white horse of Mananaun," said Ballor's Son promptly.

"The Horse of Mananaun carries a rider," said the Cat.

"Maybe it's the wind," said Ballor's Son.

"It's not the wind," said the Cat.

"I know what it is," said Flame of Joy, "a thing that I have seen often, sliding from hillside to lake. *It is the shadow of a cloud.*"

"Your eyes have served you well," said the Cat. "You have answered my riddle. I will set you down within a stone's throw of the Wood of Pomegranates. Climb on my shoulders."

They climbed and took a joyous neck-grip.

The cat balanced himself for a spring, and with a sinewy, space-devouring leap launched his bulk against the sky.

When his feet touched earth, he was on the verge of the Wood of Pomegranates. The sun slanted low among the ruby-colored fruits. It was late afternoon.

Gently he lowered Ballor's Son and Flame of Joy from his shoulders. Speechless they were because of their delight in the swift motion and in the homecoming.

"My benison on both of you," said the Cat of Cruachan. "Do not harass the Sacred Beasts. Do not disregard the advice of your elders. Be good and you will be happy. Farewell."

In a flash he was gone.

"I wish he hadn't hurried off like that," said Flame of Joy. "I was thinking out a farewell wish to say to him."

"So was I," said Ballor's Son. "We'll keep it till we see him again."

Grimm and Perrault

THE SLEEPING BEAUTY

ADAPTED BY *Pauline Rosenberg*

ILLUSTRATED BY *Marie Lawson*

ONCE upon a time there lived a King and Queen who had everything in the world they wanted, except one thing. They had no children. They wished and wished for a son or a daughter.

At last a beautiful baby daughter was born, and they were as happy as could be. The King showed his delight by giving a christening feast, the like of which had never been seen before.

He sent messengers out to invite all the fairies in the kingdom to be godmothers to the Princess. Seven good fairies were found, and they all came to honor the royal baby.

After the christening the guests returned to the castle for the banquet. Before each fairy was placed a plate, knife, and spoon of pure gold set with diamonds and rubies. But just as they were sitting down an unexpected guest appeared—an ugly old fairy who had not been invited because no one had heard of her for more than fifty years. The King ordered another cover to be placed for her, but he had no more gold dishes, so hers had to be ordinary ones. She felt slighted, and one of the younger fairies heard her muttering angry threats. When they rose from the table, the young fairy hid behind the hangings so she could help the Princess if the old fairy tried to harm her.

Now the fairies came forward to present their gifts to the Princess. These were good wishes that were sure to come true. The first fairy said, "My gift to the Princess is that she shall become the most beautiful woman in the world." The second fairy said, "She shall be graceful in everything she does." The third fairy said, "She shall be as good as she is beautiful." The fourth said, "She shall be a perfect dancer." The fifth, "She shall sing like a nightingale." The sixth fairy said, "My wish is that she shall be able to play any musical instrument perfectly."

Then came the turn of the old fairy. Spitefully she said, "My wish is that when the Princess is grown she shall have her hand pierced with a spindle and die of the wound."

The parents were almost beside themselves with grief.

Just then the fairy who had hidden behind the hangings came out and said:

"O King and Queen, do not weep! Your daughter shall not die of this misfortune. I cannot undo entirely the evil wished by the old fairy. The Princess shall indeed pierce her hand with a spindle, but instead of dying she shall fall into a deep sleep. She shall sleep for a hundred years, until a king's son shall come and awaken her."

To prevent the misfortune foretold by the fairy, the King commanded that no one, on pain of death, should spin with a spindle or even have one in his home.

All the good wishes of the fairies came true. The Princess grew up so beautiful and graceful, so good and kind that everyone loved her.

One day when she was just fifteen years old her parents were away, and she was left in the castle alone. Wandering about, she came to the top of a tall tower, where she found a very old woman—so deaf that she had never heard the King's command—busy at her spinning wheel.

"What are you doing, Granny?" asked the Princess.

"I'm spinning, my pretty child," said the woman.

"Let me see if I can do it," said the Princess.

So saying she picked up the spindle, and then—she pierced her finger with the point, and at once fell into a deep sleep.

At the same time everyone and everything in the palace fell asleep. The King and Queen had just come home, and they at once fell asleep, and with them the courtiers, the pages, the footmen, and all the servants. The cook, who was just about to box the kitchen boy's ears because he had made a mistake, fell asleep, and the boy did, too. The horses went to sleep in the stable, the dogs in the yard, the doves on the roof, and the flies on the wall. Even the fire flickering on the hearth grew still, and the meat stopped roasting. On the trees about the castle not a leaf stirred.

All around the castle there now grew up a hedge of briars, thorny and so thick that no one could get through it. Nothing could be seen of the castle but the high tower where the lovely princess slept.

From time to time princes heard of the Sleeping Beauty and tried to reach the castle, but they could not get through the thorny hedge.

At last a hundred years had passed. A king's son came riding through the land, and when he heard the story of the Sleeping Beauty, he made up his mind that he would awaken her.

As he came to the thorny hedge, the branches gave way and let him pass. When he entered the courtyard, what a sight met his eyes! The dogs were asleep, and so were the horses in their stalls, and the doves that perched, with heads under their wings, on the roof. In the kitchen the cook was asleep, with his hand raised as if to strike the sleeping kitchen boy beside him. All the guards about the castle slept quietly, and in the throne room the king and queen and all the ladies and gentlemen of the court as well were sound asleep.

At last the Prince reached the tower and opened the door of the little room where the Princess slept. There she lay, as fresh and lovely as the day she fell asleep. The Prince bent down and kissed her. She opened her eyes and smiled. "Is it you, Prince?" she murmured; "I have waited for you a long time."

Hand in hand they went down the tower stairs. And now the whole castle awoke. The King and Queen and all their attendants rubbed their eyes and looked about them. The horses in the stable got up and shook themselves. The dogs began to bark and leap about. The doves on the roof lifted their heads from under their wings and began to coo. The flies on the wall began to crawl again. In the kitchen the cook boxed the boy's ears so that he cried out. The fire on the hearth blazed up, and the meat went on roasting.

The wedding of the Prince and the Princess was celebrated with all splendor, and they lived happily ever after.

THE STORY OF ALADDIN; or, THE WONDERFUL LAMP

ILLUSTRATED BY *Henry C. Pitz*

IN ONE of the large and rich cities of China there once lived a tailor named Mustapha. He was so poor that by the hardest daily labor he could barely support himself and his family, which consisted only of his wife and a son.

This son, Aladdin, was a very careless, idle, and disobedient fellow. He would leave home early in the morning and play all day in the streets and public places. When he was old enough, his father tried to teach him the tailor's trade, but Mustapha no sooner turned his back than the boy was gone for the day. He was frequently punished, but in vain; and at last the father gave him up as a hopeless idler and in a few months died of the grief Aladdin caused him.

The boy, now free from restraint, became worse than ever. Until he was fifteen, he spent all his time with idle companions, never thinking how useless a man this would make of him. Playing thus with his evil mates one day, a stranger passing by stood to observe him.

The stranger was a person known as the African magician. Only two days before, he had arrived from Africa, his native country; and, seeing in Aladdin's face something that showed the boy to be well fitted for his purposes, he had taken pains to learn all that he could find out about him.

"Child," he said to Aladdin, calling him aside, "was not your father called Mustapha the tailor?"

"Yes, sir," answered the boy; "but he has been dead a long time."

Then the African magician embraced Aladdin and kissed him, saying with tears in his eyes, "I am your uncle. I knew you at first sight; you are so like my dear brother." Then he gave the boy a handful of money and said, "Give my love to your mother and tell her that I will visit her tomorrow, that

I may see where my good brother lived and died."

"You have no uncle," said Aladdin's mother when she had heard his story. "Neither your father nor I ever had a brother."

Again the next day the magician found Aladdin playing in the streets and embraced him as before, and put two pieces of gold into his hand, saying, "Carry this to your mother. Tell her I shall come to sup with you tonight; but show me first where you live."

This done, Aladdin ran home with the money, and all day his mother made ready to receive their guest. Just as they began to fear that he might not find the house, the African magician knocked at the door and came in, bringing wine and fruits of every sort. After words of greeting to them both, he asked only to be placed where he might face the sofa on which Mustapha used to sit.

"My poor brother!" he exclaimed. "How unhappy am I, not to have come soon enough to give you one last embrace!"

Then he told Aladdin's mother how he had left their native land of China forty years ago, had traveled in many lands, and finally settled in Africa. The desire had seized him to see his brother and his home once more, and therefore he had come, alas! too late.

When the widow wept at the thought of her husband, the African magician turned to Aladdin and asked, "What business do you follow? Are you of any trade?"

The boy hung his head, and his mother added to his shame by saying, "Aladdin is an idle fellow. He would not learn his father's trade, and now will not heed me, but spends his time where you found him, in the streets. Unless you can persuade him to mend his ways, some day I must turn him out to shift for himself."

Again the widow wept, and the magician said,—

"This is not well, nephew. But there are many trades beside your father's. What say you to having a shop, which I will furnish for you with fine stuffs and linens? Tell me freely."

This seemed an easy life, and Aladdin, who hated work, jumped at the plan. "Well, then," said the magician, "come

Instantly a genie appeared and said, "What wouldst thou have?"

with me tomorrow, and, after clothing you handsomely, we will open the shop."

Soon after supper the stranger took his leave. On the next day he bought the boy his promised clothes and entertained him with a company of merchants at his inn. When he brought Aladdin home to his mother at night, she called down many blessings on his head for all his kindness.

Early the next morning the magician came for Aladdin, saying they would spend that day in the country, and on the next would buy the shop. So away they walked through the gardens and palaces outside one of the gates of the city. Each palace seemed more beautiful than the last, and they had gone far before Aladdin thought the morning half gone. By the brink of a fountain they rested, and ate the cakes and fruit which the magician took from his girdle. At the same time he gave the boy good advice about the company he should keep. On they went again after their repast, still farther into the country, till they nearly reached the place, between two mountains, where the magician intended to do the work that had brought him from Africa to China.

"We will go no farther now," said he to Aladdin. "I will show you here some strange things. While I strike a light, gather me all the loose, dry sticks you can see, to kindle a fire with."

There was soon a great heap of them, and when they were in a blaze the magician threw in some incense, and spoke magical words which Aladdin did not understand.

This was scarcely done when the earth opened just before the magician, and they both saw a stone with a brass ring fixed in it. Aladdin was so frightened that he would have run away, but the magician seized him and gave him a box on the ear that knocked him down.

"What have I done, to be treated so?" cried Aladdin, trembling.

"I am your uncle," was the answer; "I stand in your father's place; make no replies. But, child," he added, softening, "do not be afraid. I shall ask nothing but that you obey me promptly, if you would have the good things I intend for you. Know, then, that under this stone there is a treasure that will make you richer than the greatest monarch on earth. No one but yourself may lift this stone or enter the cave; so you must do instantly whatever I command, for this is a matter of great importance to both of us."

"Well, uncle, what is to be done?" said Aladdin, losing his fear.

"Take hold of the ring and lift up that stone."

"Indeed, uncle, I am not strong enough; you must help me."

"No," said the magician; "if I help you we can do nothing. Lift it yourself, and it will come easily." Aladdin obeyed, raised the stone with ease, and laid it on one side.

When the stone was pulled up, there appeared a staircase about three or four feet deep, leading to a door. "Descend, my son," said the magician, "and open that door. It will lead you into a palace divided into three great halls. Before you enter the first, tuck up your robe with care. Pass through the three halls, but never touch the walls, even with your clothes. If you do you will die instantly. At the end of the third hall you

will find a door opening into a garden planted with trees loaded with fine fruit Walk directly across the garden to a terrace, where you will see a niche before you, and in the niche a lighted lamp. Take it down and put it out. Throw away the wick and pour out the liquor, which is not oil and will not hurt your clothes; then put the lamp into your waistband and bring it to me."

The magician then took a ring from his finger and put it on Aladdin's, saying, "This is a talisman against all evil, so long as you obey me. Go, therefore, boldly, and we shall both be rich all our lives."

Aladdin descended, found all to be as the magician had said, and carefully obeyed his orders. When he had put the lamp into his waistband, he wondered at the beauty of the fruit in the garden, white, red, green, blue, purple, yellow, and of all other colors, and gathered some of every sort. The fruits were really precious jewels; but Aladdin, ignorant of their immense value, would have preferred figs, grapes, or pomegranates. Nevertheless, he filled two purses his uncle had given him, besides the skirts of his vest, and crammed his bosom as full as it would hold.

Then he returned with extreme care and found the magician anxiously waiting.

"Pray, uncle," he said, "lend me your hand to help me out."

"Give me the lamp first," replied the magician. "It will be troublesome to you."

"Indeed, uncle, I cannot now, but I will as soon as I am up."

The magician was bent on taking it at once from his hand, but the boy was so laden with his fruit that he flatly refused to give it over before getting out of the cave. This drove the magician into such a passion that he threw more incense into the fire, spoke two magical words, and instantly the stone moved back into its place, with the earth above it, as it had been when they first reached the spot.

Aladdin now saw that he had been deceived by one who was not his uncle, but a cruel enemy. In truth, this man had learned from his magic books about the secret and value of the wonderful lamp, which would make him richer than any earthly ruler if he could but receive it freely given into his hands by another person. He had chosen Aladdin for this purpose, and when it failed he set out immediately on his return to Africa, but avoided the town, that none might ask him what had become of the boy.

Aladdin was indeed in a sorry plight. He called for his uncle, but in vain. The earth was closed above him, and the palace door at the foot of the steps. His cries and tears brought him no help. At last he said, "There is no strength or power but in the great and high God"; and in joining his hands to pray he rubbed the ring which the magician had put on his finger. Instantly a genie of frightful aspect appeared and said, "What wouldst thou have? I am ready to obey thee. I serve him who possesses the ring on thy finger,—I and the other slaves of that ring."

At another time Aladdin would have been frightened at the sight of such a figure; but his danger gave him courage to say, "Whoever thou art, deliver me from this place."

He had no sooner spoken these words than he found himself outside the cave, of which no sign was to be seen on the surface of the earth. He lost no time in making his way home, where he fainted from weakness, and afterwards told his mother of his strange adventure. They were both very bitter against the cruel magician, but this did not prevent Aladdin from sleeping soundly until late the next morning. As there was nothing for breakfast, he bethought him of selling the lamp in order to buy food. "Here it is," said his mother, "but it is very dirty. If I rub it clean I believe it will bring more."

No sooner had she begun to rub it than a hideous genie of gigantic size appeared before her, and said in a voice of thunder, "What wouldst thou have? I am ready to obey thee as thy slave, and the slave of all those who have the lamp in their hands,—I and the other slaves of the lamp."

In terror at the sight, Aladdin's mother fainted; but the boy, who had already seen a genie, said boldly, "I am hungry; bring me something to eat."

The genie disappeared and returned in an instant with a large silver tray, holding twelve covered silver dishes filled with tempting viands, six large white bread cakes on two plates, two flagons of wine, and two silver cups. All these he placed upon a carpet and disappeared before Aladdin's mother had come out of her swoon.

When she was herself again, they satisfied their hunger, and still there was enough food for the rest of that day and two meals on the next. This they put aside, and Aladdin's mother made him tell of all that had passed between him and the genie during her swoon. The simple woman thought it all a dangerous and wicked business and begged Aladdin to sell both the lamp and the ring; but he persuaded her to let him keep them both, on the condition that she should have nothing to do with genies again.

When they had eaten all the food left from the feast the genie brought, Aladdin sold the silver plates one by one to a dishonest merchant, who cheated him by paying but a small part of their value, and yet made the boy think himself rich. The tray he sold last, and when the money it brought was spent he rubbed the lamp again, and again the genie appeared and provided the mother and son with another feast and other silver dishes. These kept them in funds for some time longer, especially as Aladdin had the good fortune to meet with an honest goldsmith, who paid him the full value of the metal. Aladdin, all the while, by visiting the shops of merchants, was gaining knowledge of the world and a desire to improve himself. From the jewelers he came to know that the fruits he had gathered when he got the lamp were not merely colored glass, but stones of untold value, the rarest in the city. This, however, he had the prudence not to tell to anyone, even his mother.

One day, as Aladdin was walking about the town, he heard an order proclaimed that the people should close their shops and houses and keep within doors while the Princess Buddir al Buddoor, the Sultan's daughter, should go to the bath and return. Aladdin was filled with an eager desire to see the face of the princess and contrived to place himself behind the door of the bath. When she was a few paces away from it she removed her veil, and Aladdin saw for a moment one of the most beautiful faces in the world. When she passed by him he quitted his hiding-place and went home thoughtful and grave.

"Are you ill?" asked his mother.

"No," he answered, "but I love the princess more than I can express and am resolved that I will ask her in marriage of the Sultan."

His mother thought him mad, but Aladdin said, "I have the slaves of the lamp and the ring to help me," and then told her for the first time what riches he possessed in the jewels brought from the underground palace. "These," he said, "will secure the favor of the Sultan. You have a large porcelain dish fit to hold them; fetch it, and let us see how they will look when we have arranged them according to their different colors."

Their eyes were dazzled by the splendor of the jewels when they were arranged in the dish, and Aladdin's mother consented at once to take them to the Sultan, and ask his daughter's hand for her son.

Early the next morning she wrapped the dish in two fine napkins and set out for the palace. Though the crowd was great, she made her way into the divan, or audience hall, and placed herself just before the Sultan, the Grand Vizier, and other lords who sat beside him. But there were many cases for him to hear and judge, and her turn did not come that day. She told Aladdin she was sure the Sultan saw her and she would try again.

For six days more she carried the jewels to the divan and stood in the same place. On the sixth the Sultan, as he was leaving the hall, said to the Grand Vizier, "For some time I have observed a certain woman standing near me every day with something wrapped in a napkin. If she comes again, do not fail to call her, that I may hear what she has to say."

On the next day, therefore, she was called forward. She bowed her head till it touched the carpet on the platform of the throne. Then the Sultan bade her rise and said,—

"Good woman, I have observed you many days. What business brings you here?"

"Monarch of monarchs," she replied, "I beg you to pardon the boldness of my petition."

"Well," said the Sultan, "I will forgive you, be it what it may, and no hurt shall come to you. Speak boldly."

This gave her heart to tell the errand on which her son had sent her. The Sultan listened without anger till she was done and then asked what she had brought tied up in the napkin. She took the china dish, which she had set down at the foot of the throne, untied it, and presented it to the Sultan.

His wonder knew no bounds when he looked upon the jewels. Not until he received the gift from the woman's hands could he find words to say, "How rich! how beautiful!"

Then he turned to the Grand Vizier and said, "Behold, admire, wonder! and confess that your eyes never beheld jewels so rich and beautiful before. What sayest thou to such a present? Is it not worthy of the princess, my daughter? Ought I not to bestow her on one who values her at so great a price?"

"I cannot but own," replied the Grand Vizier, "that the present is worthy of the princess. But wait for three months. Before that time I hope my son, whom you regard with favor, will be

able to make a nobler present than this Aladdin, of whom your majesty knows nothing."

The Sultan granted this request and said to Aladdin's mother,—

"Good woman, go home and tell your son that I agree to what you have proposed, but I cannot marry the princess, my daughter, for three months. At the end of that time come again."

The news which Aladdin's mother brought home filled him and her with joy. From that time forth he counted every week, day, and hour as they passed. When two of the three months were gone, Aladdin's mother went out one evening to buy some oil and found the streets full of joyful people, and officers busy with preparations for some festival.

"What does it mean?" she asked the oil merchant.

"Whence came you, good woman," said he, "that you do not know that the Grand Vizier's son is to marry the Princess Buddir al Buddoor, the Sultan's daughter, tonight?"

Home she ran to Aladdin and cried, "Child, you are undone! the Sultan's fine promises will come to nought. This night the Grand Vizier's son is to marry the Princess Buddir al Buddoor."

Aladdin was thunderstruck but wasted no time in idle words against the Sultan. He went at once to his chamber, took the lamp, rubbed it in the same place as before, when instantly the genie appeared, and said to him,—

"What wouldst thou have? I am ready to obey thee as thy slave,—I and the other slaves of the lamp."

"Hear me," said Aladdin; "thou hast hitherto obeyed me, but now I am about to impose on thee a harder task. The Sultan's daughter, who was promised me as my bride, will this night be wed to the son of the Grand Vizier. Bring them both hither to me when they are married."

"Master," replied the genie, "I obey you."

Aladdin did not have to wait long after supping with his mother and going to his chamber to be shown again that the genie was indeed his faithful slave. On this night and the next the princess and the Grand Vizier's son were borne away from the Sultan's palace in a manner which none could understand, not even they themselves. The strange event was told to few, but the Sultan was one of them. He consulted with the Grand Vizier, and, as both of these parents feared to expose the young couple to further dangers from unseen foes, the marriage was canceled, and all the merrymaking in honor of it was stopped. None but Aladdin knew the cause of all the trouble, and he kept his secret to himself. Least of all did the Sultan and Grand Vizier, who had quite forgotten Aladdin, suspect that he had a hand in the matter.

Of course Aladdin had not forgotten the Sultan's promise, and on the very day which ended the three months, his mother came again to the divan and stood in her old place. When the Sultan saw her she was called forward, and, having bowed to the floor, she said,—

"Sire, I come at the end of three months to ask you to fulfill the promise you made to my son."

The Sultan could hardly believe the request had been made in earnest, and, after a few words with the Grand Vizier, decided to propose terms which one of Aladdin's humble position could not possibly fulfill.

"Good woman," he said, "it is true that sultans ought to abide by their word, and I am ready to keep mine. But as I cannot marry my daughter without further proof that your son will be able to support her in royal state, you may tell him that I will fulfill my promise so soon as he shall send me forty trays of massy gold, full of the same sort of jewels you have already given me and carried by forty black slaves, who shall be led by as many young and handsome white slaves, all dressed magnificently. When this is done, I will bestow my daughter, the princess, upon him. Go, good woman, and tell him so, and I will wait till you bring me his answer."

As Aladdin's mother hurried home she laughed to think how far the Sultan's demand would be beyond her son's power. "He awaits your answer," she said to Aladdin when she had told him all, and added, laughing, "I believe he may wait long."

"Not so long as you think," replied Aladdin. "This demand is a mere trifle. I will prepare to answer it at once."

In his own chamber he summoned the genie of the lamp, who appeared without delay and promised to carry out Aladdin's commands. Within a very short time, a train of forty black slaves, led by as many white slaves, appeared opposite the house in which Aladdin lived. Each black slave carried on his head a basin of massy gold, full of pearls, diamonds, rubies, and emeralds. Aladdin then said to his mother,—

"Madam, pray lose no time. Go to the Sultan before he leaves the divan and make this gift to him, that he may see how ardently I desire his daughter's hand."

With Aladdin's mother at its head, the procession began to move through the streets, which were soon filled with people praising the beauty and bearing of the slaves, splendidly dressed and walking at an equal distance from one another. At the palace nothing so brilliant had ever been seen before. The richest robes of the court looked poor beside the dresses of these slaves. When they had all entered they formed a half-circle around the Sultan's throne; the black slaves laid the golden trays on the carpet, touched it with their foreheads, and at the same time the white slaves did likewise. When they rose the black slaves uncovered the trays, and then all stood with their arms crossed over their breasts.

This done, Aladdin's mother advanced to the throne, bowed to the floor, and said,—

"Sire, my son knows that this present is much below the notice of the Princess Buddir al Buddoor, but hopes that your majesty will accept of it and make it pleasing to the princess. His hope is the greater because he has tried to carry out your own wish."

With delight the Sultan replied,—

"Go and tell your son that I wait with open arms to embrace him; and the more haste he makes to come and receive the princess, my daughter, from my hands, the greater pleasure he will give me."

While he showed the slaves and the jewels to the princess, Aladdin's mother carried the good news to her son. "My son," she said, "you may rejoice, for the Sultan has declared that you shall marry the Princess Buddir al Buddoor. He waits for you with impatience."

Aladdin was overjoyed, but, saying little, retired to his chamber. He rubbed the lamp, and when its slave appeared said,—

"Genie, convey me at once to a bath, and give me the richest robe ever worn by a monarch."

This was soon done, and he found himself again in his own chamber, where the genie asked if he had any other commands.

"Yes," answered Aladdin, "bring me a charger better than the best in the Sultan's stables. Fit him with trappings worthy of his value. Furnish twenty slaves, clothed as richly as those who carried the presents to the Sultan, to walk by my side and follow me, and twenty more to go before me in two ranks. Besides these, bring my mother six women slaves, as richly dressed as any of the Princess Buddir al Buddoor's, each carrying a complete dress fit for a Sultan's wife. I want also ten thousand pieces of gold in ten purses: go, and make haste."

The commands were instantly fulfilled, and Aladdin gave

the six women slaves to his mother, with the six dresses they had brought, wrapped in silver tissue. Of the ten purses he gave four to his mother, and the other six he left in the hands of the slaves who brought them, saying that they must march before him and throw the money by handfuls into the crowd as the procession moved to the Sultan's palace. Mounted on his horse, Aladdin, though he had never ridden before, appeared with a grace which the most practiced horseman might have envied. It was no wonder that the people made the air echo with their shouts, especially when the slaves threw out the handfuls of gold.

The Sultan met him at the palace with joy and surprise that the son of so humble a mother as the woman he had seen should have such dignity and good looks, and should be dressed more richly than he himself had ever been. He embraced Aladdin, held him by the hand, and made him sit near the throne. Then there was a great feast, and after it the contract of marriage between the princess and Aladdin was drawn up. When the Sultan asked him if he would stay in the palace and complete the marriage that day, Aladdin answered,—

"Sire, though my impatience is great to enter on the honor your majesty has granted, yet I beg first to be allowed to build a palace worthy of the princess, your daughter. I pray you to give me ground enough near your own, and I will have it finished with the utmost speed."

The request was granted, and Aladdin took his leave with as much politeness as if he had always lived at court. Again, as he passed through the streets, the people shouted and wished him joy. In his own chamber once more, he took the lamp, rubbed it, and there was the genie.

"Genie," said Aladdin, "build me a palace fit to receive the Princess Buddir al Buddoor. Let its materials be of the rarest. Let its walls be of massive gold and silver bricks. Let each front contain six windows, and let the lattices of these (except one, which must be left unfinished) be enriched with diamonds, rubies, and emeralds, beyond anything of the kind ever seen in the world. Let there be courts and a spacious garden, kitchens, storehouses, stables,—well equipped,—offices, servants, and slaves. Above all, provide a safe treasure-house, and fill it with gold and silver. Go, and fulfill my wishes."

Early the next morning the genie returned and bore Aladdin to the place where the palace had been built. Everything was done as Aladdin had commanded. The officers, slaves, and grooms were at their work in hall and stable. The hall, with the twenty-four windows, was beyond his fondest hopes.

"Genie," he said, "there is but one thing wanting,—a fine carpet for the princess to walk upon from the Sultan's palace to mine. Lay one down at once."

In an instant the desire was fulfilled. Then the genie carried Aladdin to his own home.

When the Sultan looked out of his windows in the morning, he was amazed to see a shining building where there had been but an empty garden. "It must be Aladdin's palace," he said, "which I gave him leave to build for my daughter. He has wished to surprise us, and let us see what wonders can be done in a single night."

He was only a little less surprised when Aladdin's mother, dressed more richly than ever his own daughter had been, appeared at the palace. So good a son, he thought, must make a good husband. And soon the son himself appeared; and when in royal pomp he left his humble house for the last time, he did not fail to take with him the wonderful lamp which had brought him all his good fortune, or to wear the ring.

His marriage to the princess was performed with the utmost splendor. There was feasting and music and dancing, and when the princess was brought to her new palace she was so dazzled by its richness that she said to Aladdin, "I thought, prince, there was nothing so beautiful in the world as my father's palace, but now I know that I was deceived."

The next day Aladdin with a troop of slaves went himself to the Sultan and asked him to come with the Grand Vizier and lords of the court to a repast in the palace of the princess. The Sultan gladly consented, and the nearer he came to the building the more he marveled at its grandeur. When he entered the hall of the twenty-four windows he exclaimed,—

"This palace is one of the wonders of the world. Where else shall we find walls built of gold and silver, and windows of diamonds, rubies, and emeralds? But tell me this. Why, in a hall of such beauty, was one window left incomplete?"

"Sire," said Aladdin, "I left it so, that you should have the glory of finishing this hall."

"I take your wish kindly," said the Sultan, "and will give orders about it at once."

When the jewelers and goldsmiths were called they undertook to finish the window, but needed all the jewels the Sultan could give and the Grand Vizier lend for the work. Even the jewels of Aladdin's gift were used, and after working for a month the window was not half finished. Aladdin therefore dismissed them all one day, bade them undo what they had done, and take the jewels back to the Sultan and Vizier. Then he rubbed his lamp, and there was the genie.

"Genie," he said, "I ordered thee to leave one of the four and twenty windows imperfect, and thou hast obeyed me. Now I would have thee make it like the rest." And in a moment the work was done.

The Sultan was greatly surprised when the chief jeweler brought back the stones and said that their work had been stopped, he could not tell why. A horse was brought, and the Sultan rode at once to Aladdin's palace to ask what it all meant. One of the first things he saw there was the finished window. He could hardly believe it to be true, and looked very closely at all the four and twenty to see if he was deceived. When he was convinced he embraced Aladdin and said,—

"My son, what a man you are to do such things in the twinkling of an eye! there is not your fellow in the world; the more I know of you the more I admire you."

Aladdin won not only the love of the Sultan, but also of the people. As he went to one mosque or another to prayers or paid visits to the Grand Vizier and lords of the court, he caused two slaves who walked by the side of his horse to throw handfuls of money to the people in the streets. Thus he lived for several years, making himself dear to all.

About this time the African magician, who had supposed Aladdin to be dead in the cave where he had left him, learned by magic art that he had made his escape, and by the help of the genie of the wonderful lamp was living in royal splendor.

On the very next day the magician set out for the capital of China, where on his arrival he took up his lodging in an inn. There he quickly learned about Aladdin's wealth and goodness and popularity. As soon as he saw the palace he knew that none but genies, the slaves of the lamp, could have built it, and he returned to his inn all the more angry at Aladdin for having got what he wanted himself. When he learned by his magic that Aladdin did not carry the lamp about with him but left it in the palace, he rubbed his hands, and said, "Well, I shall have it now, and I shall make Aladdin return to his low estate."

The next morning he learned that Aladdin had gone with a hunting party, to be absent eight days, three of which had passed. He needed to know no more, and quickly formed his plans. He went to a shop and asked for a dozen copper lamps. The master of the shop had not so many then, but promised them the next day, and said he would have them, as the magician wished, handsome and well polished.

When the magician came back and paid for them, he put them in a basket and started directly for Aladdin's palace. As he drew near he began crying, "Who will change old lamps for new ones?" The children and people who crowded around scoffed at him as a fool, but he heeded them not, and went on crying, "Who will change old lamps for new ones?"

The princess was in the hall with the four and twenty windows, and, seeing a crowd outside, sent one of her women slaves to find out what the man was crying. The slave returned laughing and told of the foolish offer. Another slave, hearing it, said, "Now you speak of lamps, I know not whether the princess may have observed it, but there is an old one upon a shelf of the Prince Aladdin's robing room. Whoever owns it will not be sorry to find a new one in its stead. If the princess chooses, she may have the pleasure of seeing whether this old man is silly enough to make the exchange."

The princess, who knew not the value of this lamp, thought it would be a good joke to do as her slave suggested, and in a few moments it was done. The magician did not stop to cry, "New lamps for old ones!" again, but hurried to his inn and out of the town, setting down his basket of new lamps where nobody saw him.

When he reached a lonely spot he pulled the old lamp out of his breast, and, to make sure that it was the one he wanted, rubbed it. Instantly the genie appeared and said, "What wouldst thou have? I am ready to obey thee as thy slave, and the slave of all those who have that lamp in their hands,—both I and the other slaves of the lamp."

"I command thee," replied the magician, "to bear me and the palace which thou and the other slaves of the lamp have built in this city, with all the people in it, at once to Africa."

The genie made no reply, but in a moment he and the other slaves of the lamp had borne the magician and the palace entire to the spot where he wished it to stand.

Early the next morning, when the Sultan went as usual to gaze upon Aladdin's palace, it was nowhere to be seen. How so large a building that had been standing for some years could disappear so completely, and leave no trace behind, he could not understand. The Grand Vizier was summoned to explain it. In secret he bore no good will to Aladdin, and was glad to suggest that the very building of the palace had been by magic, and that the hunting party had been merely an excuse for the removal of the palace by the same means. The Sultan was persuaded, therefore, to send a body of his guards to seize Aladdin as a prisoner of state. When he appeared the Sultan would hear no word from him, but ordered him put to death. This displeased the people so much that the Sultan, fearing a riot, granted him his life and let him speak.

"Sire," said Aladdin, "I pray you to let me know the crime by which I have lost thy favor?"

"Your crime!" answered the Sultan; "wretched man! do you not know it? Follow me, and I will show you."

Then he led Aladdin to a window and said, "You ought to

know where your palace stood; look, and tell me what has become of it."

Aladdin was as much amazed as the Sultan had been. "True, it is vanished," he said after a speechless pause, "but I have had no concern in its removal. I beg you to give me forty days, and if in that time I cannot restore it, I will offer my head to be disposed of at your pleasure."

"I give you the time you ask," answered the Sultan, "but at the end of forty days forget not to present yourself before me."

The lords, who had courted Aladdin in his better days, paid him no heed as he left the palace in extreme shame. For three days he wandered about the city, exciting the pity of all he met by asking if they had seen his palace, or could tell where it was. On the third day he wandered into the country. As he approached a river he slipped and fell down a bank. Clutching at a rock to save himself, he rubbed his ring, and instantly the genie whom he had seen in the cave appeared before him. "What wouldst thou have?" said the genie. "I am ready to obey thee as thy slave, and the slave of all those that have that ring on their finger,—both I and the other slaves of the ring."

Aladdin had never thought of help from this quarter, and said with delight,—

"Genie, show me where the palace I caused to be built now stands, or bring it back where it first stood."

"Your command," answered the genie, "is not wholly in my power; I am only the slave of the ring, and not of the lamp."

"I command thee, then," replied Aladdin, "by the power of the ring, to bear me to the spot where my palace stands, wherever it may be."

These words were no sooner out of his mouth than he found himself in the midst of a large plain, where his palace stood, not far from a city, and directly above him was the window of his wife's chamber. Just then one of her household happened to look out and see him, and told the good news to the Princess Buddir al Buddoor. She could not believe it to be true, and hastening to the window, opened it herself with a noise which made Aladdin look up. Seeing the princess, he saluted her with

an air that expressed his joy, and in a moment he had entered by a private door and was in her arms.

After shedding tears of joy, they sat down, and Aladdin said, "I beg of you, princess, to tell me what is become of an old lamp which stood upon a shelf in my robing chamber."

"Alas!" answered the princess, "I was afraid our misfortune might be owing to that lamp; and what grieves me most is that I have been the cause of it. I was foolish enough to change the old lamp for a new one, and the next morning I found myself in this unknown country, which I am told is Africa."

"Princess," said Aladdin, "you have told me all by telling me we are in Africa. Now, only tell me where the old lamp is."

"The African magician," answered the princess, "carries it carefully wrapped up in his bosom. This I know, because one day he pulled it out before me, and showed it to me in triumph."

Aladdin quickly formed and carried out a plan to leave the palace, disguise himself, buy of a druggist a certain powder which he named, and return to the princess. He told her what she must do to help his purposes. When the magician should come to the palace, she must assume a friendly manner and ask him to sup with her. "Before he leaves," said Aladdin, "ask him to exchange cups with you. This he will gladly do, and you must give him the cup containing this powder. On drinking it he will instantly fall asleep, and we shall obtain the lamp, whose slaves will do our bidding, and bear us and the palace back to the capital of China."

It was not long before the magician came to the palace, and the princess did exactly as Aladdin had bidden her. When, at the end of the evening, she offered her guest the drugged cup, he drank it, to the last drop, and fell back lifeless on the sofa.

Aladdin was quickly called and said, "Princess, retire, and let me be left alone while I try to take you back to China as speedily as you were brought thence." On the body of the magician he found the lamp, carefully hidden in his garments. Aladdin rubbed it, and the genie stood before him.

"Genie," said Aladdin, "I command thee to bear this palace instantly back to the place whence it was brought hither." The genie bowed his head and departed. In a moment the palace was again in China.

Early the next day the Sultan was looking from his window and mourning his daughter's fate. He could not believe his eyes when first he saw her palace standing in its old place. But as he looked more closely he was convinced, and joy came to his heart instead of the grief that had filled it. At once he ordered a horse and was on his way, when Aladdin, looking from the hall of twenty-four windows, saw him coming and hastened to help him dismount. He was brought at once to the princess, and both wept tears of joy. When the strange events had been partly explained, he said to Aladdin,—

"My son, be not displeased at the harshness I showed towards you. It rose from a father's love, and therefore you will forgive it."

"Sire," said Aladdin, "I have not the least reason to complain of your conduct, since you did nothing but what your duty required. This wicked magician was the sole cause of all."

Only once again were Aladdin and his palace in danger from magic arts. A younger brother of the African magician learned of what had happened, and, in the guise of a holy woman, Fatima, whom he killed that he might pretend to take her place, came to live in the palace. The princess, thinking him really the holy woman, heeded all that he said. One day, admiring the beauty of the hall, he told her that nothing could surpass it if only a roc's egg were hung from the middle of the dome. "A roc," he said, "is a bird of enormous size which lives at the summit of Mount Caucasus. The architect who built your palace can get you an egg."

When the princess told Aladdin of her desire, he summoned the genie of the lamp and said to him,—

"Genie, I command thee in the name of this lamp, bring a roc's egg to be hung in the middle of the dome of the hall of the palace."

No sooner were these words spoken than the hall shook as if ready to fall, and the genie told Aladdin that he had asked him to bring his own master and hang him up in the midst of the hall; it was enough to reduce Aladdin and the princess and the palace all to ashes; but he should be spared, because the request had really come from another. Then he told Aladdin who was the true author of it, and warned him against the pretended Fatima, whom till then he had not known as the brother of the African magician. Aladdin saw his danger, and on that very day he killed his wicked enemy with the dagger which was meant to be his own death.

Thus was Aladdin delivered from the two brothers who were magicians. Within a few years the Sultan died at a good old age, and, as he left no male children, the Princess Buddir al Buddoor came to the throne, and she and Aladdin reigned together many years.

Oscar Wilde

THE SELFISH GIANT

ILLUSTRATED BY *Clara Ernst*

EVERY afternoon, as they were coming from school, the children used to go and play in the Giant's garden.

It was a large lovely garden, with soft green grass. Here and there over the grass stood beautiful flowers like stars, and there were twelve peach trees that in the springtime broke out into delicate blossoms of pink and pearl, and in the autumn bore rich fruit. The birds sat on the trees and sang so sweetly that the children used to stop their games in order to listen to them. "How happy we are here!" they cried to each other.

One day the Giant came back. He had been to visit his friend the Cornish ogre and had stayed with him for seven years. After the seven years were over he had said all that he had to say, for his conversation was limited and he determined to return to his own castle. When he arrived he saw the children playing in the garden.

"What are you doing there?" he cried in a very gruff voice, and the children ran away.

"My own garden is my own garden," said the Giant; "anyone can understand that, and I will allow nobody to play in it but myself." So he built a high wall all around it, and put up a notice-board.

TRESPASSERS
WILL BE
PROSECUTED

He was a very selfish Giant.

The poor children had now nowhere to play. They tried to play on the road, but the road was very dusty and full of hard stones, and they did not like it. They used to wander round the high wall when their lessons were over and talk about the beautiful garden inside. "How happy we were there," they said to each other.

Then the Spring came, and all over the country there were little blossoms and little birds. Only in the garden of the Selfish Giant it was still winter. The birds did not care to sing in it as there were no children, and the trees forgot to blossom. Once a beautiful flower put its head out from the grass, but when it saw the notice-board it was so sorry for the children that it slipped back into the ground again, and went off to sleep. The only people who were pleased were the Snow and the Frost. "Spring has forgotten this garden," they cried, "so we will live here all the year round." The Snow covered up the grass with her great white cloak, and the Frost painted all the trees silver. Then they invited the North Wind to stay with them, and he came. He was wrapped in furs, and he roared all day about the garden and blew the chimney-pots down. "This is a delightful spot," he said, "we must ask the Hail on a visit." So the Hail came. Every day for three hours he rattled on the roof of the castle till he broke most of the slates, and then he ran round and round the garden as fast as he could go. He was dressed in gray, and his breath was like ice.

"I cannot understand why the Spring is so late in coming," said the Selfish Giant, as he sat at the window and looked out at his cold white garden; "I hope there will be a change in the weather."

But the Spring never came, nor the Summer. The Autumn gave golden fruit to every garden, but to the Giant's garden she gave none. "He is too selfish," she said. So it was always Winter there, and the North Wind, and the Hail, and the Frost, and the Snow danced about through the trees.

One morning the Giant was lying awake in bed when he heard some lovely music. It sounded so sweet to his ears that he thought it must be the King's musicians passing by. It was really only a little linnet singing outside his window, but it was so long since he had heard a bird sing in his garden that it seemed to him to be the most beautiful music in the world. Then the Hail stopped dancing over his head, and the North Wind ceased roaring, and a delicious perfume came to him through the open casement. "I believe the Spring has come at last," said the Giant; and he jumped out of bed and looked out.

What did he see?

He saw a most wonderful sight. Through a little hole in the wall the children had crept in, and they were sitting in the branches of the trees. In every tree that he could see there was a little child. And the trees were so glad to have the children back again that they had covered themselves with blossoms, and were waving their arms gently above the children's heads. The birds were flying about and twittering with delight, and the flowers were looking up through the green grass and laughing. It was a lovely scene, only in one corner it was still winter. It was the farthest corner of the garden, and in it was standing a little boy. He was so small that he could not reach up to the branches of the tree, and he was wandering all round it, crying bitterly. The poor tree was still quite covered with frost and snow, and the North Wind was blowing and roaring above it. "Climb up! little boy," said the Tree, and it bent its branches down as low as it could; but the boy was too tiny.

And the Giant's heart melted as he looked out. "How selfish I have been!" he said; "now I know why the Spring would not come here. I will put that poor little boy on the top of the tree, and then I will knock down the wall, and my garden shall be the children's playground for ever and ever." He was really very sorry for what he had done.

So he crept downstairs and opened the front door quite softly, and went out into the garden. But when the children saw him they were so frightened that they all ran away, and the garden became winter again. Only the little boy did not run, for his eyes were so full of tears that he did not see the Giant coming. And the Giant stole up behind him and took him gently in his hand, and put him up into the tree. And the tree broke at once into blossom, and the birds came and sang on it, and the little boy stretched out his two arms and flung them round the Giant's

ERNST

neck and kissed him. And the other children, when they saw that the Giant was not wicked any longer, came running back, and with them came the Spring. "It is your garden now, little children," said the Giant, and he took a great axe and knocked down the wall. And when the people were going to market at twelve o'clock they found the Giant playing with the children in the most beautiful garden they had ever seen.

All day long they played, and in the evening they came to the Giant to bid him good-bye.

"But where is your little companion?" he said: "the boy I put into the tree." The Giant loved him the best because he had kissed him.

"We don't know," answered the children; "he has gone away."

"You must tell him to be sure and come here tomorrow," said the Giant. But the children said that they did not know where he lived, and had never seen him before; and the Giant felt very sad.

Every afternoon, when school was over, the children came and played with the Giant. But the little boy whom the Giant loved was never seen again. The Giant was very kind to all the children, yet he longed for his first little friend and often spoke of him. "How I would like to see him!" he used to say.

Years went over, and the Giant grew very old and feeble. He could not play about any more, so he sat in a huge armchair, and watched the children at their games, and admired his garden. "I have many beautiful flowers," he said; "but the children are the most beautiful flowers of all."

One winter morning he looked out of his window as he was dressing. He did not hate the Winter now, for he knew that it was merely the Spring asleep, and that the flowers were resting.

Suddenly he rubbed his eyes in wonder, and looked and looked. It certainly was a marvellous sight. In the farthest corner of the garden was a tree quite covered with lovely white blossoms. Its branches were all golden, and silver fruit hung down from them, and underneath it stood the little boy he had loved.

Downstairs ran the Giant in great joy, and out into the gar-

den. He hastened across the grass, and came near the child. And when he came quite close his face grew red with anger, and he said, "Who hath dared to wound thee?" For on the palms of the child's hands were the prints of two nails, and the prints of two nails were on the little feet.

"Who hath dared to wound thee?" cried the Giant; "tell me, that I may take my sword and slay him."

"Nay!" answered the child; "but these are the wounds of Love."

"Who art thou?" said the Giant, and a strange awe fell on him, and he knelt before the little child.

And the child smiled on the Giant, and said to him, "You let me play once in your garden, today you shall come with me to my garden, which is Paradise."

And when the children ran in that afternoon, they found the Giant lying dead under the tree, all covered with white blossoms.

Frank R. Stockton

THE REFORMED PIRATE

ILLUSTRATED BY *Jill Elgin*

IT WAS a very delightful country where little Corette lived. It seemed to be almost always summer there, for the winters were just long enough to make people glad when they were over. When it rained, it mostly rained at night, and so the fields and gardens had all the water they wanted, while the people were generally quite sure of a fine day. And as they lived a great deal out-of-doors, this was a great advantage to them.

The principal business of the people of this country was the raising of sweet marjoram. The soil and climate were admirably adapted to the culture of the herb, and fields and fields of it were to be seen in every direction. At that time, and this was a good while ago, very little sweet marjoram was raised in other parts of the world, so this country had the trade nearly all to itself.

The great holiday of the year was the day on which the harvest of this national herb began. It was called "Sweet Marjoram Day," and the people, both young and old, thought more of it than of any other holiday in the year.

On that happy day everybody went out into the fields. There was never a person so old or so young, or so busy, that he or she could not go to help in the harvest. Even when there were sick people, which was seldom, they were carried out to the fields and stayed there all day. And they generally felt much better in the evening.

There were always patches of sweet marjoram planted on purpose for the very little babies to play in on the great day.

They must be poor, indeed, these people said, if they could not raise sweet marjoram for their own needs and for exportation, and yet have enough left for the babies to play in.

So all this day the little youngsters rolled and tumbled and kicked and crowed in the soft green and white beds of the fragrant herb, and pulled it up by the roots, and laughed and chuckled, and went to sleep in it, and were the happiest babies in the world.

They needed no care, except at the dinner hour, so the rest of the people gave all their time to gathering in the crop and having fun. There was always lots of fun on this great harvest day, for everybody worked so hard that the whole crop was generally in the sweet marjoram barns before breakfast, so that they had nearly the whole day for games and jollity.

In this country where little Corette lived, there were fairies. Not very many of them, it is true, for the people had never seen but two. These were sisters, and there were never fairies more generally liked than these two little creatures, neither of them over four inches high. They were very fond of the company of human beings and were just as full of fun as anybody.

They often used to come to spend an hour or two, and sometimes a whole day, with the good folks and they seemed always glad to see and to talk to everybody.

These sisters lived near the top of a mountain in a fairy cottage. This cottage had never been seen by any of the people, but the sisters had often told them all about it. It must have been a charming place.

The house was not much bigger than a bandbox, and it had two stories and a garret, with a little portico running all around it. Inside was the dearest little furniture of all kinds—beds, tables, chairs, and all the furniture that could possibly be needed.

Everything about the house and grounds was on the same small scale. There was a little stable and a little barn, with a little old man to work the little garden and attend to the two little cows. Around the house were garden-beds ever so small, and little graveled paths; and a kitchen-garden, where the peas climbed up little sticks no bigger than pins, and where the little chickens, about the size of flies, sometimes got in and scratched up the little vegetables. There was a little meadow for pasture, and a grove of little trees; and there was also a small field of sweet marjoram, where the blossoms were so tiny that you could hardly have seen them without a magnifying glass.

It was not very far from this cottage to the sweet marjoram country, and the fairy sisters had no trouble at all in running down there whenever they felt like it, but none of the people had ever seen this little home. They had looked for it, but could not find it, and the fairies would never take any of them to it. They said it was no place for human beings. Even the smallest boy, if he were to trip his toe, might fall against their house and knock it over, and as to any of them coming into the fairy grounds, that would be impossible, for there was no spot large enough for even a common-sized baby to creep about in.

On Sweet Marjoram Day the fairies never failed to come. Every year they taught the people new games and all sorts of new ways of having fun. The good folks would never have even thought of having such fine times if it had not been for these fairies.

One delightful afternoon, about a month before Sweet Marjoram Day, Corette, who was a little girl just old enough, and not a day too old (which is exactly the age all little girls ought to be), was talking about the fairy cottage to some of her companions.

"We never can see it," said Corette sorrowfully.

"No," said one of the other girls, "we are too big. If we were little enough, we might go."

"Are you sure the sisters would be glad to see us, then?" asked Corette.

"Yes, I heard them say so. But it doesn't matter at all, as we are not little enough."

"No," said Corette, and she went off to take a walk by herself.

She had not walked far before she reached a small house which stood by the seashore. This house belonged to a Reformed Pirate who lived there all by himself. He had entirely

given up a seafaring life so as to avoid all temptation, and he employed his time in the mildest pursuits he could think of.

When Corette came to his house, she saw him sitting in an easy chair in front of his door, near the edge of a small bluff which overhung the sea, busily engaged in knitting a tidy.

When he saw Corette, he greeted her kindly and put aside his knitting, which he was very glad to do, for he hated knitting tidies, though he thought it was his duty to make them.

"Well, my little maid," he said in a strange, muffled voice, which sounded as if he were speaking under water, for he tried to be as gentle in every way as he could, "how do you do? You don't look quite as gay as usual. Has anything run afoul of you?"

"Oh, no!" said Corette, and she came and stood by him, and, taking up his tidy, she looked it over carefully and showed him when he had dropped a lot of stitches and where he had made some too tight and others a great deal too loose. He did not know how to knit very well.

When she had shown him as well as she could how he ought to do it, she sat down on the grass by his side, and after a while she began to talk to him about the fairy cottage and what a great pity it was that it was impossible for her ever to see it.

"It *is* a pity," said the Reformed Pirate. "I've heard of that cottage, and I'd like to see it myself. In fact, I'd like to go to see almost anything that was proper and quiet, so as to get rid of the sight of this everlasting knitting."

"There are other things you might do besides knit," said Corette.

"Nothing so depressing and suitable," said he, with a sigh.

"It would be of no use for you to think of going there," said Corette. "Even I am too large, and you are ever and ever so much too big. You couldn't get one foot into any of their paths."

"I've no doubt that's true," he replied; "but the thing might be done. Almost anything can be done if you set about it in the right way. But you see, little maid, that you and I don't know enough. Now, years ago, when I was in a different line of business, I often used to get puzzled about one thing or another, and then I went to somebody who knew more than myself."

"Were there many such persons?" asked Corette.

"Well, no. I always went to one old fellow who was a Practicing Wizard. He lived, and still lives, I reckon, on an island about fifty miles from here, right off there to the sou'-sou'-west. I've no doubt that if we were to go to him, he'd tell us just how to do this thing."

"But how could we get there?" asked Corette.

"Oh! I'd manage that," said the Reformed Pirate, his eyes flashing with animation. "I've an old sailboat back there in the creek that's as good as ever she was. I could fix her up, and get everything all shipshape in a couple of days, and then you and I could scud over there in no time. What do you say? Wouldn't you like to go?"

"Oh, I'd like to go ever so much!" cried Corette, clapping her hands, "if they'd let me."

"Well, run and ask them," said he, rolling up his knitting and stuffing it under the cushion of his chair, "and I'll go and look at that boat right away."

So Corette ran home to her father and mother and told them all about the matter. They listened with great interest, and her father said:

"Well now, our little girl is not looking quite as well as usual. I have noticed that she is somewhat pale. A sea-trip might be the very thing for her."

"I think it would do her a great deal of good," said her mother, "and as to that Reformed Pirate, she'd be just as safe with him as if she was on dry land."

So it was agreed that Corette should go. Her father and mother were always remarkably kind.

The Reformed Pirate was perfectly delighted when he heard this, and he went hard to work to get his little vessel ready. To sail again on the ocean seemed to him the greatest of earthly joys, and as he was to do it for the benefit of a good little girl, it was all perfectly right and proper.

When they started, the next day but one, all the people who lived near enough came down to see them off. Just as they were about to sail, the Reformed Pirate said:

"Hello! I wonder if I hadn't better run back to the house and get my sword! I only wear the empty scabbard now, but it might be safer, on a trip like this, to take the sword along."

So he ran back and got it, and then he pushed off amid the shouts of all the good people on the beach.

The boat was quite a good-sized one, and it had a cabin and everything neat and comfortable. The Reformed Pirate managed it beautifully, all by himself, and Corette sat in the stern and watched the waves and the sky and the sea birds, and was very happy indeed.

As for her companion, he was in a state of ecstasy. As the breeze freshened, and the sails filled, and the vessel went dashing over the waves, he laughed and joked and sang snatches of old sea songs, and was the jolliest man afloat.

After a while, as they went thus sailing merrily along, a distant ship appeared in sight. The moment his eyes fell upon it, a sudden change came over the Reformed Pirate. He sprang to his feet, and, with his hand still upon the helm, he leaned forward and gazed at the ship. He gazed and he gazed and he gazed without saying a word. Corette spoke to him several times, but he answered not. And as he gazed he moved the helm so that his little craft gradually turned from her course and sailed to meet the distant ship.

As the two vessels approached each other, the Reformed Pirate became very much excited. He tightened his belt and loosened his sword in its sheath. Hurriedly giving the helm to Corette, he went forward and jerked a lot of ropes and hooks from a cubbyhole where they had been stowed away. Then he pulled out a small, dark flag, with bits of skeleton painted on it, and hoisted it to the topmast.

By this time he had nearly reached the ship, which was a large three-masted vessel. There seemed to be a great commotion on board; sailors were running this way and that; women were screaming; and officers could be heard shouting, "Put her about! Clap on more sail!"

But steadily on sailed the small boat, and the moment it came alongside the big ship, the Reformed Pirate threw out grapnels and made the two vessels fast together. Then he hooked a rope ladder to the side of the ship, and, rushing up it, sprang with a yell on the deck of the vessel, waving his flashing sword around his head!

"Down, dastards! varlets! hounds!" he shouted. "Down upon your knees! Throw down your arms! SURRENDER!"

Then every man went down upon his knees, and threw down his arms and surrendered.

"Where is your Captain?" roared their conqueror.

The Captain came trembling forward.

"Bring to me your gold and silver, your jewels and your precious stones, and your rich stuffs!"

The Captain ordered these to be quickly brought and placed before the Reformed Pirate, who continued to stride to and fro across the deck waving his glittering blade, and who, when he saw the treasures placed before him, shouted again:

"Prepare for scuttling!" and then, while the women got down on their knees and begged that he would not sink the ship, and the children cried, and the men trembled so that they could hardly kneel straight, and the Captain stood pale and shaking before him, he glanced at the pile of treasure and touched it with his sword.

"Aboard with this, my men!" he said. "But first I will divide this into—into—into *one* part. Look here!" and then he paused, glanced around, and clapped his hand to his head. He looked

at the people, the treasure, and the ship. Then suddenly he sheathed his sword, and, stepping up to the Captain, extended his hand.

"Good sir," said he, "you must excuse me. This is a mistake. I had no intention of taking this vessel. It was merely a temporary absence of mind. I forgot I had reformed, and seeing this ship, old scenes and my old business came into my head, and I just came and took the vessel without really thinking what I was doing. I beg you will excuse me. And these ladies —I am very sorry to have inconvenienced them. I ask them to overlook my unintentional rudeness."

"Oh, don't mention it!" cried the Captain, his face beaming with joy as he seized the hand of the Reformed Pirate. "It is of no importance, I assure you. We are delighted, sir, delighted!"

"Oh, yes!" cried all the ladies. "Kind sir, we are charmed! We are charmed!"

"You are all very good indeed," said the Reformed Pirate, "but I really think I was not altogether excusable. And I am very sorry that I made your men bring up all these things."

"Not at all! not at all!" cried the Captain. "No trouble whatever to show them. Very glad indeed to have the opportunity. By the by, would you like to take a few of them, as a memento of your visit?"

"Oh, no, I thank you," said the Reformed Pirate, "I would rather not."

"Perhaps, then, some of your men might like a trinket or a bit of cloth—"

"Oh, I have no men! There is no one on board but myself—excepting a little girl, who is a passenger. But I must be going. Good-bye, Captain!"

"I am sorry you are in such a hurry," said the Captain. "Is there anything at all that I can do for you?"

"No, thank you. But stop!—there may be something. Do you sail to any port where there is a trade in tidies?"

"Oh, yes! To several such," said the Captain.

"Well, then, I would be very much obliged to you," said the Reformed Pirate, "if you would sometimes stop off that point of land that you see there and send a boat ashore to my house for a load of tidies."

"You manufacture them by the quantity, then?" asked the Captain.

"I expect to," said the other, sadly.

The Captain promised to stop, and after shaking hands with every person on deck, the Reformed Pirate went down the side of the ship, and taking in his ladder and his grapnels, he pushed off.

As he slowly sailed away, having lowered his flag, the Captain looked over the side of his ship and said,—

"If I had only known that there was nobody but a little girl on board! I thought, of course, he had a boatload of pirates."

Corette asked a great many questions about everything that had happened on the ship, for she had heard the noise and confusion as she sat below in the little boat; but her companion was disposed to be silent, and said very little in reply.

When the trip was over and they had reached the island, the Reformed Pirate made his boat fast, and, taking little Corette by the hand, he walked up to the house of the Practicing Wizard.

This was a queer place. It was a great rambling house, one story high in some places and nine or ten in other places; and then, again, it seemed to run into the ground and reappear at a short distance—the different parts being connected by cellars and basements, with nothing but flower-gardens over them.

Corette thought she had never seen such a wonderful building; but she had not long to look at the outside of it, for her companion, who had been there before and knew the ways of the place, went up to a little door in a two-story part of the house and knocked. Our friends were admitted by a dark cream-colored slave, who informed them that the Practicing Wizard was engaged with other visitors, but that he would soon be at leisure.

So Corette and the Reformed Pirate sat down in a handsome room full of curious and wonderful things, and in a short time they were summoned into the Practicing Wizard's private office.

"Glad to see you," said he, as the Reformed Pirate entered. "It has been a long time since you were here. What can I do for you, now? Want to know something about the whereabouts of any ships, or the value of any cargoes?"

"Oh, no! I'm out of that business now," said the other. "I've come this time for something entirely different. But I'll let this little girl tell you what it is. She can do it better than I can."

So Corette stepped up to the Practicing Wizard, who was a pleasant elderly man with a smooth white face and a constant

smile, which seemed to have grown on his face instead of a beard, and she told him the whole story of the fairy sisters and their cottage, of her great desire to see it, and of the difficulties in the way.

"I know all about those sisters," he said; "I don't wonder you want to see their house. You both wish to see it?"

"Yes," said the Reformed Pirate; "I might as well go with her, if the thing can be done at all."

"Very proper," said the Practicing Wizard, "very proper indeed. But there is only one way in which it can be done. You must be condensed."

"Does that hurt?" asked Corette.

"Oh, not at all! You'll never feel it. For the two it will be one hundred and eighty ducats," said he, turning to the Reformed Pirate; "we make a reduction when there are more than one."

"Are you willing?" asked the Reformed Pirate of Corette, as he put his hand in his breeches' pocket.

"Oh, yes!" said Corette, "If that's the only way."

Whereupon her good friend said no more but pulled out a hundred and eighty ducats and handed them to the Practicing Wizard, who immediately commenced operations.

Corette and the Reformed Pirate were each seated in a large easy chair, and upon each of their heads the old white-faced gentleman placed a little pink ball, about the size of a pea. Then he took a position in front of them.

"Now, then," said he, "sit perfectly still. It will be over in a few minutes," and he lifted up a long thin stick, and, pointing it toward the couple, he began to count: "One, two, three, four—"

As he counted, the Reformed Pirate and Corette began to shrink, and by the time he had reached fifty, they were no bigger than cats. But he kept on counting until Corette was about three and a half inches high, and her companion about five inches.

Then he stopped and knocked the pink ball from each of their heads with a little tap of his long stick.

"There we are," said he, and he carefully picked up the little creatures and put them on a table in front of a looking-glass, that they might see how they liked his work.

It was admirably done. Every proportion had been perfectly kept.

"It seems to me that it couldn't be better," said the Condensed Pirate, looking at himself from top to toe.

"No," said the Practicing Wizard, smiling rather more than usual, "I don't believe it could."

"But how are we to get away from here?" said Corette to her friend. "A little fellow like you can't sail that big boat."

"No," said he ruefully, "that's true. I couldn't do it. But perhaps, sir, you could condense the boat."

"Oh, no!" said the old gentleman, "that would never do. Such a little boat would be swamped before you reached shore, if a big fish didn't swallow you. No, I'll see that you get away safely."

So saying, he went to a small cage that stood in a window and took from it a pigeon.

"This fellow will take you," said he. "He is very strong and swift and will go ever so much faster than your boat."

Next he fastened a belt around the bird, and to the lower part of this he hung a little basket with two seats in it. He then lifted Corette and the Condensed Pirate into the basket, where they sat down opposite one another.

"Do you wish to go directly to the cottage of the fairy sisters?" said the gentleman.

"Oh, yes!" said Corette.

So he wrote the proper address on the bill of the pigeon and, opening the window, carefully let the bird fly.

"I'll take care of your boat," he cried to the Condensed Pirate, as the pigeon rose in the air. "You'll find it all right when you come back."

And he smiled worse than ever.

The pigeon flew up to a great height, and then he took flight in a straight line for the Fairy Cottage, where he arrived before his passengers thought they had half finished their journey.

The bird alighted on the ground, just outside of the boundary fence; and when Corette and her companion had jumped from the basket, he rose and flew away home as fast as he could go.

The Condensed Pirate now opened a little gate in the fence, and he and Corette walked in. They went up the graveled path, and under the fruit trees, where the ripe peaches hung as big as peas, and they knocked at the door of the fairy sisters.

When these two little ladies came to the door, they were amazed to see Corette.

"Why, how did you ever?" they cried. "And if there isn't our old friend, the Reformed Pirate!"

"Condensed Pirate, if you please," said that individual. "There's no use of my being reformed while I'm so small as this. I couldn't hurt anybody if I wanted to."

"Well, come right in," said the sisters, "and tell us all about it."

So they went in and sat in the little parlor and told their story. The fairies were delighted with the whole affair and insisted on a long visit, to which our two friends were not at all opposed.

They found everything at this cottage exactly as they had been told. They ate the daintiest little meals off the daintiest little dishes, and they thoroughly enjoyed all the delightful little things in the little place. Sometimes, Corette and the fairies would take naps in little hammocks under the tree, while the Condensed Pirate helped the little man drive up the little cows or work in the little garden.

On the second day of their visit, when they were all sitting on the little portico after supper, one of the sisters, thinking that the Condensed Pirate might like to have something to do and knowing how he used to occupy himself, took from her basket a little half-knit tidy, with the needles in it, and asked him if he cared to amuse himself with that.

"No, *Ma'am!*" said he, firmly but politely. "Not at present. If I find it necessary to reform again, I may do something of the kind, but not now. But I thank you, all the same."

After this, they were careful not to mention tidies to him.

Corette and her companion stayed with the fairies for more than a week. Corette knew that her father and mother did not expect her at home for some time, and so she felt quite at liberty to stay as long as she pleased.

As to the sisters, they were delighted to have their visitors with them.

But one day the Condensed Pirate, finding Corette alone, led her with great secrecy to the bottom of the pasture field, the very outskirts of the fairies' domain.

"Look here," said he, in his lowest tones. "Do you know, little Corette, that things are not as I expected them to be here? Everything is very nice and good, but nothing appears very small to me. Indeed, things seem to be just about the right size. How does it strike you?"

"Why, I have been thinking the same thing," said Corette. "The sisters used to be such dear, cunning little creatures, and now they're bigger than I am. But I don't know what can be done about it."

"I know," said the Condensed Pirate.

"What?" asked Corette.

"Condense 'em," answered her companion, solemnly.

"Oh! But you couldn't do that!" exclaimed Corette.

"Yes, but I can—at least, I think I can. You remember those two pink condensing balls?"

"Yes," said Corette.

"Well, I've got mine."

"You have!" cried Corette. "How did you get it?"

"Oh! when the old fellow knocked it off my head, it fell on the chair beside me, and I picked it up and put it in my coat pocket. It would just go in. He charges for the balls, and so I thought I might as well have it."

"But do you know how he works them?"

"Oh, yes!" replied the Condensed Pirate. "I watched him. What do you say? Shall we condense this whole place?"

"It won't hurt them," said Corette, "and I don't really think they would mind it."

"Mind it! No!" said the other. "I believe they'd like it."

So it was agreed that the Fairy Cottage, inmates and grounds should be condensed until they were, relatively, as small as they used to be.

That afternoon, when the sisters were taking a nap and the little man was at work in the barn, the Condensed Pirate went up into the garret of the cottage and got out on the roof. Then he climbed to the top of the tallest chimney, which overlooked everything on the place, and there he laid his little pink ball.

He then softly descended and, taking Corette by the hand (she had been waiting for him on the portico), he went down to the bottom of the pasture field.

When he was quite sure that he and Corette were entirely outside of the fairies' grounds, he stood up, pointed to the ball with a long, thin stick which he had cut, and began to count: "One, two, three—"

And as he counted the cottage began to shrink. Smaller and smaller it became, until it got to be very little indeed.

"Is that enough?" said the Condensed Pirate, hurriedly, between two counts.

"No," replied Corette. "There is the little man, just come out of the barn. He ought to be as small as the sisters used to be. I'll tell you when to stop."

So the counting went on until Corette said "Stop!" and the cottage was really not much bigger than a thimble. The little man stood by the barn and seemed to Corette to be just about the former size of the fairy sisters; but, in fact, he was not quite a quarter of an inch high. Everything on the place was small in proportion, so that when Corette said "Stop!" the Condensed Pirate easily leaned over and knocked the pink ball from the chimney with his long stick. It fell outside the grounds, and he picked it up and put it in his pocket.

Then he and Corette stood and admired everything! It was charming! It was just what they had imagined before they came there. While they were looking with delight at the little fields and trees and chickens—so small that really big people could not have seen them—and at the cute little house with its vines and portico, the two sisters came out on the little lawn.

When they saw Corette and her companion, they were astounded.

"Why, when did you grow big again?" they cried. "Oh! how sorry we are! Now you cannot come into our house and live with us any longer."

Corette and the Condensed Pirate looked at each other, as much as to say, "They don't know they have been made so little."

Then Corette said, "We are sorry too. I suppose we shall have to go away now. But we have had a delightful visit."

"It has been a charming one for us," said one of the sisters, "and if we only had known, we would have had a little party before you went away; but now it is too late."

The Condensed Pirate said nothing. He felt rather guilty about the matter. He might have waited a little, and yet he could not have told them about it. They might have objected to being condensed.

"May we stay awhile and look at things?" asked Corette.

"Yes," replied one of the fairies; "but you must be very careful not to step inside the grounds, or to stumble over on our place. You might do untold damage."

So the two little big people stood and admired the fairy cottage and all about it, for this was indeed the sight they came to see; and then they took leave of their kind entertainers, who would have been glad to have them stay longer but were really trembling with apprehension lest some false step or careless movement might ruin their little home.

As Corette and the Condensed Pirate took their way through the woods to their home, they found it very difficult to get along, they were so small. When they came to a narrow stream which Corette would once have jumped over with ease, the Condensed Pirate had to make a ferryboat of a piece of bark and paddle himself and the little girl across.

"I wonder how the fairies used to come down to us," said Corette, who was struggling along over the stones and moss, hanging on to her companion's hand.

"Oh! I expect they have a nice smooth path somewhere through the woods, where they can run along as fast as they please; and bridges over the streams."

"Why didn't they tell us of it?" asked Corette.

"They thought it was too little to be of any use to us. Don't you see?—they think we're big people and wouldn't need their path."

"Oh, yes!" said Corette.

In time, however, they got down the mountain and out of the woods, and then they climbed up on one of the fences and ran along the top of it toward Corette's home.

When the people saw them, they cried out: "Oh, here come our dear little fairies, who have not visited us for so many days!" But when they saw them close at hand and perceived that they were little Corette and the Pirate who had reformed, they were dumbfounded.

Corette did not stop to tell them anything; but still holding her companion's hand she ran on to her parents' house, followed by a crowd of neighbors.

Corette's father and mother could hardly believe that this little being was their daughter, but there was no mistaking her face and her clothes, and her voice, although they were all so small; and when she had explained the matter to them, and to the people who filled the house, they understood it all. They were overcome with joy to have their daughter back again.

When the Condensed Pirate went to his house, he found the door locked, as he had left it, but he easily crawled in through a crack. He found everything of an enormous size. It did not look like the old place. He climbed up the leg of a chair and got on the table, by the help of the tablecloth, but it was hard work. He found something to eat and drink, and all his possessions were in order, but he did not feel at home.

Days passed on, and while the Condensed Pirate did not feel any better satisfied, a sadness seemed to spread over the country, and particularly over Corette's home. The people grieved that they never saw the fairy sisters, who indeed had made two or three visits, with infinite trouble and toil, but who could not make themselves observed, their bodies and their voices being so very small.

And Corette's father and mother grieved. They wanted their daughter to be as she was before. They said that Sweet Marjoram Day was very near, but that they could not look forward to it with pleasure. Corette might go out to the fields, but she could only sit upon some high place, as the fairies used to sit. She could not help in the gathering. She could not even be with the babies; they would roll on her and crush her. So they mourned.

It was now the night before the great holiday. Sweet Marjoram Eve had not been a very gay time, and the people did not expect to have much fun the next day. How could they if the fairy sisters did not come? Corette felt badly, for she had never told that the sisters had been condensed, and the Condensed Pirate, who had insisted on her secrecy, felt worse. That night he lay in his great bed, really afraid to go to sleep on account of rats and mice.

He was so extremely wakeful that he lay and thought, and thought, and thought for a long time, and then he got up and dressed and went out.

It was a beautiful moonlight night, and he made his way directly to Corette's house. There, by means of a vine, he climbed up to her window and gently called her. She was not sleeping well, and she soon heard him and came to the window.

He then desired her to bring him two spools of fine thread.

Without asking any questions, she went for the thread, and very soon made her appearance at the window with one spool in her arms, and then she went back for another.

"Now, then," said the Condensed Pirate, when he had thrown the spools down to the ground, "Will you dress yourself and wait here at the window until I come and call for you?"

Corette promised, for she thought he had some good plan in his head, and he hurried down the vine, took up a spool under each arm, and made his way to the church. This building had a high steeple which overlooked the whole country. He left one of his spools outside, and then, easily creeping with the other under one of the great doors, he carried it with infinite pains and labor up into the belfry.

There he tied it on his back and, getting out of the window, began to climb up the outside of the steeple.

It was not hard for him to do this, for the rough stones gave him plenty of foothold, and he soon stood on the very tiptop of the steeple. He then took tight hold of one end of the thread of his spool and let the spool drop. The thread rapidly unwound until the spool soon touched the ground.

Now our friend took from his pocket the pink ball and, passing the end of the thread through a little hole in the middle of it, he tied it firmly. Placing the ball in a small depression on the top of the steeple, he left it there with the thread hanging from it, and rapidly descended to the ground. There he took the other spool and tied the end of its thread to that which was hanging from the steeple.

He now put down the spool and ran to call Corette. When she heard his voice, she clambered down the vine to him.

"Now, Corette," he said, "run to my house and stand on the beach, near the water, and wait for me."

Corette ran off as he had asked, and he went back to his spool. He took it up and walked slowly to his house, carefully unwinding the thread as he went. The church was not very far from the seashore, so he soon joined Corette. With her assistance he then unwound the rest of the thread and made a little coil. He next gave the coil to Corette to hold, cautioning her to be very careful, and then he ran off to where some bits of wood were lying, close to the water's edge. Selecting a little piece of thin board, he pushed it into the water, and taking a small stick in his hand he jumped on it and poled it along to where Corette was standing. The ocean here formed a little bay where the water was quite smooth.

"Now, Corette," said the Condensed Pirate, "we must be very careful. I will push this ashore, and you must step on board, letting out some of the thread as you come. Be sure not to pull it tight. Then I will paddle out a little way, and as I push, you must let out more thread."

Corette did as she was directed, and very soon they were standing on the little raft a few yards from the shore. Then her companion put down his stick and took the coil of thread.

"What are you going to do?" asked Corette. She had wanted to ask before, but there did not seem to be time.

"Well," he said, "we can't make ourselves any bigger—at least, I don't know how to do it, and so I'm going to condense the whole country. The little pink ball is on top of the steeple, which is higher than anything else about here, you know. I can't knock the ball off at the proper time, so I've tied a thread to it to pull it off. You and I are outside of the place, on the water, so we won't be made any smaller. If the thing works, everybody will be our size, and all will be right again."

"Splendid!" cried Corette. "But how will you know when things are little enough?"

"Do you see that door in my house, almost in front of us? Well, when I was of the old size, I used just to touch the top of that door with my head, if I didn't stoop. When you see that the door is about my present height, tell me to stop. Now then!"

The Condensed Pirate began to count, and instantly the whole place, church, houses, fields, and of course the people who were in bed, began to shrink! He counted a good while before Corette thought his door would fit him. At last she called to him to stop. He glanced at the door to feel sure, counted one more, and pulled the thread. Down came the ball, and the size of the place was fixed!

The whole of the sweet marjoram country was now so small that the houses were like bandboxes, and the people not more than four or five inches high—excepting some very tall people who were six inches.

Drawing the ball to him, the Condensed Pirate pushed out some distance, broke it from the thread, and threw it into the water.

"No more condensing!" said he. He then paddled himself and Corette ashore, and running to his cottage, threw open the door and looked about him. Everything was just right! Everything fitted! He shouted with joy.

It was just daybreak when Corette rushed into her parents' house. Startled, her father and mother sprang out of bed.

"Our daughter! Our darling daughter!" they shouted, "and she has her proper size again!"

In an instant she was clasped in their arms.

When the first transports of joy were over, Corette sat down and told them the whole story—told them everything.

"It is all right," said her mother, "so that we are all of the same size," and she shed tears of joy.

Corette's father ran out to ring the church bell, so as to wake up the people and tell them the good news of his daughter's restoration. When he came in, he said:

"I see no difference in anything. Everybody is all right."

There never was such a glorious celebration of Sweet Marjoram Day as took place that year.

But the best thing of all was the appearance of the fairy sisters. When they came among the people, they all shouted as if they had gone wild. And the good little sisters were so overjoyed that they could scarcely speak.

"What a wonderful thing it is to find that we have grown to our old size again! We were here several times lately, but somehow or other we seemed to be so very small that we couldn't make you see or hear us. But now it's all right. We have forty-two new games!"

And at that, the crop being all in, the whole country with a shout of joy went to work to play.

There were no gayer people to be seen than Corette and the Condensed Pirate. Some of his friends called this good man by his old name, but he corrected them.

"I am reformed, all the same," he said, "but do not call me by that name. I shall never be able to separate it from its association with tidies. And with *them* I am done forever. Owing to circumstances, I do not need to be depressed."

The captain of the ship never stopped off the coast for a load of tidies. Perhaps he did not care to come near the house of his former captor, for fear that he might forget himself again and take the ship a second time. But if the captain had come, it is not likely that his men would have found the cottage of the Condensed Pirate, unless they had landed at the very spot where it stood.

And so it happened that no one ever noticed this country after it was condensed. Passing ships could not come near enough to see such a very little place, and there never were any very good roads to it by land.

But the people continued to be happy and prosperous, and they kept up the celebration of Sweet Marjoram Day as gayly as when they were all ordinary-sized people.

In the whole country there were only two persons, Corette and the Pirate, who really believed that they were condensed.

Oscar Wilde

THE HAPPY PRINCE

ILLUSTRATED BY *Henry C. Pitz*

HIGH above the city, on a tall column, stood the statue of the Happy Prince. He was gilded all over with thin leaves of fine gold, for eyes he had two bright sapphires, and a large red ruby glowed on his sword hilt.

He was very much admired indeed. "He is as beautiful as a weathercock," remarked one of the Town Councillors who wished to gain a reputation for having artistic tastes; "only not quite so useful," he added, fearing lest people should think him unpractical, which he really was not.

"Why can't you be like the Happy Prince?" asked a sensible mother of her little boy who was crying for the Moon. "The Happy Prince never dreams of crying for anything."

"I am glad there is someone in the world who is quite happy," muttered a disappointed man as he gazed at the wonderful statue.

"He looks just like an angel," said the Charity Children as they came out of the cathedral in their bright scarlet cloaks and their clean white pinafores.

"How do you know?" said the Mathematical Master, "you have never seen one."

"Ah! but we have, in our dreams," answered the children; and the Mathematical Master frowned and looked very severe, for he did not approve of children dreaming.

One night there flew over the city a little Swallow. His friends had gone away to Egypt six weeks before, but he had stayed behind, for he was in love with the most beautiful Reed.

He had met her early in the spring as he was flying down the river after a big yellow moth, and had been so attracted by her slender waist that he had stopped to talk to her.

"Shall I love you?" said the Swallow, who liked to come to the point at once, and the Reed made him a low bow. So he flew round and round her, touching the water with his wings, and making silver ripples. This was his courtship, and it lasted all through the summer.

"It is a ridiculous attachment," twittered the other Swallows; "she has no money and far too many relations"; and indeed the river was quite full of Reeds. Then, when the autumn came, they all flew away.

After they had gone he felt lonely and began to tire of his lady-love. "She has no conversation," he said, "and I am afraid that she is a coquette, for she is always flirting with the wind." And certainly, whenever the wind blew, the Reed made the most graceful curtseys. "I admit that she is domestic," he continued, "but I love traveling, and my wife, consequently, should love traveling also."

"Will you come away with me?" he said finally to her; but the Reed shook her head, she was so attached to her home.

"You have been trifling with me," he cried. "I am off to the Pyramids. Good-bye!" and he flew away.

All day long he flew, and at nighttime he arrived at the city.

"Where shall I put up?" he said. "I hope the town has made preparations."

Then he saw the statue on the tall column.

"I will put up there," he cried; "it is a fine position with plenty of fresh air." So he alighted just between the feet of the Happy Prince.

"I have a golden bedroom," he said softly to himself as he looked round, and he prepared to go to sleep; but just as he was putting his head under his wing a large drop of water fell on him. "What a curious thing!" he cried; "there is not a single cloud in the sky, the stars are quite clear and bright, and yet it is raining. The climate in the north of Europe is really dreadful. The Reed used to like the rain, but that was merely her selfishness."

Then another drop fell.

"What is the use of a statue if it cannot keep the rain off?" he said; "I must look for a good chimney pot," and he determined to fly away.

But before he had opened his wings, a third drop fell, and he looked up, and saw—Ah! what did he see?

The eyes of the Happy Prince were filled with tears, and tears were running down his golden cheeks. His face was so beautiful in the moonlight that the little Swallow was filled with pity.

"Who are you?" he said.

"I am the Happy Prince."

"Why are you weeping then?" asked the Swallow; "you have quite drenched me."

"When I was alive and had a human heart," answered the statue, "I did not know what tears were, for I lived in the Palace of Sans-Souci, where sorrow is not allowed to enter. In the daytime I played with my companions in the garden, and in the evening I led the dance in the Great Hall. Round the garden ran a very lofty wall, but I never cared to ask what lay beyond it, everything about me was so beautiful. My courtiers called me the Happy Prince, and happy indeed I was, if pleasure be happiness. So I lived, and so I died. And now that I am dead they have set me up here so high that I can see all the ugliness and all the misery of my city, and though my heart is made of lead yet I cannot choose but weep."

"What! is he not solid gold?" said the Swallow to himself. He was too polite to make any personal remarks out loud.

"Far away," continued the statue in a low musical voice, "far away in a little street there is a poor house. One of the windows is open, and through it I can see a woman seated at a table. Her face is thin and worn, and she has coarse, red hands, all pricked by the needle, for she is a seamstress. She is embroidering passion flowers on a satin gown for the loveliest of the Queen's maids of honor to wear at the next Court ball. In a bed in the corner of the room her little boy is lying ill. He has a fever and is asking for oranges. His mother has nothing to give him but river water, so he is crying. Swallow, Swallow, little Swallow, will you not bring her the ruby out of my sword hilt? My feet are fastened to this pedestal, and I cannot move."

"I am waited for in Egypt," said the Swallow. "My friends are flying up and down the Nile and talking to the large lotus-flowers. Soon they will go to sleep in the tomb of the great King. The King is there himself in his painted coffin. He is wrapped in yellow linen and embalmed with spices. Round his

neck is a chain of pale green jade, and his hands are like withered leaves."

"Swallow, Swallow, little Swallow," said the Prince, "will you not stay with me for one night and be my messenger? The boy is so thirsty, and the mother so sad."

"I don't think I like boys," answered the Swallow. "Last summer, when I was staying on the river, there were two rude boys, the miller's sons, who were always throwing stones at me. They never hit me, of course; we swallows fly far too well for that, and besides, I come of a family famous for its agility; but still, it was a mark of disrespect."

But the Happy Prince looked so sad that the little Swallow was sorry. "It is very cold here," he said; "but I will stay with you for one night and be your messenger."

"Thank you, little Swallow," said the Prince.

So the Swallow picked out the great ruby from the Prince's sword and flew away with it in his beak over the roofs of the town.

He passed by the cathedral tower, where the white marble angels were sculptured. He passed by the palace and heard the sound of dancing. A beautiful girl came out on the balcony with her lover. "How wonderful the stars are," he said to her, "and how wonderful is the power of love!"

"I hope my dress will be ready in time for the State-ball," she answered; "I have ordered passion flowers to be embroidered on it; but the seamstresses are so lazy."

He passed over the river, and saw the lanterns hanging to the masts of the ships. . . . At last he came to the poor house and looked in. The boy was tossing feverishly on his bed, and the mother had fallen asleep, she was so tired. In he hopped, and laid the great ruby on the table beside the woman's thimble. Then he flew gently round the bed, fanning the boy's forehead with his wings. "How cool I feel," said the boy, "I must be getting better"; and he sank into a delicious slumber.

Then the Swallow flew back to the Happy Prince, and told him what he had done. "It is curious," he remarked, "but I feel quite warm now, although it is so cold."

"That is because you have done a good action," said the Prince. And the little Swallow began to think, and then he fell asleep. Thinking always made him sleepy.

When day broke he flew down to the river and had a bath. "What a remarkable phenomenon," said the Professor of Ornithology as he was passing over the bridge. "A swallow in winter!" And he wrote a long letter about it to the local newspaper. Everyone quoted it, it was full of so many words that they could not understand.

"Tonight I go to Egypt," said the Swallow, and he was in high spirits at the prospect. He visited all the public monuments, and sat a long time on top of the church steeple. Wherever he went the Sparrows chirruped, and said to each other: "What a distinguished stranger!" so he enjoyed himself very much.

When the moon rose he flew back to the Happy Prince. "Have you any commissions for Egypt?" he cried; "I am just starting."

"Swallow, Swallow, little Swallow," said the Prince, "will you not stay with me one night longer?"

"I am waited for in Egypt," answered the Swallow. "To-morrow my friends will fly up to the Second Cataract. The river-horse couches there among the bulrushes, and on a great granite throne sits the God Memnon. All night long he watches the stars, and when the morning star shines he utters one cry of joy, and then he is silent. At noon the yellow lions come down to the water's edge to drink. They have eyes like green beryls, and their roar is louder than the roar of the cataract."

"Swallow, Swallow, little Swallow," said the Prince, "far away across the city I see a young man in a garret. He is leaning over a desk covered with papers, and in a tumbler by his side there is a bunch of withered violets. His hair is brown and crisp, and his lips are red as a pomegranate, and he has large and dreamy eyes. He is trying to finish a play for the Director of the Theater, but he is too cold to write any more. There is no fire in the grate, and hunger has made him faint."

"I will wait with you one night longer," said the Swallow, who really had a good heart. "Shall I take him another ruby?"

"Alas! I have no ruby now," said the Prince; "my eyes are all that I have left. They are made of rare sapphires, which were brought out of India a thousand years ago. Pluck out one of them and take it to him. He will sell it to the jeweller, and buy food and firewood, and finish his play."

"Dear Prince," said the Swallow, "I cannot do that"; and he began to weep.

"Swallow, Swallow, little Swallow," said the Prince, "do as I command you."

So the Swallow plucked out the Prince's eye, and flew away to the student's garret. It was easy enough to get in, as there was a hole in the roof. Through this he darted and came into

the room. The young man had his head buried in his hands, so he did not hear the flutter of the bird's wings, and when he looked up he found the beautiful sapphire lying on the withered violets.

"I am beginning to be appreciated," he cried; "this is from some great admirer. Now I can finish my play," and he looked quite happy.

The next day the Swallow flew down to the harbor. He sat on the mast of a large vessel and watched the sailors hauling big chests out of the hold with ropes. "Heave ahoy!" they shouted as each chest came up. "I am going to Egypt," cried the Swallow, but nobody minded, and when the Moon rose he flew back to the Happy Prince.

"I am come to bid you good-bye," he cried.

"Swallow, Swallow, little Swallow," said the Prince, "will you not stay with me one night longer?"

"It is winter," answered the Swallow, "and the chill snow will soon be here. In Egypt the sun is warm on the green palm trees, and the crocodiles lie in the mud and look lazily about them. My companions are building a nest in the Temple of Baalbec, and the pink and white doves are watching them, and cooing to each other. Dear Prince, I must leave you, but I will never forget you, and next spring I will bring you back two beautiful jewels in place of those you have given away. The ruby shall be redder than a red rose, and the sapphire shall be as blue as the great sea."

"In the square below," said the Happy Prince, "there stands a little match-girl. She has let her matches fall in the gutter, and they are all spoiled. Her father will beat her if she does not bring home some money, and she is crying. She has no shoes or stockings, and her little head is bare. Pluck out my other eye and give it to her, and her father will not beat her."

"I will stay with you one night longer," said the Swallow, "but I cannot pluck out your eye. You would be quite blind then."

"Swallow, Swallow, little Swallow," said the Prince, "do as I command you."

So he plucked out the Prince's other eye, and darted down with it. He swooped past the match-girl and slipped the jewel into the palm of her hand. "What a lovely bit of glass," cried the little girl; and she ran home, laughing.

Then the Swallow came back to the Prince. "You are blind now," he said, "so I will stay with you always."

"No, little Swallow," said the poor Prince, "you must go away to Egypt."

"I will stay with you always," said the Swallow, and he slept at the Prince's feet.

All the next day he sat on the Prince's shoulder and told him stories of what he had seen in strange lands. He told him of the red ibises, who stand in long rows on the banks of the Nile, and catch goldfish in their beaks; of the Sphinx, who is as old as the world itself, and lives in the desert, and knows everything; of the merchants, who walk slowly by the side of their camels and carry amber beads in their hand; of the King of the Mountains of the Moon, who is as black as ebony and worships a large crystal; of the great green snake that sleeps in a palm tree and has twenty priests to feed it with honeycakes; and of the pygmies who sail over a big lake on large flat leaves and are always at war with the butterflies.

"Dear little Swallow," said the Prince, "you tell me of marvelous things, but more marvelous than anything is the suffering of men and of women. There is no Mystery so great as Misery. Fly over my city, little Swallow, and tell me what you see there."

So the Swallow flew over the great city, and saw the rich making merry in their beautiful houses, while the beggars were sitting at the gates. He flew into dark lanes and saw the white faces of starving children looking out listlessly at the black streets. Under the archway of a bridge two little boys were lying in one another's arms to try and keep themselves warm. "How hungry we are!" they said. "You must not lie here," shouted the Watchman, and they wandered out into the rain.

Then he flew back and told the Prince what he had seen.

"I am covered with fine gold," said the Prince, "you must take it off, leaf by leaf, and give it to my poor; the living always think that gold can make them happy."

Leaf after leaf of the fine gold the Swallow picked off, till the Happy Prince looked quite dull and gray. Leaf after leaf of the fine gold he brought to the poor, and the children's faces grew rosier, and they laughed and played games in the street. "We have bread now!" they cried.

Then the snow came, and after the snow came the frost. The streets looked as if they were made of silver, they were so bright and glistening; long icicles like crystal daggers hung down from the eaves of the houses, everybody went about in furs, and the little boys wore scarlet caps and skated on the ice.

The poor little Swallow grew colder and colder, but he would not leave the Prince, he loved him too well. He picked up crumbs outside the baker's door when the baker was not looking, and tried to keep himself warm by flapping his wings.

But at last he knew that he was going to die. He had just strength to fly up to the Prince's shoulder. "Good-bye, dear Prince!" he murmured, "will you let me kiss your hand?"

"I am glad that you are going to Egypt at last, little Swallow," said the Prince, "you have stayed too long here; but you must kiss me on the lips, for I love you."

"It is not to Egypt that I am going," said the Swallow. "I am going to the House of Death. Death is the brother of Sleep, is he not?"

And he kissed the Happy Prince on the lips, and fell down dead at his feet.

At that moment a curious crack sounded inside the statue, as if something had broken. The fact is that the leaden heart had snapped right in two. It certainly was a dreadfully hard frost.

Early the next morning the Mayor was walking in the square below in company with the Town Councillors. As they passed the column he looked up at the statue: "Dear me! how shabby the Happy Prince looks!" he said.

"How shabby indeed!" cried the Town Councillors, who always agreed with the Mayor; and they went up to look at it.

"The ruby has fallen out of his sword, his eyes are gone, and he is golden no longer," said the Mayor; "in fact, he is little better than a beggar!"

"Little better than a beggar," said the Town Councillors.

"And here is actually a dead bird at his feet!" continued the Mayor. "We must really issue a proclamation that birds are not to be allowed to die here." And the Town Clerk made a note of the suggestion.

So they pulled down the statue of the Happy Prince. "As he is no longer beautiful he is no longer useful," said the Art Professor at the University.

Then they melted the statue in a furnace, and the Mayor held a meeting of the Corporation to decide what was to be done with the metal. "We must have another statue, of course," he said, "and it shall be a statue of myself."

"Of myself," said each of the Town Councillors, and they quarrelled. When I last heard of them they were quarrelling still.

"What a strange thing!" said the overseer of the workmen at the foundry. "This broken lead heart will not melt in the furnace. We must throw it away." So they threw it on a dust-heap where the dead Swallow was also lying.

"Bring me the two most precious things in the city," said God to one of His Angels; and the Angel brought Him the leaden heart and the dead bird.

"You have rightly chosen," said God, "for in my garden of Paradise this little bird shall sing forevermore, and in my city of gold the Happy Prince shall praise me."

THE ENCHANTED GARDEN

Ruth Dixon

Ding! Dong! The moon is gleaming;
  Tiptoe through a faery glade
To a little garden dreaming
  In a green and silver shade.

Hush! Hush! A wood-wind's creeping
  Past the place where poppies dwell,
Where the nightingale is sleeping
  In a bower of asphodel,

Where the King of Faery's daughter
  And an Elf with magic lute
Play beside the trembling water
  Of a fountain that is mute,

While in silver silence, flowers,
  Rose and gold and amethyst,
Sleep away the moonlit hours,
  Vanish in the morning mist.

Ding! Dong! The moon is gleaming;
  Tiptoe through a faery glade
To a little garden dreaming
  In a green and silver shade.

THE NIGHTINGALE

ADAPTED FROM *Hans Christian Andersen*

ILLUSTRATED BY *Lynd Ward*

IN CHINA, you must know, the emperor is a Chinaman, and all those about him are Chinamen, too. The story I am going to tell you happened a great many years ago, so it is well to hear it now before it is forgotten. The emperor's palace was the most beautiful in the world. It was built entirely of porcelain, and very costly, but so delicate and brittle than one had to take care how one touched it. In the garden could be seen the most wonderful flowers, with silver bells tied to them, which tinkled so that everyone who passed could not help noticing the flowers. Indeed, everything in the emperor's garden was remarkable, and it extended so far that the gardener himself did not know where it ended. Those who traveled beyond the garden came into a noble forest, with lofty trees, sloping down to the deep blue sea, and the great ships sailed under the shadow of its branches. In one of these trees lived a nightingale, who sang so beautifully that even the poor fishermen, who had so many other things to do, would stop and listen. Sometimes, when they went at night to spread their nets, they would hear her sing, and say, "Oh, is not that beautiful?" But when they returned to their fishing, they forgot the bird until the next night. Then they would hear it again and exclaim, "Oh, how beautiful is the nightingale's song!"

Suddenly there came a lovely song. It was the little nightingale.

Travelers from every country in the world came to the city of the emperor, which they admired very much. They admired also the palace and gardens. And when they heard the nightingale, they said that it was the best of all. And the travelers, on their return home, related what they had seen; and learned men wrote books, containing descriptions of the town, the palace, and the gardens; but they did not forget the nightingale, which was really the greatest wonder. And those who could write poetry composed beautiful verses about the nightingale, who lived in a forest near the deep sea. The books traveled all over the world, and some of them came into the hands of the emperor; and he sat in his golden chair, and, as he read, he nodded his approval every moment, for it pleased him to find such a beautiful description of the city, his palace, and his gardens. But when he came to the words, "the nightingale is the most beautiful of all," he exclaimed, "What is this? I know nothing of any nightingale. Is there such a bird in my empire? And even in my garden? I have never heard of it. Something, it appears, may be learnt from books."

Then he called one of his cavaliers, who was so highbred that when any in an inferior rank to himself spoke to him, or asked him a question, he would answer, "Pooh," which means nothing.

"There is a very wonderful bird mentioned here, called a nightingale," said the emperor; "they say it is the best thing in my large kingdom. Why have I not been told of it?"

"I have never heard the name," replied the cavalier; "she has not been present at court."

"It is my pleasure that she shall appear at court this evening," said the emperor; "the whole world knows what I possess better than I do myself."

"I have never heard of her," said the cavalier; "yet I will seek for her and I will find her."

But where was the nightingale to be found? The nobleman went upstairs and down, through halls and passages; yet none of those whom he met had heard of the bird. So he returned to the emperor and said that it must be a fable, invented by those who had written the book. "Your Imperial Majesty," he said, "cannot believe everything contained in books; sometimes they are only fiction, or what is called the black art.

"But the book in which I have read this account," said the emperor, "was sent to me by the great and mighty emperor of Japan, and therefore it cannot contain a falsehood. I will hear the nightingale; she must be here this evening; she has my highest favor; and if she does not come, the whole court shall be trampled upon after supper is ended."

"Tsing-pe!" cried the cavalier, and again he ran up and down stairs, through all the halls and corridors; and half the court ran with him, for they they did not like the idea of being trampled upon. There was a great inquiry about this wonderful nightingale, whom all the world knew, but who was unknown to the court.

At last they met with a poor girl in the kitchen, who said, "Oh yes, I know the nightingale quite well; indeed, she can sing. Every evening I have permission to take home to my poor sick mother some scraps from the table; she lives down by the seashore, and as I come back I feel tired, and I sit down in the

wood to rest, and listen to the nightingale's song. Then the tears come to my eyes, and it is just as if my mother kissed me."

"Little maiden," said the cavalier, "I will obtain for you constant employment in the kitchen, and you shall have permission to see the emperor dine, if you will lead us to the nightingale; for she is invited for this evening to the palace." So she went into the wood where the nightingale sang, and half the court followed her. As they went along, a cow began to low.

"Oh," said a young courtier, "now we have found her; what wonderful power for such a small creature; I have certainly heard it before."

"No, that is only a cow lowing," said the little girl; "we are a long way from the place yet."

Then some frogs began to croak in the marsh.

"Beautiful," said the young courtier again. "Now I hear it, tinkling like the little church bells."

"No, those are frogs," said the maiden; "but I think we shall hear her soon"; and presently the nightingale began to sing.

"Hark, hark! there she is," said the girl, "and there she sits," she added, pointing to a little gray bird who was perched on a bough.

"Is it possible?" said the cavalier, "I never imagined it would be a little, plain, simple thing like that. She has certainly changed color at seeing so many grand people around her."

"Little nightingale," cried the girl, raising her voice, "our most gracious emperor wishes you to sing before him."

"With the greatest pleasure," said the nightingale, and began to sing most delightfully.

"It sounds like tiny glass bells," said the cavalier, "and see how her little throat works! It is surprising that we have never heard this before; she will be a great success at court."

"Shall I sing once more before the emperor?" asked the nightingale, who thought he was present.

"My excellent little nightingale," said the cavalier, "I have the great pleasure of inviting you to a court festival this evening, where you will charm His Imperial Majesty by your beautiful song."

"My song sounds best in the green wood," said the bird, but still she came willingly when she heard the emperor's wish.

The palace was festively adorned for the occasion. The wall and floors of porcelain glittered in the light of a thousand lamps. Beautiful flowers, round which little bells were tied, stood in the corridors: what with the running to and fro and the draught, these bells tinkled so loudly that no one could be heard. In the center of the great hall, a golden perch had been fixed for the nightingale to sit on. The whole court was present, and the little kitchenmaid had received permission to stand by the door. She was now installed as a real court cook. All were in full dress, and every eye was turned to the little gray bird when the emperor nodded to her to begin. The nightingale sang so sweetly that the tears came into the emperor's eyes and then rolled down his cheeks as her song became still more touching and went to everyone's heart. The emperor was so delighted that he declared the nightingale should have his gold slipper to wear around her neck, but she declined the honor with thanks: she had been sufficiently rewarded already. "I have seen tears in an emperor's eyes," she said, "that is my richest reward. An emperor's tears have wonderful power and are quite sufficient honor for me"; and then she sang again and more enchantingly than ever.

"That singing is a lovely gift," said the ladies of the court to each other; and then they took water in their mouths to make them utter the gurgling sounds of the nightingale when they spoke to anyone, so that they might fancy themselves nightingales. And the footmen and chambermaids also expressed their satisfaction, which is saying a great deal, for they are very

difficult to please. In fact, the nightingale's visit was most successful. She was now to remain at court, to have her own cage, with liberty to go out twice a day, and once during the night. Twelve servants were appointed to attend her on these occasions, who each held her by a silken thread fastened to her leg. There was certainly not much pleasure in this kind of flying.

The whole city spoke of the wonderful bird, and when two people met, one said "nightin," and the other said "gale," and they understood what was meant, for nothing else was talked of. Eleven peddlers' children were named after her, but not one of them could sing a note.

One day the emperor received a large packet on which was written "The Nightingale." "Here is no doubt a new book about our celebrated bird," said the emperor. But instead of a book, it was a work of art contained in a casket, an artificial nightingale made to look like a living one, and covered all over with diamonds, rubies, and sapphires. As soon as the artificial bird was wound up, it could sing like the real one, and could move its tail up and down, which sparkled with silver and gold. Round its neck hung a piece of ribbon, on which was written, "The Emperor of China's nightingale is poor compared with that of the Emperor of Japan's."

"This is very beautiful," exclaimed all who saw it, and he who had brought the artificial bird received the title of "Imperial Nightingale-bringer-in-chief."

"Now they must sing together," said the court, "and what a duet it will be." But they did not get on well, for the real nightingale sang in its own natural way, but the artificial bird sang only waltzes.

"That is not a fault," said the music-master, "it is quite perfect to my taste," so then it had to sing alone, and was as successful as the real bird; besides, it was so much prettier to look at, for it sparkled like bracelets and breastpins. Three and thirty times did it sing the same tunes without being tired; the people would gladly have heard it again, but the emperor said the living nightingale ought to sing something. But where was she?

No one had noticed her when she flew out at the open window, back to her own green woods.

"What has become of her?" said the emperor, when her flight had been discovered; and all the courtiers blamed her and said she was a very ungrateful creature.

"But we have the best bird after all," said one, and then they would have the artificial bird sing again, although it was the thirty-fourth time they had listened to the same piece, and even then they had not learnt it, for it was rather difficult. But the music-master praised the bird in the highest degree, and even asserted that it was better than a real nightingale, not only in dress and the beautiful diamonds, but also in its musical power. "For you must perceive, My Chief Lord and Emperor, that with a real nightingale we can never tell what is going to be sung, but with this bird everything is settled. It can be opened and explained, so that people may understand how the waltzes are formed, and why one note follows upon another."

"This is exactly what we think," they all replied, and then the music-master received permission to exhibit the bird to the people on the following Sunday, and the emperor commanded that they should be present to hear it sing. When they heard it, they were like people intoxicated; however, it must have been with drinking tea, which is quite a Chinese custom. They all said "Oh!" and held up their forefingers and nodded, but a poor fisherman, who had heard the real nightingale, said, "It sounds prettily enough, and the melodies are all alike; yet there seems something wanting, I cannot exactly explain what."

And after this the real nightingale was banished from the empire, and the artificial bird placed on a silk cushion close to the emperor's bed. The presents of gold and precious stones which had been received with it were round the bird, and it was now advanced to the title of "Highest Imperial After-Dinner Singer," and to the rank of No. 1 on the left hand, for the emperor considered the left side, on which the heart lies, as the most noble, and the heart of an emperor is in the same place as that of other people.

The music-master wrote a work, in twenty-five volumes,

which was very learned and very long, and full of the most difficult Chinese words about the artificial bird: yet all the people said they had read it and understood it, for fear of being thought stupid and having their bodies trampled upon.

So a year passed, and the emperor, the court, and all the other Chinese knew every little twitter in the artificial bird's song; and for that same reason it pleased them better. They could sing with the bird, which they often did. The street boys sang, "Zi-zi-zi, cluck, cluck, cluck," and the emperor himself could sing it also. It was really most amusing.

One evening, when the artificial bird was singing its best, and the emperor lay in bed listening to it, something inside the bird sounded "whizz." Then a spring cracked. "Whir-r-r-r" went all the wheels, running round, and then the music stopped. The emperor immediately sprang out of bed, and called for his physician; but what could he do? Then they sent for a watchmaker; and, after a great deal of talking and examination, the bird was put into something like order; but he said that it must be used carefully, as the barrels were worn, and it would be impossible to put in new ones without injuring the music. Now there was great sorrow, as the bird could only be allowed to play once a year; and even that was dangerous for the works inside it. Then the music-master made a little speech, full of hard words, and declared that the bird was as good as ever; and, of course, no one contradicted him.

Five years passed, and then a real grief came upon the land. The Chinese really were fond of their emperor, and he now lay so ill that he was not expected to live. Already a new emperor had been chosen, and the people who stood in the street asked the cavalier how the old emperor was; but he only said, "Pooh!" and shook his head.

Cold and pale lay the emperor in his royal bed; the whole court thought he was dead, and everyone ran away to pay homage to the new ruler. The chamberlains went out to have a talk on the matter, and the ladies' maids invited company to take coffee. Cloth had been laid down on the halls and passages, so that not a footstep should be heard, and all was silent and still. But the emperor was not yet dead, although he lay white and stiff on his gorgeous bed, with the long velvet curtains and heavy gold tassels. A window stood open, and the moon shone in upon the emperor and the artificial bird. The poor emperor, finding he could scarcely breathe with a strange weight on his chest, opened his eyes, and saw Death sitting there. He had put on the emperor's golden crown and held in one hand his sword of state and in the other his beautiful banner. All around the bed, and peeping through the long velvet curtains, were a number of strange heads, some ugly and others lovely and gentle-looking. These were the emperor's good and bad deeds.

"Do you remember this?" "Do you recollect that?" they asked one after another, thus bringing to his remembrance circumstances that made the perspiration stand on his brow.

"I know nothing about it," said the emperor. "Music! music!" he cried; "the large Chinese drum! that I may not hear what they say." But still they went on, and Death nodded like a Chinaman to all they said. "Music! music!" shouted the emperor. "You little, precious golden bird, sing, pray sing! I have given you gold and costly presents; I have even hung my golden slipper round your neck. Sing! sing!" But the bird remained silent. There was no one to wind it up, and therefore it could not sing a note.

Death continued to stare at the emperor with his cold, hollow eyes, and the room was fearfully still. Suddenly there came through the open window a lovely song. It was the little live nightingale that sat on a spray. She had heard of the emperor's sad plight and had come to sing to him of comfort and hope. And as she sang, the shadows grew paler and paler; the blood in the emperor's veins flowed more rapidly, and gave life to his weak limbs; and even Death himself listened, and said, "Go on, little nightingale, go on!"

"Then will you give me the beautiful golden sword and that rich banner? and will you give me the emperor's crown?" said the bird.

So Death gave up each of these treasures for a song; and the nightingale sang on and on. She sang the quiet churchyard music—the churchyard where the white roses grow, where elder blossoms send forth perfume on the breeze. Then Death longed to go and see his garden, and floated out through the window in the form of a cold, white mist.

"Thanks, thanks," said the emperor. "You heavenly little bird, I know you well. I banished you from my kingdom once, and yet you have charmed away the evil faces from my bed and banished Death from my heart, with your sweet song. How can I reward you?"

"You have already rewarded me," said the nightingale. "I shall never forget the tears I drew from your eyes the first time I sang to you. These are the jewels that rejoice a singer's heart. But now sleep, and grow strong and well again. I will sing to you again."

And as she sang, the emperor fell into a sweet slumber; and how mild and refreshing that sleep was! When he awoke, strengthened and restored, the sun shone brightly through the window; but not one of his servants had returned—they all believed he was dead; only the nightingale still sat beside him and sang.

"You must always remain with me," said the emperor. "You shall sing only when it pleases you; and I will break the artificial bird into a thousand pieces."

"No, do not do that," replied the nightingale; "the bird did very well as long as it could. Keep it here still. I cannot live in the palace and build my nest, but let me come when I like. I will sit on a bough outside your window, in the evening, and sing to you, so that you may be happy, and have thoughts full of joy. I will sing to you of those who are happy, and those who suffer; of the good and the evil, who are hidden around you. The little bird flies far from your court and from you to the homes of the fishermen and the peasant's cot. I love your heart better than your crown; and yet something holy lingers round that also. I will come, I will sing to you; but you must promise me one thing."

"Everything," said the emperor, who, having dressed himself in his imperial robes, stood with the hand that held the heavy golden sword pressed to his heart.

"I only ask one thing," she replied; "let no one know that you have a little bird who tells you everything. It will be best to conceal it." So saying, the nightingale flew away.

The servants now came in to look after the dead emperor; when, yes, there he stood! And the emperor said, "Good morning."

Index

PALACE